MILTON

Poetry & Prose

With Essays by

JOHNSON   HAZLITT

MACAULAY

With an Introduction by

A. M. D. HUGHES

and Notes by various scholars

OXFORD

AT THE CLARENDON PRESS

The notes in this edition are based mainly on the notes in the Clarendon Press editions of Johnson's *Life of Milton* by C. H. Firth, Macaulay's *Essay on Milton* by P. T. Creswell, Milton's *Poems* by R. C. Browne, revised by Henry Bradley, and Milton's *Areopagitica* by J. W. Hales.

FIRST EDITION 1920
REPRINTED 1922, 1925, 1930, 1955

PRINTED IN GREAT BRITAIN
AT THE UNIVERSITY PRESS, OXFORD
BY CHARLES BATEY, PRINTER TO THE UNIVERSITY

CONTENTS

INTRODUCTION

THE process of assaying and valuing the works of Milton has been long and gradual, and not without a fluctuation in the estimate, for Milton is dominated, both as an artist and as a thinker, by the fashion of his age, and is also solitary and remote. His earlier writings are characteristic of the period when English poetry, after the great Elizabethan flood, was silting up in learned fancy and curious wit, but here or there still ran with a lively current. The Hymn on the Nativity is 'metaphysical' poetry in the style of Donne and Cowley, in which, as Johnson has judicially phrased it, 'if the conceits were far-fetched, they were sometimes worth the carriage'. *L'Allegro* and *Il Penseroso*, recovering, as they do, some of the supreme felicities of Elizabethan verse, the ease and magic of words and the serenity of heart, are among the things that are never stale or strange. But in *Comus* and *Lycidas* the poet has taken up the masque and the pastoral from the fashion of his day, each of them a form of poetry which only a true poet could redeem from artifice, and then only if the reader should connive. Down to almost the end of this period he is apparently at home in the Merry England of his youth. His theme is the beauty of holiness, and he takes his 'pleasure unreproved' in 'pomp and feast and revelry' and in the comeliness of Anglican worship. But *Lycidas* suddenly gives voice to the spirit which parted him from the Church, plunged him into twenty years of political contention, and suspended his lifelong purpose of leaving a work to posterity 'so written that they should not willingly let it die '. He returned to poetry a lonely prophet in an evil time; and resuming from *Comus* his great theme of temptation, sang of the Fall in Eden as the kernel of man's history, and of man's history as the critical encounter in a war of Heaven and Hell—a subject beyond example high, and bare, and difficult. If the earlier poems call for some compliance from the reader in respect of the style, so do the later in respect of the spirit and the thought. In all the three great poems of his old age there is a temper which, whether it breathes in the grand style of *Paradise Lost* or the bloomless severity of *Paradise Regained*, whether triumphant or stoically assured, is always self-centred, and often imperious and a little harsh.

Three important factors of the long debate are represented by the essays in this book. The first is a famous document of the academic criticism of the eighteenth century. The second is in the manner of the imaginative submission which restored so much of our literary heritage in the romantic era. The third was the earliest and best of the critical estimates written for the Reviews. Somewhat deficient, as all Macaulay's work is, in analytic power, it abounded in good observations, and its fervid panegyric proclaimed his political sympathy with Milton's creed.

In Johnson's time the spirit of man looked back to the literature of the sixteenth and early seventeenth centuries with the feeling of maturity for the adventures of youth. The vernal hours of the Renaissance were gone, when the language, much more pliant than it afterwards became, and richer from day to day, flowed freely in new music and rhythm, when imagination 'ran to and fro' and nested in all manner of lore and myth, and the half of life was pageant and play. The faculty of make-believe and the ear for numbers weakened together, and the mythology of Greece and Rome, to Milton a living dialect of the heart, was now only a cold embellishment. It was Johnson's

merit that in these circumstances he stood for honesty.
He was far from niggardly in his admiration. His force
of mind and his sensibility together made his criticism,
not indeed an accomplice of the original creation, as the
best kind is, but on its own plane luminous and liberal.
It is eminently a judicial criticism, a methodized endeavour
to balance impartially the merits and demerits of its subject.
But his strength, and also his weakness, are most conspicuous in the attack. As Landor has remarked, he ' is
seldom erroneous in his censures, but not sufficiently
moved to admiration by what is highest and purest in
poetry '. The pastoral was no longer a medium of real
emotion ; he would have done with it. The masque was
a spurious form, neither music nor architecture nor drama,
but a mixture of the three. As printed in a book, however,
it was drama ; and he would test it accordingly. Hardly
less spurious was the literary play of the type of *Samson
Agonistes* ; that, too, must be taken as it purported to be.
In all this he took his stand on sincerity and truth, and on
the axiom that matter must be one with form. That in
Comus ' the language is too luxuriant for dialogue ', and
the dialogue at times ' tediously instructive , is a true
observation, and Macaulay's rejoinder, that, being dramatic
only in semblance, ' the speeches must be read as magnificent soliloquies ', is simply an avowal of its truth. Simi-
larly, the complaint that the middle part of *Samson Agonistes*
' neither hastens nor retards the catastrophe ' is no more
or less than Macaulay's indictment in a slightly different
form. Johnson's only fault in these instances is in not
displaying the redeeming and glorifying beauty of either
poem in due degree. But in the strictures on *Lycidas* his
insensitiveness has amounted to positive disablement ; for
here all depends on the ear of the reader, on the fascination
of the literary models, and on a poetic piety for the legends
of the ancient world. What was once the most penetrative

spell in the classical literatures had so far palled with time
that to Johnson, scholar as he was, the poets of the Renaissance had erred in mingling the Christian story and the
pagan myths.   And so far had the ear for the music of verse
declined upon an emphatic rhyming and 'the stated recur-
rence of settled numbers' that Johnson may be said to
have almost forfeited a whole dimension of poetic sense.
Under such disabilities it was natural to see in *Lycidas*
only another pastoral, and to argue that a grief embodied
in so much fiction was itself fictitious.   The logical meaning of a poem may be only the least of its elements, and it
is the music of this noble elegy that expresses most inti-
mately its quiet and tender memories though not such
passion as throbs fierce and sudden in the lines on the
'blind mouths' and the 'Wolf with privy paw'.   The same
critical deficiency is at the root of his strange judgement
that of Milton's sonnets the best are only not bad.   Partly,
as we may infer, he thought the sonnet too small for its
matter, but mainly, as he tells us, it foiled his craving for
simple metre and frequent rhyme.

Milton is one of the poets who have set up great differences between the learned and the simple among their
readers, between the men of letters and the rest.   This is
especially true of *Paradise Regained.*   The three essayists
cited in this book agree with Milton himself in blaming the
popular distaste for it, though it remained for Coleridge to
formulate expressly the defence which Johnson has here
implied : that it must pass, not for an epic, but for a great
didactic poem, and is therefore justified in its 'narrow
basis' of incident and its frugal style.   But on several
topics of *Paradise Lost* the common instinct has been truer
to Milton than the critical wit, and in the course of the
debate the instinct has won the wit to its side.   The chief
subjects of the debate may be brought under four heads :
design and management, the hero, the human characters,

and the ultimate value of *Paradise Lost* as a poem ; and
what is now the canonical view may be briefly noted.

(*a*) Johnson's friends used to tell him that he should
have been a lawyer, and his forensic quality is very use-
fully, if rather excessively, let loose on the consistency of
Paradise Lost—on the propriety of the detail in the battle
in Heaven, on the bridge over Chaos, on the figures of Sin
and Death, and on the divided conception of the angelic
beings as now material and now immaterial. The crucial
item of the inquiry is the last of these. If there is no
reason why Satan should not go through the eye of a
needle as easily as into the body of a toad, why does any
material thing embarrass him—his armour or the walls of
Paradise ? The answer to the objection involves the
greater question of Milton's imagination, and it is here
especially that Macaulay avails us. The substance of his
argument is decisive ; namely, that unless the angelic
beings could assume different forms the story was not to
be told. Milton's masterly tact has kept them in the
twilight between the tangible and the inapparent, and
made them loom and waver, appear and vanish. Forensic
acuteness is here out of place. Poetry, says Johnson,
' calls imagination to the aid of reason '. But reason may
be a fractious ally, and far too chary of that 'willing sus-
pension of disbelief' which is the poet's need and due.

(*b*) Addison would have had us read the poem by the
intention of its author, and see the ' hero ' in the Messiah.
Johnson's piety recoils from the question, but his dubious
vote is given at last to Adam. Hazlitt was among the
first of the critics who freely recognized that the ' hero ',
in the sense of the appealing character, is Satan, and his
fine appraisement of that ' clouded ruin of a God ' has lifted
this part of his essay to the poetic plane. Macaulay and
the more recent critics have followed him. For we shall
never more read *Paradise Lost* as Milton wished we

should. He dug a channel for our sympathies, but the river has made its own bed. He built a house, but we who enter in do not use it by his plan. Men's judgements on the poem have conflicted because its imagination is at variance with its theology, and the theology has but gradually loosened its hold. There was, moreover, in Milton himself an unconscious sympathy with the majesty of the fallen angel and the resolute leadership in a hopeless cause that coloured his purpose and almost put a contradiction into the heart of the poem.

(c) More recent writers have noted in Adam and Eve a finer differentiation than is pointed out by our essayists. But Hazlitt has splendidly parried the objection that they and the life they lead are poor in interest. ' Was there nothing in this scene,' he asks, ' which God and Nature alone witnessed, to interest a modern critic ? What need was there of action, where the heart was full of bliss and innocence without it ? . . . All things seem to acquire fresh sweetness, and to be clothed with fresh beauty in their sight. They tasted as it were for themselves and us, of all that there ever was pure in human bliss.'

(d) Milton's poetry, says Hazlitt, was written with labour and thought, and never gushed, like Shakespeare's, as from abundant springs. No one, says Johnson, ever wished that *Paradise Lost* was longer than it is. Its sublimity leaves us hungering for the mind's daily food. But Milton's strength was in self-reserve ; nor was he, either as poet or saint, one of those who, in Ruskin's words, ' are content to receive rather than to earn their salvation '. His love of beauty and his rich sensuousness required a protective estrangement from many of the ways of men, and he ' mixed with action ', as the political pamphlets abundantly show, an idealist and a solitary still. His song first and last is of the moral core of life, of the militant will, and the victory in the soul preceding and determining the 'strenuous liberty' of the state. As in *Paradise Lost* over against the awful war in Heaven and its great resolves of heart there is set the peace and 'bowery loveliness' of Eden, so in Milton's own nature, and indeed in the best mind of English Puritanism, there is an alternation or rhythm of 'earnest melancholy' and serene delight. The strenuousness and stern majesty of the moral being generated a peculiar pureness and freshness in the sense of beauty and a peculiar depth in the sense of rest. A book, says Milton, preserves 'as in a vial' the pure essence of him that wrote it; and that is why *Paradise Lost* is one of the great things that man has made.

MILTON'S LIFE

1608. Milton born in London (December 9).

1625–32. At Christ's College, Cambridge.

1629. *On the Morning of Christ's Nativity.*

1632–38. At Horton, Buckinghamshire.

1632(?) *L'Allegro, Il Penseroso.*

1634. *Comus* acted ; published 1637.

1637. *Lycidas* written (November) ; published 1638.

1638. Leaves England for Italy (April).

1639. Returns to England (August).
Begins to reside in London.

1641–42. His five anti-episcopal pamphlets.

1643–45. His four divorce pamphlets.

1644. *Areopagitica.*

1645. *Poems* (collected edition of early poems).

1649. *Tenure of Kings and Magistrates* (first republican pamphlet).
Appointed Latin Secretary to the Council.

1651. *Pro Populo Anglicano Defensio* ; 1654 *Defensio Secunda.*

1652. His blindness becomes total.

1660. The Restoration.

1667. *Paradise Lost* (ten books); 'revised and augmented' (twelve books) 1674.

1671. *Paradise Regained.*
Samson Agonistes.

1673. *Poems* (new edition of 1645 volume, with additions).

1674. Dies in London (November 8).

I

From JOHNSON'S LIFE OF MILTON

First published 1779 ; the extract is from the revised edition of 1783

In the examination of Milton's poetical works, I shall pay so much regard to time as to begin with his juvenile productions. For his early pieces he seems to have had a degree of fondness not very laudable : what he has once written he resolves to preserve, and gives to the public an unfinished poem, which he broke off because he was *nothing satisfied with what he had done,* supposing his readers less nice than himself. These preludes to his future labours are in Italian, Latin, and English. Of the Italian I cannot pretend to speak as a critic ; but I have heard them com- 10 mended by a man well qualified to decide their merit. The Latin pieces are lusciously elegant ; but the delight which they afford is rather by the exquisite imitation of the ancient writers, by the purity of the diction, and the harmony of the numbers, than by any power of invention, or vigour of sentiment. They are not all of equal value ; the elegies excel the odes ; and some of the exercises on Gunpowder Treason might have been spared.

The English poems, though they make no promises of *Paradise Lost,* have this evidence of genius, that they have 20 a cast original and unborrowed. But their peculiarity is not excellence : if they differ from verses of others, they differ for the worse ; for they are too often distinguished by repulsive harshness ; the combinations of words are

new, but they are not pleasing; the rhymes and epithets
seem to be laboriously sought, and violently applied.

That in the early parts of his life he wrote with much
care appears from his manuscripts, happily preserved at
Cambridge, in which many of his smaller works are found
as they were first written, with the subsequent corrections.
Such relics show how excellence is required ; what we hope
ever to do with ease, we may learn first to do with diligence.

Those who admire the beauties of this great poet, some-
10 times force their own judgment into false approbation of
his little pieces, and prevail upon themselves to think that
admirable which is only singular.   All that short compositions can commonly attain is neatness and elegance.
Milton never learned the art of doing little things with
grace ; he overlooked the milder excellence of suavity and
softness ; he was a *Lion* that had no skill *in dandling the Kid.*

One of the poems on which much praise has been
bestowed is *Lycidas*; of which the diction is harsh, the
rhymes uncertain, and the numbers unpleasing.   What
20 beauty there is, we must therefore seek in the sentiments
and images.   It is not to be considered as the effusion of
real passion ; for passion runs not after remote allusions
and obscure opinions.   Passion plucks no berries from
the myrtle and ivy, nor calls upon Arethuse and Mincius,
nor tells of rough *satyrs* and *fauns with cloven heel.*   Where
there is leisure for fiction, there is little grief.

In this poem there is no nature, for there is no truth;
there is no art, for there is nothing new.   Its form is that
of a pastoral, easy, vulgar, and therefore disgusting : what-
30 ever images it can supply, are long ago exhausted ; and its
inherent improbability always forces dissatisfaction on the
mind.   When Cowley tells of Hervey that they studied
together, it is easy to suppose how much he must miss the
companion of his labours, and the partner of his discoveries;
but what image of tenderness can be excited by these lines !

We drove a field, and both together heard
What time the grey fly winds her sultry horn.
Battening our flocks with the fresh dews of night.

We know that they never drove a field, and that they had
no flocks to batten; and though it be allowed that the
representation may be allegorical, the true meaning is so
uncertain and remote, that it is never sought because it
cannot be known when it is found.

Among the flocks, and copses, and flowers, appear the
heathen deities ; Jove and Phoebus, Neptune and Aeolus, 10
with a long train of mythological imagery, such as a College
easily supplies. Nothing can less display knowledge, or
less exercise invention, than to tell how a shepherd has
lost his companion, and must now feed his flocks alone,
without any judge of his skill in piping ; and how one god
asks another god what is become of Lycidas, and how neither
god can tell. He who thus grieves will excite no sympathy;
he who thus praises will confer no honour.

This poem has yet a grosser fault. With these trifling
fictions are mingled the most awful and sacred truths, 20
such as ought never to be polluted with such irreverent
combinations. The shepherd likewise is now a feeder of
sheep, and afterwards an ecclesiastical pastor, a superin-
tendent of a Christian flock. Such equivocations are
always unskilful ; but here they are indecent, and at least
approach to impiety, of which, however, I believe the
writer not to have been conscious.

Such is the power of reputation justly acquired, that its
blaze drives away the eye from nice examination. Surely
no man could have fancied that he read *Lycidas* with 30
pleasure, had he not known its author.

Of the two pieces, *L'Allegro* and *Il Penseroso*, I believe
opinion is uniform ; every man that reads them, reads
them with pleasure. The author's design is not, what
Theobald has remarked, merely to show how objects

derive their colours from the mind, by representing the operation of the same things upon the gay and the melancholy temper, or upon the same man as he is differently disposed ; but rather how, among the successive variety of appearances, every disposition of mind takes hold on those by which it may be gratified.

The *cheerful* man hears the lark in the morning; the *pensive* man hears the nightingale in the evening. The *cheerful* man sees the cock strut, and hears the horn and 10 hounds echo in the wood ; then walks, *not unseen*, to observe the glory of the rising sun, or listen to the singing milkmaid, and view the labours of the ploughman and the mower ; then casts his eyes about him over scenes of smiling plenty, and looks up to the distant tower, the residence of some fair inhabitant ; thus he pursues rural gaiety through a day of labour or of play, and delights himself at night with the fanciful narratives of superstitious ignorance.

The *pensive* man, at one time, walks *unseen* to muse at midnight; and at another hears the sullen curfew. If the 20 weather drives him home, he sits in a room lighted only by *glowing embers*; or by a lonely lamp outwatches the North Star, to discover the habitation of separate souls, and varies the shades of meditation, by contemplating the magnificent or pathetic scenes of tragic and epic poetry. When the morning comes, a morning gloomy with rain and wind, he walks into the dark trackless woods, falls asleep by some murmuring water, and with melancholy enthusiasm expects some dream of prognostication, or some music played by aërial performers.

30 Both Mirth and Melancholy are solitary, silent inhabitants of the breast that neither receive nor transmit communication ; no mention is therefore made of a philosophical friend, or a pleasant companion. The seriousness does not arise from any participation of calamity, nor the gaiety from the pleasures of the bottle.

The man of *cheerfulness,* having exhausted the country, tries what *towered cities* will afford, and mingles with scenes of splendour, gay assemblies, and nuptial festivities; but he mingles a mere spectator, as, when the learned comedies of Jonson, or the wild dramas of Shakspeare, are exhibited, he attends the theatre.

The *pensive* man never loses himself in crowds, but walks the cloister, or frequents the cathedral. Milton probably had not yet forsaken the Church.

Both his characters delight in music; but he seems to 10 think that cheerful notes would have obtained from Pluto a complete dismission of Eurydice, of whom solemn sounds only procured a conditional release.

For the old age of Cheerfulness he makes no provision; but Melancholy he conducts with great dignity to the close of life. His Cheerfulness is without levity, and his Pensiveness without asperity.

Through these two poems the images are properly selected, and nicely distinguished; but the colours of the diction seem not sufficiently discriminated. I know not 20 whether the characters are kept sufficiently apart. No mirth can, indeed, be found in his melancholy; but I am afraid that I always meet some melancholy in his mirth. They are two noble efforts of imagination.

The greatest of his juvenile performances is the *Mask of Comus;* in which may very plainly be discovered the dawn or twilight of *Paradise Lost.* Milton appears to have formed very early that system of diction, and mode of verse, which his maturer judgment approved, and from which he never endeavoured nor desired to deviate. 30

Nor does *Comus* afford only a specimen of his language; it exhibits likewise his power of description and his vigour of sentiment, employed in the praise and defence of virtue. A work more truly poetical is rarely found; allusions, images, and descriptive epithets, embellish almost every

period with lavish decoration. As a series of lines, therefore, it may be considered as worthy of all the admiration
with which the votaries have received it.

As a drama it is deficient. The action is not probable.
A Masque, in those parts where supernatural intervention
is admitted, must indeed be given up to all the freaks of
imagination; but so far as the action is merely human, it
ought to be reasonable, which can hardly be said of the
conduct of the two brothers; who, when their sister sinks
10 with fatigue in a pathless wilderness, wander both away
together in search of berries too far to find their way back,
and leave a helpless Lady to all the sadness and danger
of solitude. This however is a defect overbalanced by its
convenience.

What deserves more reprehension is, that the prologue
spoken in the wild wood by the attendant Spirit is
addressed to the audience; a mode of communication so
contrary to the nature of dramatic representation, that no
precedents can support it.

20 The discourse of the Spirit is too long; an objection
that may be made to almost all the following speeches:
they have not the sprightliness of a dialogue animated
by reciprocal contention, but seem rather declamations
deliberately composed, and formally repeated, on a moral
question. The auditor therefore listens as to a lecture,
without passion, without anxiety.

The song of Comus has airiness and jollity; but, what
may recommend Milton's morals as well as his poetry, the
invitations to pleasure are so general, that they excite no
30 distinct images of corrupt enjoyment, and take no dangerous
hold on the fancy.

The following soliloquies of Comus and the Lady are
elegant, but tedious. The song must owe much to the
voice, if it ever can delight. At last the Brothers enter,
with too much tranquillity; and when they have feared lest

their sister should be in danger, and hoped that she is not in danger, the Elder makes a speech in praise of chastity, and the Younger finds how fine it is to be a philosopher.

Then descends the Spirit in form of a shepherd; and the Brother, instead of being in haste to ask his help, praises his singing, and inquires his business in that place. It is remarkable, that at this interview the Brother is taken with a short fit of rhyming. The Spirit relates that the Lady is in the power of Comus; the Brother moralizes again; and the Spirit makes a long narration, of no use 10 because it is false, and therefore unsuitable to a good Being.

In all these parts the language is poetical, and the sentiments are generous; but there is something wanting to allure attention.

The dispute between the Lady and Comus is the most animated and affecting scene of the drama, and wants nothing but a brisker reciprocation of objections and replies, to invite attention, and detain it.

The songs are vigorous, and full of imagery; but they 20 are harsh in their diction, and not very musical in their numbers.

Throughout the whole, the figures are too bold, and the language too luxuriant for dialogue. It is a drama in the epic style, inelegantly splendid, and tediously instructive.

The *Sonnets* were written in different parts of Milton's life, upon different occasions. They deserve not any particular criticism; for of the best it can only be said, that they are not bad; and perhaps only the eighth and twenty-first are truly entitled to this slender commendation. 30 The fabric of a sonnet, however adapted to the Italian language, has never succeeded in ours, which, having greater variety of termination, requires the rhymes to be often changed.

Those little pieces may be dispatched without much

anxiety; a greater work calls for greater care.   I am now
to examine *Paradise Lost*; a poem which, considered with
respect to design, may claim the first place, and with
respect to performance the second, among the productions
of the human mind.

By the general consent of critics, the first praise of genius
is due to the writer of an epic poem, as it requires an
assemblage of all the powers which are singly sufficient
for other compositions.   Poetry is the art of uniting
10 pleasure with truth, by calling imagination to the help of
reason.   Epic poetry undertakes to teach the most important truths by the most pleasing precepts, and therefore
relates some great event in the most affecting manner.
History must supply the writer with the rudiments of
narration, which he must improve and exalt by a nobler
art, must animate by dramatic energy, and diversify by
retrospection and anticipation; morality must teach him
the exact bounds, and different shades, of vice and virtue;
from policy, and the practice of life, he has to learn the
20 discriminations of character, and the tendency of the
passions, either single or combined; and physiology must
supply him with illustrations and images.   To put these
materials to poetical use, is required an imagination capable
of painting nature, and realizing fiction.   Nor is he yet
a poet till he has attained the whole extension of his
language, distinguished all the delicacies of phrase, and
all the colours of words, and learned to adjust their
different sounds to all the varieties of metrical modera-
tion.

30   Bossu is of opinion that the poet's first work is to find
a *moral*, which his fable is afterwards to illustrate and
establish.   This seems to have been the process only of
Milton; the moral of other poems is incidental and con-
sequent; in Milton's only it is essential and intrinsic.
His purpose was the most useful and the most arduous:
to vindicate the ways of God to man; to show the reasonable-

ness of religion, and the necessity of obedience to the Divine Law.

To convey this moral, there must be a *fable*, a narration artfully constructed, so as to excite curiosity, and surprise expectation. In this part of his work, Milton must be confessed to have equalled every other poet. He has involved in his account of the Fall of Man the events which preceded, and those that were to follow it: he has interwoven the whole system of theology with such propriety, that every part appears to be necessary; and 10 scarcely any recital is wished shorter for the sake of quickening the progress of the main action.

The subject of an epic poem is naturally an event of great importance. That of Milton is not the destruction of a city, the conduct of a colony, or the foundation of an empire. His subject is the fate of worlds, the revolutions of heaven and of earth; rebellion against the Supreme King, raised by the highest order of created beings; the overthrow of their host, and the punishment of their crime; the creation of a new race of reasonable creatures; their 20 original happiness and innocence, their forfeiture of immortality, and their restoration to hope and peace.

Great events can be hastened or retarded only by persons of elevated dignity. Before the greatness displayed in Milton's poem, all other greatness shrinks away. The weakest of his agents are the highest and noblest of human beings, the original parents of mankind; with whose actions the elements consented; on whose rectitude, or deviation of will, depended the state of terrestrial nature, and the condition of all the future inhabitants of the globe. 30

Of the other agents in the poem, the chief are such as it is irreverence to name on slight occasions. The rest were lower powers;

> — of which the least could wield
> Those elements, and arm him with the force
> Of all their regions;

powers, which only the control ot Omnipotence restrains from laying creation waste, and filling the vast expanse of space with ruin and confusion. To display the motives and actions of beings thus superior, so far as human reason can examine them, or human imagination represent them, is the task which this mighty poet has undertaken and performed.

In the examination of epic poems much speculation is commonly employed upon the *characters*. The characters in the *Paradise Lost*, which admit of examination, are those of angels and of man ; of angels good and evil ; of man in his innocent and sinful state.

Among the angels, the virtue of Raphael is mild and placid, of easy condescension and free communication ; that of Michael is regal and lofty, and, as may seem, attentive to the dignity of his own nature. Abdiel and Gabriel appear occasionally, and act as every incident requires ; the solitary fidelity of Abdiel is very amiably painted.

Of the evil angels the characters are more diversified. To Satan, as Addison observes, such sentiments are given as suit *the most exalted and most depraved being*. Milton has been censured, by Clarke,[1] for the impiety which some-times breaks from Satan's mouth. For there are thoughts, as he justly remarks, which no observation of character can justify, because no good man would willingly permit them to pass, however transiently, through his own mind. To make Satan speak as a rebel, without any such expressions as might taint the reader's imagination, was indeed one of the great difficulties in Milton's undertaking, and I cannot but think that he has extricated himself with great happiness. There is in Satan's speeches little that can give pain to a pious ear. The language of rebellion

---

[1] Essay on Study.

cannot be the same with that of obedience. The malignity of Satan foams in haughtiness and obstinacy; but his expressions are commonly general, and no otherwise offensive than as they are wicked.

The other chiefs of the celestial rebellion are very judiciously discriminated in the first and second books; and the ferocious character of Moloch appears, both in the battle and the council, with exact consistency.

To Adam and to Eve are given, during their innocence, such sentiments as innocence can generate and utter. 10 Their love is pure benevolence and mutual veneration; their repasts are without luxury, and their diligence without toil. Their addresses to their Maker have little more than the voice of admiration and gratitude. Fruition left them nothing to ask, and Innocence left them nothing to fear.

But with guilt enter distrust and discord, mutual accusation, and stubborn self-defence; they regard each other with alienated minds, and dread their Creator as the avenger of their transgression. At last they seek shelter in his mercy, soften to repentance, and melt in supplication. 20 Both before and after the Fall, the superiority of Adam is diligently sustained.

Of the *probable* and the *marvellous*, two parts of a vulgar epic poem, which immerge the critic in deep consideration, the *Paradise Lost* requires little to be said. It contains the history of a miracle, of Creation and Redemption; it displays the power and the mercy of the Supreme Being; the probable therefore is marvellous, and the marvellous is probable. The substance of the narrative is truth; and, as truth allows no choice, it is, like necessity, superior to 30 rule. To the accidental or adventitious parts, as to everything human, some slight exceptions may be made. But the main fabric is immovably supported.

It is justly remarked by Addison, that this poem has, by the nature of its subject, the advantage above all others, that it is universally and perpetually interesting. All mankind will, through all ages, bear the same relation to Adam and to Eve, and must partake of that good and evil which extend to themselves.

Of the *machinery*, so called from Θεὸς ἀπὸ μηχανῆς, by which is meant the occasional interposition of supernatural power, another fertile topic of critical remarks, here is no room to speak, because everything is done under the immediate and visible direction of Heaven ; but the rule is
10 so far observed, that no part of the action could have been accomplished by any other means.

Of *episodes*, I think there are only two, contained in Raphael's relation of the war in Heaven, and Michael's prophetic account of the changes to happen in this world. Both are closely connected with the great action ; one was necessary to Adam as a warning, the other as a consolation.

To the completeness or *integrity* of the design nothing can be objected ; it has distinctly and clearly what Aristotle requires, a beginning, a middle, and an end. There is
20 perhaps no poem, of the same length, from which so little can be taken without apparent mutilation. Here are no funeral games, nor is there any long description of a shield. The short digressions at the beginning of the third, seventh, and ninth books, might doubtless be spared ; but super-fluities so beautiful, who would take away ? or who does not wish that the author of the *Iliad* had gratified succeeding ages with a little knowledge of himself ? Perhaps no pas-sages are more frequently or more attentively read than those extrinsic paragraphs ; and, since the end of poetry
30 is pleasure, that cannot be unpoetical with which all are pleased.

The questions, whether the action of the poem be strictly *one*, whether the poem can be properly termed *heroic*, and who is the hero, are raised by such readers as draw their principles of judgement rather from books than from reason.

Milton, though he entitled *Paradise Lost* only a *poem*, yet calls it himself *heroic song*. Dryden, petulantly and indecently, denies the heroism of Adam, because he was overcome; but there is no reason why the hero should not be unfortunate, except established practice, since success and virtue do not go necessarily together. Cato is the hero of Lucan; but Lucan's authority will not be suffered by Quintilian to decide. However, if success be necessary, Adam's deceiver was at last crushed; Adam was restored to his Maker's favour, and therefore may 10 securely resume his human rank.

After the scheme and fabric of the poem, must be considered its component parts, the sentiments and the diction.

The *sentiments*, as expressive of manners, or appropriated to characters, are, for the greater part, unexceptionably just.

Splendid passages, containing lessons of morality, or precepts of prudence, occur seldom. Such is the original formation of this poem, that as it admits no human manners 20 till the Fall, it can give little assistance to human conduct. Its end is to raise the thoughts above sublunary cares or pleasures. Yet the praise of that fortitude, with which Abdiel maintained his singularity of virtue against the scorn of multitudes, may be accommodated to all times; and Raphael's reproof of Adam's curiosity after the planetary motions, with the answer returned by Adam, may be confidently opposed to any rule of life which any poet has delivered.

The thoughts which are occasionally called forth in the 30 progress, are such as could only be produced by an imagination in the highest degree fervid and active, to which materials were supplied by incessant study and unlimited curiosity. The heat of Milton's mind might be said to sublimate his learning, to throw off into his work the spirit of science, unmingled with its grosser parts.

He had considered creation in its whole extent, and his descriptions are therefore learned. He had accustomed his imagination to unrestrained indulgence, and his conceptions therefore were extensive. The characteristic quality of his poem is sublimity. He sometimes descends to the elegant, but his element is the great. He can occasionally invest himself with grace ; but his natural port is gigantic loftiness.[1] He can please when pleasure is required ; but it is his peculiar power to astonish.

10 He seems to have been well acquainted with his own genius, and to know what it was that Nature had bestowed upon him more bountifully than upon others ; the power of displaying the vast, illuminating the splendid, enforcing the awful, darkening the gloomy, and aggravating the dreadful : he therefore chose a subject on which too much could not be said, on which he might tire his fancy without the censure of extravagance.

The appearances of nature, and the occurrences of life, did not satiate his appetite of greatness. To paint things 20 as they are, requires a minute attention, and employs the memory rather than the fancy. Milton's delight was to sport in the wide regions of possibility ; reality was a scene too narrow for his mind. He sent his faculties out upon discovery, into worlds where only imagination can travel, and delighted to form new modes of existence, and furnish sentiment and action to superior beings, to trace the counsels of hell, or accompany the choirs of heaven.

But he could not be always in other worlds : he must sometimes revisit earth, and tell of things visible and 30 known. When he cannot raise wonder by the sublimity of his mind, he gives delight by its fertility.

Whatever be his subject, he never fails to fill the imagination. But his images and descriptions of the scenes or

---

[1] Algarotti terms it *gigantesca sublimità Miltoniana.*

operations of Nature do not seem to be always copied
from original form, nor to have the freshness, raciness,
and energy of immediate observation. He saw Nature, as
Dryden expresses it, *through the spectacles of books*; and
on most occasions calls learning to his assistance. The
garden of Eden brings to his mind the vale of *Enna*,
where Proserpine was gathering flowers. Satan makes
his way through fighting elements, like *Argo* between the
Cyanean rocks, or *Ulysses* between the two *Sicilian* whirl-
pools, when he shunned *Charybdis* on the *larboard*. The 10
mythological allusions have been justly censured, as not
being always used with notice of their vanity; but they
contribute variety to the narration, and produce an alternate
exercise of the memory and the fancy.

His similes are less numerous, and more various, than
those of his predecessors. But he does not confine himself
within the limits of rigorous comparison : his great excellence is amplitude, and he expands the adventitious image
beyond the dimensions which the occasion required.
Thus, comparing the shield of Satan to the orb of the 20
Moon, he crowds the imagination with the discovery of
the telescope, and all the wonders which the telescope
discovers.

Of his moral sentiments it is hardly praise to affirm that
they excel those of all other poets ; for this superiority he
was indebted to his acquaintance with the sacred writings.
The ancient epic poets, wanting the light of Revelation,
were very unskilful teachers of virtue : their principal
characters may be great, but they are not amiable. The
reader may rise from their works with a greater degree of 30
active or passive fortitude, and sometimes of prudence ;
but he will be able to carry away few precepts of justice,
and none of mercy.

From the Italian writers it appears, that the advantages
of even Christian knowledge may be possessed in vain.

Ariosto's pravity is generally known; and though the *Deliverance of Jerusalem* may be considered as a sacred subject, the poet has been very sparing of moral instruction.

In Milton every line breathes sanctity of thought, and purity of manners, except when the train of the narration requires the introduction of the rebellious spirits; and even they are compelled to acknowledge their subjection to God, in such a manner as excites reverence, and confirms piety.

Of human beings there are but two; but those two are the parents of mankind, venerable before their fall for dignity and innocence, and amiable after it for repentance and submission. In their first state their affection is tender without weakness, and their piety sublime without presumption. When they have sinned, they show how discord begins in mutual frailty, and how it ought to cease in mutual forbearance; how confidence of the divine favour is forfeited by sin, and how hope of pardon may be obtained by penitence and prayer. A state of innocence we can only conceive, if indeed, in our present misery, it be possible to conceive it; but the sentiments and worship proper to a fallen and offending being, we have all to learn, as we have all to practise.

The poet, whatever be done, is always great. Our progenitors, in their first state, conversed with angels; even when folly and sin had degraded them, they had not in their humiliation *the port of mean suitors*; and they rise again to reverential regard, when we find that their prayers were heard.

As human passions did not enter the world before the Fall, there is in the *Paradise Lost* little opportunity for the pathetic; but what little there is has not been lost. That passion, which is peculiar to rational nature, the anguish arising from the consciousness of transgression, and the horrors attending the sense of the Divine Displeasure, are very justly described and forcibly impressed. But the passions are moved only on one occasion; sublimity is the general and prevailing quality in this poem; sublimity variously modified—sometimes descriptive, sometimes argumentative.

The defects and faults of *Paradise Lost*, for faults and defects every work of man must have, it is the business of impartial criticism to discover. As, in displaying the excellence of Milton, I have not made long quotations, because of selecting beauties there had been no end, I shall in the same general manner mention that which seems to deserve censure; for what Englishman can take delight in transcribing passages, which, if they lessen the reputation of Milton, diminish in some degree the honour of our country?

The generality of my scheme does not admit the frequent notice of verbal inaccuracies; which Bentley, perhaps better skilled in grammar than in poetry, has often found, though he sometimes made them, and which he imputed to the obtrusions of a reviser whom the author's blindness obliged him to employ. A supposition rash and groundless, if he thought it true; and vile and pernicious, if, as is said, he in private allowed it to be false.

The plan of *Paradise Lost* has this inconvenience, that it comprises neither human actions nor human manners. The man and woman who act and suffer, are in a state which no other man or woman can ever know. The reader finds no transaction in which he can be engaged; beholds no condition in which he can by any effort of imagination place himself; he has, therefore, little natural curiosity or sympathy.

We all, indeed, feel the effects of Adam's disobedience; we all sin like Adam, and like him must all bewail our offences; we have restless and insidious enemies in the fallen angels, and in the blessed spirits we have guardians and friends; in the Redemption of mankind we hope to be included : in the description of heaven and hell we are surely interested, as we are all to reside hereafter either in the regions of horror or bliss.

But these truths are too important to be new; they have been taught to our infancy ; they have mingled with our solitary thoughts and familiar conversations, and are habitually interwoven with the whole texture of life. Being therefore not new, they raise no unaccustomed emotion in the mind ; what we knew before, we cannot learn ; what is not unexpected, cannot surprise.

Of the ideas suggested by these awful scenes, from some we recede with reverence, except when stated hours require their association ; and from others we shrink with horror, or admit them only as salutary inflictions, as counterpoises to our interests and passions. Such images rather obstruct the career of fancy than incite it.

Pleasure and terror are indeed the genuine sources of poetry; but poetical pleasure must be such as human imagination can at least conceive, and poetical terror such as human strength and fortitude may combat. The good and evil of Eternity are too ponderous for the wings of wit ; the mind sinks under them in passive helplessness, content with calm belief and humble adoration.

Known truths, however, may take a different appearance, and be conveyed to the mind by a new train of intermediate images. This Milton has undertaken, and performed with pregnancy and vigour of mind peculiar to himself. Whoever considers the few radical positions which the Scriptures afforded him, will wonder by what energetic operation he expanded them to such extent, and ramified them to so much variety, restrained as he was by religious reverence from licentiousness of fiction.

Here is a full display of the united force of study and

genius; of a great accumulation of materials, with judgement to digest, and fancy to combine them : Milton was able to select from nature, or from story, from an ancient fable, or from modern science, whatever could illustrate or adorn his thoughts. An accumulation of knowledge impregnated his mind, fermented by study, and exalted by imagination.

It has been therefore said, without an indecent hyper-bole, by one of his encomiasts, that in reading *Paradise Lost* we read a book of universal knowledge.

But original deficiency cannot be supplied. The want of human interest is always felt. *Paradise Lost* is one of the books which the reader admires and lays down, and forgets to take up again. None ever wished it longer than it is. Its perusal is a duty rather than a pleasure. We read Milton for instruction, retire harassed and over-burdened, and look elsewhere for recreation; we desert our master, and seek for companions.

Another inconvenience of Milton's design is, that it requires the description of what cannot be described, the agency of spirits. He saw that immateriality supplied no images, and that he could not show angels acting but by instruments of action; he therefore invested them with form and matter. This, being necessary, was therefore defensible; and he should have secured the consistency of his system, by keeping immateriality out of sight, and enticing his reader to drop it from his thoughts. But he has unhappily perplexed his poetry with his philosophy. His infernal and celestial powers are sometimes pure spirit, and sometimes animated body. When Satan walks with his lance upon the *burning marl*, he has a body; when, in his passage between hell and the new world, he is in danger of sinking in the vacuity, and is supported by a gust of rising vapours, he has a body; when he animates the toad, he seems to be mere spirit, that can penetrate matter at pleasure; when he *starts up in his own shape*, he

has at least a determined form; and when he is brought
before Gabriel, he has *a spear and a shield*, which he had
the power of hiding in the toad, though the arms of the
contending angels are evidently material.

The vulgar inhabitants of Pandaemonium, being *incorporeal spirits*, are *at large, though without number*, in a
limited space; yet in the battle, when they were overwhelmed by mountains, their armour hurt them, *crushed
in upon their substance, now grown gross by sinning*. This
10 likewise happened to the uncorrupted angels, who were
overthrown *the sooner for their arms, for unarmed they
might easily as spirits have evaded by contraction or remove*.
Even as spirits they are hardly spiritual; for *contraction*
and *remove* are images of matter; but if they could have
escaped without their armour, they might have escaped
from it, and left only the empty cover to be battered.
Uriel, when he rides on a sunbeam, is material; Satan is
material when he is afraid of the prowess of Adam.

The confusion of spirit and matter which pervades the
20 whole narration of the war of heaven fills it with incongruity; and the book, in which it is related, is, I believe,
the favourite of children, and gradually neglected as
knowledge is increased.

After the operation of immaterial agents, which cannot
be explained, may be considered that of allegorical persons,
which have no real existence. To exalt causes into agents,
to invest abstract ideas with form, and animate them with
activity, has always been the right of poetry. But such
airy beings are, for the most part, suffered only to do their
30 natural office, and retire. Thus Fame tells a tale, and
Victory hovers over a general, or perches on a standard;
but Fame and Victory can do no more. To give them
any real employment, or ascribe to them any material
agency, is to make them allegorical no longer, but to shock
the mind by ascribing effects to non-entity. In the *Pro*

metheus of Aeschylus, we see *Violence* and *Strength*, and in the *Alcestis* of Euripides, we see Death, brought upon the stage, all as active persons of the drama ; but no precedents can justify absurdity.

Milton's allegory of Sin and Death is undoubtedly faulty. Sin is indeed the mother of *Death*, and may be allowed to be the portress of hell ; but when they stop the journey of Satan, a journey described as real, and when Death offers him battle, the allegory is broken. That Sin and Death should have shown the way to hell, might have been 10 allowed ; but they cannot facilitate the passage by building a bridge, because the difficulty of Satan's passage is described as real and sensible, and the bridge ought to be only figurative. The hell assigned to the rebellious spirits is described as not less local than the residence of man. It is placed in some distant part of space, separated from the regions of harmony and order by a chaotic waste and an unoccupied vacuity ; but *Sin* and *Death* worked up a *mole* of *aggregated soil*, cemented with *asphaltus* ; a work too bulky for ideal architects. 20

This unskilful allegory appears to me one of the greatest faults of the poem ; and to this there was no temptation, but the author's opinion of its beauty.

To the conduct of the narrative some objections may be made. Satan is with great expectation brought before Gabriel in Paradise, and is suffered to go away unmolested. The creation of man is represented as the consequence of the vacuity left in heaven by the expulsion of the rebels ; yet Satan mentions it as a report *rife in Heaven* before his departure. 30

To find sentiments for the state of innocence, was very difficult ; and something of anticipation perhaps is now and then discovered. Adam's discourse of dreams seems not to be the speculation of a new-created being. I know not whether his answer to the angel's reproof for curiosity does not want something of propriety : it is the speech of a man acquainted with many other men. Some philosophical notions, especially when the philosophy is false, might have been better omitted. The angel, in a comparison, speaks of *timorous deer*, before deer were yet timorous, and before Adam could understand the comparison.

Dryden remarks, that Milton has some flats among his elevations. This is only to say, that all the parts are not 10 equal. In every work, one part must be for the sake of others ; a palace must have passages ; a poem must have transitions. It is no more to be required that wit should always be blazing, than that the sun should always stand at noon. In a great work there is a vicissitude of luminous and opaque parts, as there is in the world a succession of day and night. Milton, when he has expatiated in the sky, may be allowed sometimes to revisit earth ; for what other author ever soared so high, or sustained his flight so long ?

20 Milton, being well versed in the Italian poets, appears to have borrowed often from them ; and, as every man catches something from his companions, his desire of imitating Ariosto's levity has disgraced his work with the *Paradise of Fools* ; a fiction not in itself ill-imagined, but too ludicrous for its place.

His play on words, in which he delights too often ; his equivocations, which Bentley endeavours to defend by the example of the ancients ; his unnecessary and ungraceful use of terms of art ; it is not necessary to mention, because 30 they are easily remarked, and generally censured, and at last bear so little proportion to the whole, that they scarcely deserve the attention of a critic.

Such are the faults of that wonderful performance *Paradise Lost* ; which he who can put in balance with its beauties must be considered not as nice but as dull, as less to be censured for want of candour, than pitied for want of sensibility.

Of *Paradise Regained*, the general judgement seems now to be right, that it is in many parts elegant, and everywhere instructive. It was not to be supposed that the writer of *Paradise Lost* could ever write without great effusions of fancy, and exalted precepts of wisdom. The basis of *Paradise Regained* is narrow; a dialogue without action can never please like a union of the narrative and dramatic powers. Had this poem been written not by Milton, but 10 by some imitator, it would have claimed and received universal praise.

If *Paradise Regained* has been too much depreciated, *Samson Agonistes* has in requital been too much admired. It could only be by long prejudice, and the bigotry of learning, that Milton could prefer the ancient tragedies, with their encumbrance of a chorus, to the exhibitions of the French and English stages; and it is only by a blind confidence in the reputation of Milton, that a drama can be praised in which the intermediate parts have neither cause 20 nor consequence, neither hasten nor retard the catastrophe.

In this tragedy are however many particular beauties, many just sentiments and striking lines; but it wants the power of attracting the attention which a well-connected plan produces.

Milton would not have excelled in dramatic writing; he knew human nature only in the gross, and had never studied the shades of character, nor the combinations of concurring, or the perplexity of contending passions. He had read much, and knew what books could teach; but 30 had mingled little in the world, and was deficient in the knowledge which experience must confer.

Through all his greater works there prevails an uniform peculiarity of *Diction*, a mode and cast of expression which bears little resemblance to that of any former writer, and which is so far removed from common use, that an unlearned reader, when he first opens his book, finds himself surprised by a new language.

This novelty has been, by those who can find nothing wrong in Milton, imputed to his laborious endeavours after words suitable to the grandeur of his ideas. *Our language,* says Addison, *sunk under him.* But the truth is, that, both in prose and verse, he had formed his style by a perverse and pedantic principle. He was desirous to use English
10 words with a foreign idiom. This in all his prose is discovered and condemned; for there judgment operates freely, neither softened by the beauty, nor awed by the dignity of his thoughts; but such is the power of his poetry, that his call is obeyed without resistance, the reader feels himself in captivity to a higher and a nobler mind, and criticism sinks in admiration.

Milton's style was not modified by his subject: what is shown with greater extent in *Paradise Lost* may be found in *Comus.* One source of his peculiarity was his familiarity
20 with the Tuscan poets: the disposition of his words is, I think, frequently Italian; perhaps sometimes combined with other tongues. Of him, at last, may be said what Jonson says of Spenser, that *he wrote no language,* but has formed what *Butler* calls a *Babylonish Dialect,* in itself harsh and barbarous, but made by exalted genius, and extensive learning, the vehicle of so much instruction and so much pleasure, that, like other lovers, we find grace in its deformity.

Whatever be the faults of his diction, he cannot want the
30 praise of copiousness and variety: he was master of his language in its full extent; and has selected the melodious words with such diligence, that from his book alone the Art of English Poetry might be learned.

After his diction, something must be said of his *versification.* *The measure,* he says, *is the English heroic verse without rhyme.* Of this mode he had many examples among the Italians, and some in his own country. The Earl of Surrey is said to have translated one of Virgil's books without rhyme; and, beside our tragedies, a few short poems had appeared in blank verse; particularly one tending to reconcile the nation to Raleigh's wild attempt upon Guiana, and probably written by Raleigh himself. These petty performances cannot be supposed to have much influenced Milton, who more probably took his hint from Trisino's *Italia Liberata*; and, finding blank verse 10 easier than rhyme, was desirous of persuading himself that it is better.

Rhyme, he says, and says truly, *is no necessary adjunct of true poetry.* But perhaps, of poetry as a mental operation, metre or music is no necessary adjunct : it is however by the music of metre that poetry has been discriminated in all languages; and in languages melodiously constructed with a due proportion of long and short syllables, metre is sufficient. But one language cannot communicate its rules to another; where metre is scanty and imperfect, some help 20 is necessary. The music of the English heroic line strikes the ear so faintly that it is easily lost, unless all the syllables of every line co-operate together : this co-operation can be only obtained by the preservation of every verse unmingled with another, as a distinct system of sounds; and this distinctness is obtained and preserved by the artifice of rhyme. The variety of pauses, so much boasted by the lovers of blank verse, changes the measures of an English poet to the periods of a declaimer; and there are only a few skilful and happy readers of Milton, who enable their audience 30 to perceive where the lines end or begin. *Blank verse,* said an ingenious critic, *seems to be verse only to the eye.*

Poetry may subsist without rhyme, but English poetry will not often please; nor can rhyme ever be safely spared but where the subject is able to support itself. Blank verse makes some approach to that which is called the *lapidary style*; has neither the easiness of prose, nor the melody of numbers, and therefore tires by long continuance. Of the Italian writers without rhyme, whom Milton alleges as precedents, not one is popular; what reason could urge in its defence, has been confuted by the ear.

But, whatever be the advantage of rhyme, I cannot prevail on myself to wish that Milton had been a rhymer; for I cannot wish his work to be other than it is; yet, like 10 other heroes, he is to be admired rather than imitated. He that thinks himself capable of astonishing, may write blank verse; but those that hope only to please, must condescend to rhyme.

The highest praise of genius is original invention. Milton cannot be said to have contrived the structure of an epic poem, and therefore owes reverence to that vigour and amplitude of mind to which all generations must be indebted for the art of poetical narration, for the texture of the fable, the variation of incidents, the interposition of dialogue, 20 and all the stratagems that surprise and enchain attention. But, of all the borrowers from Homer, Milton is perhaps the least indebted. He was naturally a thinker for himself, confident of his own abilities, and disdainful of help or hindrance : he did not refuse admission to the thoughts or images of his predecessors, but he did not seek them. From his contemporaries he neither courted nor received support; there is in his writings nothing by which the pride of other authors might be gratified, or favour gained; no exchange of praise, nor solicitation of support. His 30 great works were performed under discountenance, and in blindness, but difficulties vanished at his touch; he was born for whatever is arduous; and his work is not the greatest of heroic poems, only because it is not the first.

II

From HAZLITT'S LECTURE on SHAKSPEARE
AND MILTON

First published 1818 ; the extract follows the

Second Edition, 1819

SHAKSPEARE discovers in his writings little religious enthusiasm, and an indifference to personal reputation ; he had none of the bigotry of his age, and his political prejudices were not very strong. In these respects, as well as in every other, he formed a direct contrast to Milton. Milton's works are a perpetual invocation to the Muses; a hymn to Fame. He had his thoughts constantly fixed on the contemplation of the Hebrew theocracy, and of a perfect commonwealth ; and he seized the pen with a hand just warm from the touch of the ark of faith. His religious zeal infused its character into his imagination ; so that he devotes himself with the same sense of duty to the cultivation of his genius, as he did to the exercise of virtue, or the good of his country. The spirit of the poet, the patriot, and the prophet, vied with each other in his breast. His mind appears to have held equal communion with the inspired writers, and with the bards and sages of ancient Greece and Rome ;—

> ' Blind Thamyris, and blind Mæonides,
> And Tiresias, and Phineus, prophets old.'

He had a high standard, with which he was always comparing himself, nothing short of which could satisfy his jealous ambition. He thought of nobler forms and nobler things than those he found about him. He lived apart, in the solitude of his own thoughts, carefully excluding from

his mind whatever might distract its purposes or alloy its purity, or damp its zeal. 'With darkness and with dangers compassed round', he had the mighty models of antiquity always present to his thoughts, and determined to raise a monument of equal height and glory, 'piling up every stone of lustre from the brook,' for the delight and wonder of posterity. He had girded himself up, and as it were, sanctified his genius to this service from his youth. 'For after', he says, 'I had from my first years, by the ceaseless dili-
10 gence and care of my father, been exercised to the tongues, and some sciences as my age could suffer, by sundry masters and teachers, it was found that whether aught was imposed upon me by them, or betaken to of my own choice, the style by certain vital signs it had, was likely to live; but much latelier, in the private academies of Italy, perceiving that some trifles which I had in memory, composed at under twenty or thereabout, met with acceptance above what was looked for; I began thus far to assent both to them and divers of my friends here at home, and not less
20 to an inward prompting which now grew daily upon me, that by labour and intense study (which I take to be my portion in this life), joined with the strong propensity of nature, I might perhaps leave something so written to after-times as they should not willingly let it die. The accomplishment of these intentions, which have lived within me ever since I could conceive myself anything worth to my country, lies not but in a power above man's to promise; but that none hath by more studious ways endeavoured, and with more unwearied spirit that none shall, that I dare
30 almost aver of myself, as far as life and free leisure will extend. Neither do I think it shame to covenant with any knowing reader, that for some few years yet, I may go on trust with him toward the payment of what I am now indebted, as being a work not to be raised from the heat of youth or the vapours of wine; like that which flows at waste from

the pen of some vulgar amourist, or the trencher fury of
a rhyming parasite, nor to be obtained by the invocation
of Dame Memory and her Siren daughters, but by devout
prayer to that eternal spirit who can enrich with all utterance and knowledge, and sends out his Seraphim with the
hallowed fire of his altar, to touch and purify the lips of
whom he pleases: to this must be added industrious and
select reading, steady observation, and insight into all
seemly and generous arts and affairs.   Although it nothing
content me to have disclosed thus much beforehand ; but
that I trust hereby to make it manifest with what small
willingness I endure to interrupt the pursuit of no less
hopes than these, and leave a calm and pleasing solitariness,
fed with cheerful and confident thoughts, to embark in
a troubled sea of noises and hoarse disputes, from beholding the bright countenance of truth in the quiet and still air
of delightful studies.'

So that of Spenser :

'The noble heart that harbours virtuous thought,
    And is with child of glorious great intent,
Can never rest until it forth have brought
    The eternal brood of glory excellent.'

Milton, therefore, did not write from casual impulse, but
after a severe examination of his own strength, and with
a resolution to leave nothing undone which it was in his
power to do.   He always labours, and almost always
succeeds.   He strives hard to say the finest things in the
world, and he does say them.   He adorns and dignifies his
subject to the utmost : he surrounds it with every possible
association of beauty or grandeur, whether moral, intellectual, or physical.   He refines on his descriptions of beauty ;
loading sweets on sweets, till the sense aches at them ;
and raises his images of terror to a gigantic elevation, that
'makes Ossa like a wart '.   In Milton, there is always an
appearance of effort : in Shakspeare, scarcely any.

Milton has borrowed more than any other writer, and exhausted every source of imitation, sacred or profane; yet he is perfectly distinct from every other writer. He is a writer of centos, and yet in originality scarcely inferior to Homer. The power of his mind is stamped on every line. The fervour of his imagination melts down and renders malleable, as in a furnace, the most contradictory materials. In reading his works, we feel ourselves under the influence of a mighty intellect, that the nearer it approaches to others, becomes more distinct from them. The quantity of art in him shows the strength of his genius: the weight of his intellectual obligations would have oppressed any other writer. Milton's learning has the effect of intuition. He describes objects, of which he could only have read in books, with the vividness of actual observation. His imagination has the force of nature. He makes words tell as pictures.

> 'Him followed Rimmon, whose delightful seat
> Was fair Damascus, on the fertile banks
> Of Abbana and Pharphar, lucid streams.'

The word *lucid* here gives to the idea all the sparkling effect of the most perfect landscape.

And again:

> 'As when a vulture on Imaus bred,
> Whose snowy ridge the roving Tartar bounds,
> Dislodging from a region scarce of prey,
> To gorge the flesh of lambs and yeanling kids
> On hills where flocks are fed, flies towards the springs
> Of Ganges or Hydaspes, Indian streams;
> But in his way lights on the barren plains
> Of Sericana, where Chineses drive
> With sails and wind their cany waggons light.'

If Milton had taken a journey for the express purpose, he could not have described this scenery and mode of life better. Such passages are like demonstrations of natural history. Instances might be multiplied without end.

We might be tempted to suppose that the vividness
with which he describes visible objects, was owing to their
having acquired an unusual degree of strength in his mind,
after the privation of his sight ; but we find the same
palpableness and truth in the descriptions which occur in
his early poems. In Lycidas he speaks of 'the great vision
of the guarded mount', with that preternatural weight of
impression with which it would present itself suddenly to
'the pilot of some small night-foundered skiff' : and the
lines in the Penseroso, describing 'the wandering moon', 10

> ' Riding near her highest noon,
> Like one that had been led astray
> Through the heaven's wide pathless way,'

are as if he had gazed himself blind in looking at her.
There is also the same depth of impression in his descriptions of the objects of all the different senses, whether
colours, or sounds, or smells—the same absorption of his
mind in whatever engaged his attention at the time. It
has been indeed objected to Milton, by a common perversity of criticism, that his ideas were musical rather than 20
picturesque, as if because they were in the highest degree
musical, they must be (to keep the sage critical balance
even, and to allow no one man to possess two qualities at
the same time) proportionably deficient in other respects.
But Milton's poetry is not cast in any such narrow, common-
place mould ; it is not so barren of resources. His worship
of the Muse was not so simple or confined. A sound
arises 'like a steam of rich distilled perfumes' ; we hear
the pealing organ, but the incense on the altars is also
there, and the statues of the gods are ranged around ! The 30
ear indeed predominates over the eye, because it is more
immediately affected, and because the language of music
blends more immediately with, and forms a more natural
accompaniment to, the variable and indefinite associations
of ideas conveyed by words. But where the associations

of the imagination are not the principal thing, the individual
object is given by Milton with equal force and beauty.
The strongest and best proof of this, as a characteristic
power of his mind, is, that the persons of Adam and Eve,
of Satan, &c. are always accompanied, in our imagination,
with the grandeur of the naked figure ; they convey to us
the ideas of sculpture.   As an instance, take the following :

'————— He soon
Saw within ken a glorious Angel stand,
10   The same whom John saw also in the sun :
His back was turned, but not his brightness hid ;
Of beaming sunny rays a golden tiar
Circled his head, nor less his locks behind
Illustrious on his shoulders fledge with wings
Lay waving round ; on some great charge employ'd
He seem'd, or fix'd in cogitation deep.
Glad was the spirit impure, as now in hope
To find who might direct his wand'ring flight
To Paradise, the happy seat of man,
20   His journey's end, and our beginning woe.
But first he casts to change his proper shape,
Which else might work him danger or delay :
And now a stripling cherub he appears,
Not of the prime, yet such as in his face
Youth smiled celestial, and to every limb
Suitable grace diffus'd, so well he feign'd :
Under a coronet his flowing hair
In curls on either cheek play'd ; wings he wore
Of many a colour'd plume sprinkled with gold,
30   His habit fit for speed succinct, and held
Before his decent steps a silver wand.'

The figures introduced here have all the elegance and
precision of a Greek statue ; glossy and impurpled, tinged
with golden light, and musical as the strings of Memnon's
harp !

Again, nothing can be more magnificent than the por-
trait of Beelzebub :

'With Atlantean shoulders fit to bear
The weight of mightiest monarchies :'

Or the comparison of Satan, as he 'lay floating many a rood', to 'that sea beast',

> 'Leviathan, which God of all his works
> Created hugest that swim the ocean-stream!'

What a force of imagination is there in this last expression! What an idea it conveys of the size of that hugest of created beings, as if it shrunk up the ocean to a stream, and took up the sea in its nostrils as a very little thing! Force of style is one of Milton's greatest excellences. Hence, perhaps, he stimulates us more in the reading, and 10 less afterwards. The way to defend Milton against all impugners, is to take down the book and read it.

Milton's blank verse is the only blank verse in the language (except Shakspeare's) that deserves the name of verse. Dr. Johnson, who had modelled his ideas of versi-fication on the regular sing-song of Pope, condemns the Paradise Lost as harsh and unequal. I shall not pretend to say that this is not sometimes the case; for where a degree of excellence beyond the mechanical rules of art is attempted, the poet must sometimes fail. But I imagine 20 that there are more perfect examples in Milton of musical expression, or of an adaptation of the sound and movement of the verse to the meaning of the passage, than in all our other writers, whether of rhyme or blank verse, put together (with the exception already mentioned). Spenser is the most harmonious of our stanza writers, as Dryden is the most sounding and varied of our rhymists. But in neither is there anything like the same ear for music, the same power of approximating the varieties of poetical to those of musical rhythm, as there is in our great epic poet. 30 The sound of his lines is moulded into the expression of the sentiment, almost of the very image. They rise or fall, pause or hurry rapidly on, with exquisite art, but without the least trick or affectation, as the occasion seems to require.

The following are some of the finest instances:

'———— His hand was known
In Heaven by many a tower'd structure high ;—
Nor was his name unheard or unador'd
In ancient Greece : and in the Ausonian land
Men called him Mulciber : and how he fell
From Heaven, they fabled, thrown by angry Jove
Sheer o'er the chrystal battlements ; from morn
To noon he fell, from noon to dewy eve,
10 A summer's day ; and with the setting sun
Dropt from the zenith like a falling star
On Lemnos, the Ægean isle : thus they relate,
Erring.'—

'———— But chief the spacious hall
Thick swarm'd, both on the ground and in the air,
Brush'd with the hiss of rustling wings. As bees
In spring time, when the sun with Taurus rides,
Pour forth their populous youth about the hive
In clusters ; they among fresh dews and flow'rs
20 Fly to and fro : or on the smoothed plank,
The suburb of their straw-built citadel,
New rubb'd with balm, expatiate and confer
Their state affairs. So thick the airy crowd
Swarm'd and were straiten'd ; till the signal giv'n,
Behold a wonder ! They but now who seem'd
In bigness to surpass earth's giant sons,
Now less than smallest dwarfs, in narrow room
Throng numberless, like that Pygmean race
Beyond the Indian mount, or fairy elves,
30 Whose midnight revels by a forest side
Or fountain, some belated peasant sees,
Or dreams he sees, while over-head the moon
Sits arbitress, and nearer to the earth
Wheels her pale course : they on their mirth and dance
Intent, with jocund music charm his ear ;
At once with joy and fear his heart rebounds.'

I can only give another instance, though I have some
difficulty in leaving off.

'Round he surveys (and well might, where he stood
40 So high above the circling canopy

Of night's extended shade) from th' eastern point
Of Libra to the fleecy star that bears
Andromeda far off Atlantic seas
Beyond the horizon: then from pole to pole
He views in breadth, and without longer pause
Down right into the world's first region throws
His flight precipitant, and winds with ease
Through the pure marble air his oblique way
Amongst innumerable stars that shone
Stars distant, but nigh hand seem'd other worlds;   10
Or other worlds they seem'd or happy isles,' &c.

The verse, in this exquisitely modulated passage, floats
up and down as if it had itself wings. Milton has himself
given us the theory of his versification—

> 'Such as the meeting soul may pierce
> In notes with many a winding bout
> Of linked sweetness long drawn out.'

Dr. Johnson and Pope would have converted his vaulting
Pegasus into a rocking-horse. Read any other blank
verse but Milton's,—Thomson's, Young's, Cowper's, 20
Wordsworth's,—and it will be found, from the want of
the same insight into 'the hidden soul of harmony', to be
mere lumbering prose.

To proceed to a consideration of the merits of Paradise
Lost, in the most essential point of view, I mean as to the
poetry of character and passion. I shall say nothing of
the fable, or of other technical objections or excellences;
but I shall try to explain at once the foundation of the
interest belonging to the poem. I am ready to give up the
dialogues in Heaven, where, as Pope justly observes, 'God 30
the Father turns a school-divine'; nor do I consider the
battle of the angels as the climax of sublimity, or the most
successful effort of Milton's pen. In a word, the interest
of the poem arises from the daring ambition and fierce
passions of Satan, and from the account of the paradisaical
happiness, and the loss of it by our first parents. Three-

fourths of the work are taken up with these characters, and nearly all that relates to them is unmixed sublimity and beauty. The two first books alone are like two massy pillars of solid gold.

Satan is the most heroic subject that ever was chosen for a poem ; and the execution is as perfect as the design is lofty. He was the first of created beings, who, for endeavouring to be equal with the highest, and to divide the empire of heaven with the Almighty, was hurled down to
10 hell. His aim was no less than the throne of the universe ; his means, myriads of angelic armies bright, the third part of the heavens, whom he lured after him with his countenance, and who durst defy the Omnipotent in arms. His ambition was the greatest, and his punishment was the greatest; but not so his despair, for his fortitude was as great as his sufferings. His strength of mind was matchless as his strength of body ; the vastness of his designs did not surpass the firm, inflexible determination with which he submitted to his irreversible doom, and final
20 loss of all good. His power of action and of suffering was equal. He was the greatest power that was ever overthrown, with the strongest will left to resist or to endure. He was baffled, not confounded. He stood like a tower ; or

'————— As when Heaven's fire
Hath scathed the forest oaks or mountain pines.'

He was still surrounded with hosts of rebel angels, armed warriors, who own him as their sovereign leader, and with whose fate he sympathises as he views them round, far as
30 the eye can reach ; though he keeps aloof from them in his own mind, and holds supreme counsel only with his own breast. An outcast from Heaven, Hell trembles beneath his feet, Sin and Death are at his heels, and mankind are his easy prey.

'All is not lost ; th' unconquerable will,
And study of revenge, immortal hate,
And courage never to submit or yield,
And what else is not to be overcome,'

are still his. The sense of his punishment seems lost in
the magnitude of it ; the fierceness of tormenting flames is
qualified and made innoxious by the greater fierceness of
his pride ; the loss of infinite happiness to himself is com
pensated in thought, by the power of inflicting infinite
misery on others.   Yet Satan is not the principle of
malignity, or of the abstract love of evil—but of the abstract
love of power, of pride, of self-will personified, to which
last principle all other good and evil, and even his own,
are subordinate. From this principle he never once
flinches. His love of power and contempt for suffering are
never once relaxed from the highest pitch of intensity.
His thoughts burn like a hell within him ; but the power
of thought holds dominion in his mind over every other
consideration. The consciousness of a determined purpose,
of 'that intellectual being, those thoughts that wander
through eternity', though accompanied with endless pain,
he prefers to nonentity, to 'being swallowed up and lost in
the wide womb of uncreated night'. He expresses the
sum and substance of all ambition in one line. 'Fallen
cherub, to be weak is miserable, doing or suffering !'
After such a conflict as his, and such a defeat, to retreat in
order, to rally, to make terms, to exist at all, is something ;
but he does more than this—he founds a new empire in
hell, and from it conquers this new world, whither he bends
his undaunted flight, forcing his way through nether and
surrounding fires. The poet has not in all this given us
a mere shadowy outline ; the strength is equal to the
magnitude of the conception. The Achilles of Homer is
not more distinct ; the Titans were not more vast ;
Prometheus chained to his rock was not a more terrific

example of suffering and of crime. Wherever the figure
of Satan is introduced, whether he walks or flies, 'rising
aloft incumbent on the dusky air', it is illustrated with the
most striking and appropriate images : so that we see it
always before us, gigantic, irregular, portentous, uneasy,
and disturbed—but dazzling in its faded splendour, the
clouded ruins of a god. The deformity of Satan is only in
the depravity of his will ; he has no bodily deformity to
excite our loathing or disgust. The horns and tail are not
10 there, poor emblems of the unbending, unconquered spirit,
of the writhing agonies within. Milton was too magna-
nimous and open an antagonist to support his argument by
the bye-tricks of a hump and cloven foot ; to bring into the
fair field of controversy the good old catholic prejudices of
which Tasso and Dante have availed themselves, and which
the mystic German critics would restore. He relied on the
justice of his cause, and did not scruple to give the devil
his due. Some persons may think that he has carried his
liberality too far, and injured the cause he professed to
20 espouse by making him the chief person in his poem.
Considering the nature of his subject, he would be equally
in danger of running into this fault, from his faith in
religion, and his love of rebellion ; and perhaps each of
these motives had its full share in determining the choice
of his subject.

Not only the figure of Satan, but his speeches in council,
his soliloquies, his address to Eve, his share in the war
in heaven, or in the fall of man, shew the same decided
superiority of character. To give only one instance, almost
30 the first speech he makes :

'Is this the region, this the soil, the clime,
Said then the lost archangel, this the seat
That we must change for Heaven ; this mournful gloom
For that celestial light ? Be it so, since he
Who now is sov'rain can dispose and bid

What shall be right: farthest from him is best,
Whom reason hath equal'd, force hath made supreme
Above his equals. Farewel happy fields,
Where joy for ever dwells: Hail horrors, hail
Infernal world, and thou profoundest Hell,
Receive thy new possessor; one who brings
A mind not to be chang'd by place or time.
The mind is its own place, and in itself
Can make a Heav'n of Hell, a Hell of Heav'n.
What matter where, if I be still the same,   10
And what I should be, all but less than he
Whom thunder hath made greater? Here at least
We shall be free; th' Almighty hath not built
Here for his envy, will not drive us hence:
Here we may reign secure, and in my choice
To reign is worth ambition, though in Hell:
Better to reign in Hell, than serve in Heaven.'

The whole of the speeches and debates in Pandemonium
are well worthy of the place and the occasion—with Gods
for speakers, and angels and archangels for hearers. 20
There is a decided manly tone in the arguments and
sentiments, an eloquent dogmatism, as if each person spoke
from thorough conviction; an excellence which Milton
probably borrowed from his spirit of partisanship, or else
his spirit of partisanship from the natural firmness and
vigour of his mind. In this respect Milton resembles
Dante, (the only modern writer with whom he has anything
in common) and it is remarkable that Dante, as well as
Milton, was a political partisan. That approximation to
the severity of impassioned prose which has been made an 30
objection to Milton's poetry, and which is chiefly to be
met with in these bitter invectives, is one of its great excellences. The author might here turn his philippics against
Salmasius to good account. The rout in Heaven is like
the fall of some mighty structure, nodding to its base, 'with
hideous ruin and combustion down'. But, perhaps, of all
the passages in Paradise Lost, the description of the

employments of the angels during the absence of Satan, some of whom 'retreated in a silent valley, sing with notes angelical to many a harp their own heroic deeds and hapless fall by doom of battle', is the most perfect example of mingled pathos and sublimity.—What proves the truth of this noble picture in every part, and that the frequent complaint of want of interest in it is the fault of the reader, not of the poet, is that when any interest of a practical kind takes a shape that can be at all turned into this, (and
10 there is little doubt that Milton had some such in his eye in writing it), each party converts it to its own purposes, feels the absolute identity of these abstracted and high speculations ; and that, in fact, a noted political writer of the present day has exhausted nearly the whole account of Satan in the Paradise Lost, by applying it to a character whom he considered as after the devil, (though I do not know whether he would make even that exception) the greatest enemy of the human race. This may serve to show that Milton's Satan is not a very insipid personage.
20   Of Adam and Eve it has been said, that the ordinary reader can feel little interest in them, because they have none of the passions, pursuits, or even relations of human life, except that of man and wife, the least interesting of all others, if not to the parties concerned, at least to the by-standers. The preference has on this account been given to Homer, who, it is said, has left very vivid and infinitely diversified pictures of all the passions and affections, public and private, incident to human nature—the relations of son, of brother, parent, friend, citizen, and many others.
30 Longinus preferred the Iliad to the Odyssey, on account of the greater number of battles it contains ; but I can neither agree to his criticism, nor assent to the present objection. It is true, there is little action in this part of Milton's poem ; but there is much repose, and more enjoy-ment. There are none of the everyday occurrences,

contentions, disputes, wars, fightings, feuds, jealousies, trades, professions, liveries, and common handicrafts of life ; 'no kind of traffic; letters are not known ; no use of service, of riches, poverty, contract, succession, bourne, bound of land, tilth, vineyard none ; no occupation, no treason, felony, sword, pike, knife, gun, nor need of any engine.' So much the better; thank Heaven, all these were yet to come. But still the die was cast, and in them our doom was sealed. In them

> 'The generations were prepared ; the pangs, 10
> The internal pangs, were ready, the dread strife
> Of poor humanity's afflicted will,
> Struggling in vain with ruthless destiny.'

In their first false step we trace all our future woe, with loss of Eden. But there was a short and precious interval between, like the first blush of morning before the day is overcast with tempest, the dawn of the world, the birth of nature from 'the unapparent deep', with its first dews and freshness on its cheek, breathing odours. Theirs was the first delicious taste of life, and on them depended all that 20 was to come of it. In them hung trembling all our hopes and fears. They were as yet alone in the world, in the eye of nature, wondering at their new being, full of enjoy- ment and enraptured with one another, with the voice of their Maker walking in the garden, and ministering angels attendant on their steps, winged messengers from heaven like rosy clouds descending in their sight. Nature played around them her virgin fancies wild ; and spread for them a repast where no crude surfeit reigned. Was there nothing in this scene, which God and nature alone wit- 30 nessed, to interest a modern critic ? What need was there of action, where the heart was full of bliss and innocence without it ! They had nothing to do but feel their own happiness, and 'know to know no more'. 'They toiled not, neither did they spin ; yet Solomon in all his glory

was not arrayed like one of these.' All things seem to
acquire fresh sweetness, and to be clothed with fresh
beauty in their sight. They tasted as it were for themselves
and us, of all that there ever was pure in human bliss.
'In them the burthen of the mystery, the heavy and the
weary weight of all this unintelligible world, is lightened.'
They stood awhile perfect, but they afterwards fell, and
were driven out of Paradise, tasting the first fruits of
bitterness as they had done of bliss. But their pangs were
10 such as a pure spirit might feel at the sight—their tears
'such as angels weep'. The pathos is of that mild con-
templative kind which arises from regret for the loss of
unspeakable happiness, and resignation to inevitable fate.
There is none of the fierceness of intemperate passion,
none of the agony of mind and turbulence of action, which
is the result of the habitual struggles of the will with
circumstances, irritated by repeated disappointment, and
constantly setting its desires most eagerly on that which
there is an impossibility of attaining. This would have
20 destroyed the beauty of the whole picture. They had
received their unlooked-for happiness as a free gift from
their Creator's hands, and they submitted to its loss, not
without sorrow, but without impious and stubborn repining.

> 'In either hand the hast'ning angel caught
> Our ling'ring parents, and to th' eastern gate
> Led them direct, and down the cliff as fast
> To the subjected plain; then disappear'd.
> They looking back, all th' eastern side beheld
> Of Paradise, so late their happy seat,
> 30   Wav'd over by that flaming brand, the gate
> With dreadful faces throng'd, and fiery arms:
> Some natural tears they dropt, but wip'd them soon;
> The world was all before them, where to choose
> Their place of rest, and Providence their guide.'

III

From MACAULAY'S ESSAY ON MILTON

First published in the Edinburgh Review

for August 1825

IT is not our intention to attempt anything like a complete examination of the poetry of Milton. The public has long been agreed as to the merit of the most remarkable passages, the incomparable harmony of the numbers, and the excellence of that style, which no rival has been able to equal, and no parodist to degrade, which displays in their highest perfection the idiomatic powers of the English tongue, and to which every ancient and every modern language has contributed something of grace, of energy, or of music. In the vast field of criticism on 10 which we are entering, innumerable reapers have already put their sickles. Yet the harvest is so abundant that the negligent search of a straggling gleaner may be rewarded with a sheaf.

The most striking characteristic of the poetry of Milton is the extreme remoteness of the associations by means of which it acts on the reader. Its effect is produced, not so much by what it expresses, as by what it suggests ; not so much by the ideas which it directly conveys, as by other ideas which are connected with them. He electrifies the 20 mind through conductors. The most unimaginative man must understand the *Iliad*. Homer gives him no choice, and requires from him no exertion, but takes the whole upon himself, and sets the images in so clear a light, that it is impossible to be blind to them. The works of Milton cannot be comprehended or enjoyed, unless the mind of the reader co-operate with that of the writer. He does not paint a finished picture, or play for a mere passive listener.

He sketches, and leaves others to fill up the outline. He strikes the key-note, and expects his hearer to make out the melody.

We often hear of the magical influence of poetry. The expression in general means nothing: but, applied to the writings of Milton, it is most appropriate. His poetry acts like an incantation. Its merit lies less in its obvious meaning than in its occult power. There would seem, at first sight, to be no more in his words than in other words. But they are words of enchantment. No sooner are they pronounced, than the past is present and the distant near. New forms of beauty start at once into existence, and all the burial-places of the memory give up their dead. Change the structure of the sentence; substitute one synonym for another, and the whole effect is destroyed. The spell loses its power; and he who should then hope to conjure with it would find himself as much mistaken as Cassim in the Arabian tale, when he stood crying, 'Open Wheat', 'Open Barley', to the door which obeyed no sound but 'Open Sesame'. The miserable failure of Dryden in his attempt to translate into his own diction some parts of the *Paradise Lost*, is a remarkable instance of this.

In support of these observations we may remark, that scarcely any passages in the poems of Milton are more generally known or more frequently repeated than those which are little more than muster-rolls of names. They are not always more appropriate or more melodious than other names. But they are charmed names. Every one of them is the first link in a long chain of associated ideas. Like the dwelling-place of our infancy revisited in manhood, like the song of our country heard in a strange land, they produce upon us an effect wholly independent of their intrinsic value. One transports us back to a remote period of history. Another places us among the novel scenes

and manners of a distant region. A third evokes all the
dear classical recollections of childhood, the school-room,
the dog-eared Virgil, the holiday, and the prize. A fourth
brings before us the splendid phantoms of chivalrous
romance, the trophied lists, the embroidered housings, the
quaint devices, the haunted forests, the enchanted gardens,
the achievements of enamoured knights, and the smiles of
rescued princesses.

In none of the works of Milton is his peculiar manner
more happily displayed than in the *Allegro* and the 10
Penseroso. It is impossible to conceive that the mechanism
of language can be brought to a more exquisite degree of
perfection. These poems differ from others, as attar of
roses differs from ordinary rosewater, the close packed
essence from the thin diluted mixture. They are indeed
not so much poems, as collections of hints, from each of
which the reader is to make out a poem for himself.
Every epithet is a text for a stanza.

The *Comus* and the *Samson Agonistes* are works which,
though of very different merit, offer some marked points 20
of resemblance. Both are lyric poems in the form of
plays. There are perhaps no two kinds of composition so
essentially dissimilar as the drama and the ode. The
business of the dramatist is to keep himself out of sight,
and to let nothing appear but his characters. As soon as
he attracts notice to his personal feelings, the illusion is
broken. The effect is as unpleasant as that which is produced on the stage by the voice of a prompter or the
entrance of a scene-shifter. Hence it was, that the tragedies of Byron were his least successful performances. 30
They resemble those pasteboard pictures invented by the
friend of children, Mr. Newbery, in which a single mov-
able head goes round twenty different bodies, so that the
same face looks out upon us successively, from the uniform
of a hussar, the furs of a judge, and the rags of a beggar.

In all the characters, patriots and tyrants, haters and lovers, the frown and sneer of Harold were discernible in an instant. But this species of egotism, though fatal to the drama, is the inspiration of the ode. It is the part of the lyric poet to abandon himself, without reserve, to his own emotions.

Between these hostile elements many great men have endeavoured to effect an amalgamation, but never with complete success. The Greek Drama, on the model of which the *Samson* was written, sprang from the Ode. The dialogue was ingrafted on the chorus, and naturally partook of its character. The genius of the greatest of the Athenian dramatists co-operated with the circumstances under which tragedy made its first appearance. Aeschylus was, head and heart, a lyric poet. In his time, the Greeks had far more intercourse with the East than in the days of Homer; and they had not yet acquired that immense superiority in war, in science, and in the arts, which, in the following generation, led them to treat the Asiatics with contempt. From the narrative of Herodotus it should seem that they still looked up, with the veneration of disciples, to Egypt and Assyria. At this period, accordingly, it was natural that the literature of Greece should be tinctured with the Oriental style. And that style, we think, is discernible in the works of Pindar and Aeschylus. The latter often reminds us of the Hebrew writers. The book of Job, indeed, in conduct and diction, bears a considerable resemblance to some of his dramas. Considered as plays, his works are absurd; considered as choruses, they are above all praise. If, for instance, we examine the address of Clytaemnestra to Agamemnon on his return, or the description of the seven Argive chiefs, by the principles of dramatic writing, we shall instantly condemn them as monstrous. But if we forget the characters, and think only of the poetry, we shall admit that it has never

been surpassed in energy and magnificence. Sophocles
made the Greek drama as dramatic as was consistent with
its original form. His portraits of men have a sort of
similarity; but it is the similarity not of a painting, but of
a bas-relief. It suggests a resemblance; but it does not
produce an illusion. Euripides attempted to carry the
reform further. But it was a task far beyond his powers,
perhaps beyond any powers. Instead of correcting what
was bad, he destroyed what was excellent. He substituted crutches for stilts, bad sermons for good odes.   10

Milton, it is well known, admired Euripides highly,
much more highly than, in our opinion, Euripides deserved.
Indeed the caresses which this partiality leads our country-
man to bestow on 'sad Electra's poet', sometimes remind
us of the beautiful Queen of Fairyland kissing the long
ears of Bottom. At all events, there can be no doubt that
this veneration for the Athenian, whether just or not, was
injurious to the *Samson Agonistes*. Had Milton taken
Aeschylus for his model, he would have given himself up
to the lyric inspiration, and poured out profusely all the   20
treasures of his mind, without bestowing a thought on
those dramatic proprieties which the nature of the work
rendered it impossible to preserve. In the attempt to
reconcile things in their own nature inconsistent he has
failed, as every one else must have failed. We cannot
identify ourselves with the characters, as in a good play.
We cannot identify ourselves with the poet, as in a good
ode. The conflicting ingredients, like an acid and an
alkali mixed, neutralize each other. We are by no means
insensible to the merits of this celebrated piece, to the   30
severe dignity of the style, the graceful and pathetic
solemnity of the opening speech, or the wild and barbaric
melody which gives so striking an effect to the choral
passages. But we think it, we confess, the least successful
effort of the genius of Milton.

The *Comus* is framed on the model of the Italian Masque, as the *Samson* is framed on the model of the Greek Tragedy. It is certainly the noblest performance of the kind which exists in any language. It is as far superior to the *Faithful Shepherdess* as the *Faithful Shepherdess* is to the *Aminta*, or the *Aminta* to the *Pastor Fido*. It was well for Milton that he had here no Euripides to mislead him. He understood and loved the literature of modern Italy. But he did not feel for it the same veneration which he entertained for the remains of Athenian and Roman poetry, consecrated by so many lofty and endearing recollections. The faults, moreover, of his Italian predecessors were of a kind to which his mind had a deadly antipathy. He could stoop to a plain style, sometimes even to a bald style; but false brilliancy was his utter aversion. His muse had no objection to a russet attire; but she turned with disgust from the finery of Guarini, as tawdry and as paltry as the rags of a chimney-sweeper on May-day. Whatever ornaments she wears are of massive gold, not only dazzling to the sight, but capable of standing the severest test of the crucible.

Milton attended in the *Comus* to the distinction which he afterwards neglected in the *Samson*. He made his Masque what it ought to be, essentially lyrical, and dramatic only in semblance. He has not attempted a fruitless struggle against a defect inherent in the nature of that species of composition; and he has therefore succeeded, wherever success was not impossible. The speeches must be read as majestic soliloquies; and he who so reads them will be enraptured with their eloquence, their sublimity, and their music. The interruptions of the dialogue, however, impose a constraint upon the writer, and break the illusion of the reader. The finest passages are those which are lyric in form as well as in spirit. 'I should much commend', says the excellent Sir Henry Wotton in a letter to Milton, 'the tragical part if the lyrical did not ravish me with a certain Dorique delicacy in your songs and odes, whereunto, I must plainly confess to you, I have seen yet nothing parallel in our language.' The criticism was just. It is when Milton escapes from the shackles of the dialogue, when he is discharged from the labour of uniting two incongruous styles, when he is at liberty to indulge his choral raptures without reserve, that he rises even above himself. Then, like his own good Genius bursting from the earthly form and weeds of Thyrsis, he stands forth in celestial freedom and beauty; he seems to cry exultingly,

> Now my task is smoothly done,
> I can fly or I can run,

to skim the earth, to soar above the clouds, to bathe in the Elysian dew of the rainbow, and to inhale the balmy smells of nard and cassia, which the musky winds of the zephyr scatter through the cedared alleys of the Hesperides.

There are several of the minor poems of Milton on which we would willingly make a few remarks. Still more willingly would we enter into a detailed examination of that admirable poem, the *Paradise Regained*, which, strangely enough, is scarcely ever mentioned except as an instance of the blindness of the parental affection which men of letters bear towards the offspring of their intellects. That Milton was mistaken in preferring this work, excellent as it is, to the *Paradise Lost*, we readily admit. But we are sure that the superiority of the *Paradise Lost* to the *Paradise Regained* is not more decided, than the superiority of the *Paradise Regained* to every poem which has since made its appearance. Our limits, however, prevent us from discussing the point at length. We hasten on to that extraordinary production which the general suffrage of critics has placed in the highest class of human compositions.

The only poem of modern times which can be compared with the *Paradise Lost* is the *Divine Comedy*. The subject of Milton, in some points, resembled that of Dante; but he has treated it in a widely different manner. We cannot, we think, better illustrate our opinion, respecting our own great poet, than by contrasting him with the father of Tuscan literature.

The poetry of Milton differs from that of Dante, as the hieroglyphics of Egypt differed from the picture-writing of Mexico. The images which Dante employs speak for themselves; they stand simply for what they are. Those of Milton have a signification which is often discernible only to the initiated. Their value depends less on what they directly represent than on what they remotely suggest. However strange, however grotesque, may be the appearance which Dante undertakes to describe, he never shrinks from describing it. He gives us the shape, the colour, the sound, the smell, the taste; he counts the numbers; he measures the size. His similes are the illustrations of a traveller. Unlike those of other poets, and especially of Milton, they are introduced in a plain, business-like manner; not for the sake of any beauty in the objects from which they are drawn; not for the sake of any ornament which they may impart to the poem; but simply in order to make the meaning of the writer as clear to the reader as it is to himself. The ruins of the precipice which led from the sixth to the seventh circle of hell were like those of the rock which fell into the Adige on the south of Trent. The cataract of Phlegethon was like that of Aqua Cheta at the monastery of St. Benedict. The place where the heretics were confined in burning tombs resembled the vast cemetery of Arles.

Now let us compare with the exact details of Dante the dim intimations of Milton. We will cite a few examples. The English poet has never thought of taking the measure

of Satan. He gives us merely a vague idea of vast bulk.
In one passage the fiend lies stretched out huge in length,
floating many a rood, equal in size to the earth-born
enemies of Jove, or to the sea-monster which the mariner
mistakes for an island. When he addresses himself to
battle against the guardian angels, he stands like Teneriffe
or Atlas: his stature reaches the sky. Contrast with these
descriptions the lines in which Dante has described the
gigantic spectre of Nimrod. 'His face seemed to me as
long and as broad as the ball of St. Peter's at Rome; and 10
his other limbs were in proportion; so that the bank,
which concealed him from the waist downwards, nevertheless showed so much of him, that three tall Germans
would in vain have attempted to reach to his hair.' We
are sensible that we do no justice to the admirable style of
the Florentine poet. But Mr. Cary's translation is not at
hand; and our version, however rude, is sufficient to
illustrate our meaning.

Once more, compare the lazar-house in the eleventh
book of the *Paradise Lost* with the last ward of Malebolge 20
in Dante. Milton avoids the loathsome details, and takes
refuge in indistinct but solemn and tremendous imagery.
Despair hurrying from couch to couch to mock the wretches
with his attendance, Death shaking his dart over them,
but, in spite of supplications, delaying to strike. What
says Dante? 'There was such a moan there as there
would be if all the sick who, between July and September,
are in the hospitals of Valdichiana, and of the Tuscan
swamps, and of Sardinia, were in one pit together; and
such a stench was issuing forth as is wont to issue from 30
decayed limbs.'

We will not take upon ourselves the invidious office of
settling precedency between two such writers. Each in
his own department is incomparable; and each, we may
remark, has wisely, or fortunately, taken a subject adapted

to exhibit his peculiar talent to the greatest advantage. The *Divine Comedy* is a personal narrative. Dante is the eye-witness and ear-witness of that which he relates. He is the very man who has heard the tormented spirits crying out for the second death, who has read the dusky characters on the portal within which there is no hope, who has hidden his face from the terrors of the Gorgon, who has fled from the hooks and the seething pitch of Barbariccia and Draghignazzo. His own hands have
10 grasped the shaggy sides of Lucifer. His own feet have climbed the mountain of expiation. His own brow has been marked by the purifying angel. The reader would throw aside such a tale in incredulous disgust, unless it were told with the strongest air of veracity, with a sobriety even in its horrors, with the greatest precision and multiplicity in its details. The narrative of Milton in this respect differs from that of Dante, as the adventures of Amadis differ from those of Gulliver. The author of *Amadis* would have made his book ridiculous if he had introduced
20 those minute particulars which give such a charm to the work of Swift, the nautical observations, the affected delicacy about names, the official documents transcribed at full length, and all the unmeaning gossip and scandal of the court, springing out of nothing, and tending to nothing. We are not shocked at being told that a man who lived, nobody knows when, saw many very strange sights, and we can easily abandon ourselves to the illusion of the romance. But when Lemuel Gulliver, surgeon, resident at Rotherhithe, tells us of pygmies and giants, flying
30 islands, and philosophizing horses, nothing but such circumstantial touches could produce for a single moment a deception on the imagination.

Of all the poets who have introduced into their works the agency of supernatural beings, Milton has succeeded best. Here Dante decidedly yields to him : and as this is a point on which many rash and ill-considered judgements have been pronounced, we feel inclined to dwell on it a little longer. The most fatal error which a poet can possibly commit in the management of his machinery, is that of attempting to philosophize too much. Milton has been often censured for ascribing to spirits many functions of which spirits must be incapable. But these objections, though sanctioned by eminent names, originate, we venture to say, in profound ignorance of the art of poetry.

What is spirit? What are our own minds, the portion 10 of spirit with which we are best acquainted? We observe certain phenomena. We cannot explain them into material causes. We therefore infer that there exists something which is not material. But of this something we have no idea. We can define it only by negatives. We can reason about it only by symbols. We use the word; but we have no image of the thing; and the business of poetry is with images, and not with words. The poet uses words indeed; but they are merely the instruments of his art, not its objects. They are the materials which he is to dispose in 20 such a manner as to present a picture to the mental eye. And if they are not so disposed, they are no more entitled to be called poetry than a bale of canvas and a box of colours to be called a painting. . . .

From these considerations, we infer that no poet, who should affect that metaphysical accuracy for the want of which Milton has been blamed, would escape a disgraceful failure. Still, however, there was another extreme which, though far less dangerous, was also to be avoided. The imaginations of men are in a great measure under the 30 control of their opinions. The most exquisite art of poetical colouring can produce no illusion, when it is employed to represent that which is at once perceived to be incongruous and absurd. Milton wrote in an age of philosophers and theologians. It was necessary, therefore,

for him to abstain from giving such a shock to their under-
standings as might break the charm which it was his object
to throw over their imaginations. This is the real explana-
tion of the indistinctness and inconsistency with which he
has often been reproached. Dr. Johnson acknowledges
that it was absolutely necessary that the spirit should be
clothed with material forms. 'But', says he, 'the poet
should have secured the consistency of his system by
keeping immateriality out of sight, and seducing the reader
to drop it from his thoughts.' This is easily said; but
what if Milton could not seduce his readers to drop immateriality from their thoughts? What if the contrary
opinion had taken so full a possession of the minds of men
as to leave no room even for the half belief which poetry
requires? Such we suspect to have been the case. It was
impossible for the poet to adopt altogether the material
or the immaterial system. He therefore took his stand on
the debatable ground. He left the whole in ambiguity.
He has doubtless, by so doing, laid himself open to the
charge of inconsistency. But, though philosophically in
the wrong, we cannot but believe that he was poetically in
the right. This task, which almost any other writer would
have found impracticable, was easy to him. The peculiar
art which he possessed of communicating his meaning
circuitously through a long succession of associated ideas,
and of intimating more than he expressed, enabled him to
disguise those incongruities which he could not avoid.

Poetry which relates to the beings of another world
ought to be at once mysterious and picturesque. That of
Milton is so. That of Dante is picturesque indeed beyond
any that ever was written. Its effect approaches to that
produced by the pencil or the chisel. But it is picturesque
to the exclusion of all mystery. This is a fault on the
right side, a fault inseparable from the plan of Dante's
poem, which, as we have already observed, rendered the

utmost accuracy of description necessary. Still it is a
fault. The supernatural agents excite an interest; but it
is not the interest which is proper to supernatural agents.
We feel that we could talk to the ghosts and demons,
without any emotion of unearthly awe. We could, like
Don Juan, ask them to supper, and eat heartily in their
company. Dante's angels are good men with wings. His
devils are spiteful ugly executioners. His dead men are
merely living men in strange situations. The scene which
passes between the poet and Farinata is justly celebrated. 10
Still, Farinata in the burning tomb is exactly what Farinata
would have been at an *auto da fe*. Nothing can be more
touching than the first interview of Dante and Beatrice.
Yet what is it, but a lovely woman chiding, with sweet
austere composure, the lover for whose affection she is
grateful, but whose vices she reprobates? The feelings
which give the passage its charm would suit the streets of
Florence as well as the summit of the Mount of Purgatory.

The spirits of Milton are unlike those of almost all other
writers. His fiends, in particular, are wonderful creations. 20
They are not metaphysical abstractions. They are not
wicked men. They are not ugly beasts. They have no
horns, no tails, none of the fee-faw-fum of Tasso and
Klopstock. They have just enough in common with
human nature to be intelligible to human beings. Their
characters are, like their forms, marked by a certain dim
resemblance to those of men, but exaggerated to gigantic
dimensions, and veiled in mysterious gloom.

Perhaps the gods and demons of Aeschylus may best
bear a comparison with the angels and devils of Milton. 30
The style of the Athenian had, as we have remarked,
something of the Oriental character; and the same
peculiarity may be traced in his mythology. It has nothing
of the amenity and elegance which we generally find in
the superstitions of Greece. All is rugged, barbaric, and

colossal. . . . His favourite gods are those of the elder generation, the sons of heaven and earth, compared with whom Jupiter himself was a stripling and an upstart, the gigantic Titans, and the inexorable Furies. Foremost among his creations of this class stands Prometheus, half fiend, half redeemer, the friend of man, the sullen and implacable enemy of heaven. Prometheus bears undoubtedly a considerable resemblance to the Satan of Milton. In both we find the same impatience of control,
10 the same ferocity, the same unconquerable pride. In both characters also are mingled, though in very different proportions, some kind and generous feelings. Prometheus, however, is hardly superhuman enough. He talks too much of his chains and his uneasy posture : he is rather too much depressed and agitated. His resolution seems to depend on the knowledge which he possesses that he holds the fate of his torturer in his hands, and that the hour of his release will surely come. But Satan is a creature of another sphere. The might of his intellectual
20 nature is victorious over the extremity of pain. Amidst agonies which cannot be conceived without horror, he deliberates, resolves, and even exults. Against the sword of Michael, against the thunder of Jehovah, against the flaming lake, and the marl burning with solid fire, against the prospect of an eternity of unintermitted misery, his spirit bears up unbroken, resting on its own innate energies, requiring no support from anything external, nor even from hope itself.

To return for a moment to the parallel which we have
30 been attempting to draw between Milton and Dante, we would add that the poetry of these great men has in a considerable degree taken its character from their moral qualities. They are not egotists. They rarely obtrude their idiosyncrasies on their readers. They have nothing in common with those modern beggars for fame, who

extort a pittance from the compassion of the inexperienced by exposing the nakedness and sores of their minds. Yet it would be difficult to name two writers whose works have been more completely, though undesignedly, coloured by their personal feelings.

The character of Milton was peculiarly distinguished by loftiness of spirit ; that of Dante by intensity of feeling. In every line of the *Divine Comedy* we discern the asperity which is produced by pride struggling with misery. There is perhaps no work in the world so deeply and uniformly 10 sorrowful. The melancholy of Dante was no fantastic caprice. It was not, as far as at this distance of time can be judged, the effect of external circumstances. It was from within. Neither love nor glory, neither the conflicts of earth nor the hope of heaven could dispel it. It turned every consolation and every pleasure into its own nature. It resembled that noxious Sardinian soil of which the intense bitterness is said to have been perceptible even in its honey. His mind was, in the noble language of the Hebrew poet, 'a land of darkness, as darkness itself, and 20 where the light was as darkness'. The gloom of his character discolours all the passions of men, and all the face of nature, and tinges with its own livid hue the flowers of Paradise and the glories of the eternal throne. All the portraits of him are singularly characteristic. No person can look on the features, noble even to ruggedness, the dark furrows of the cheek, the haggard and woful stare of the eye, the sullen and contemptuous curve of the lip, and doubt that they belong to a man too proud and too sensitive to be happy. 30

Milton was, like Dante, a statesman and a lover ; and, like Dante, he had been unfortunate in ambition and in love. He had survived his health and his sight, the comforts of his home, and the prosperity of his party. Of the great men by whom he had been distinguished at his

entrance into life, some had been taken away from the evil
to come; some had carried into foreign climates their unconquerable hatred of oppression; some were pining in
dungeons; and some had poured forth their blood on
scaffolds. Venal and licentious scribblers, with just
sufficient talent to clothe the thoughts of a pander in the
style of a bellman, were now the favourite writers of the
Sovereign and of the public. It was a loathsome herd,
which could be compared to nothing so fitly as to the
10 rabble of *Comus*, grotesque monsters, half bestial, half
human, dropping with wine, bloated with gluttony, and
reeling in obscene dances. Amidst these that fair Muse
was placed, like the chaste lady of the Masque, lofty, spot-
less, and serene, to be chattered at, and pointed at, and
grinned at, by the whole rout of Satyrs and Goblins. If
ever despondency and asperity could be excused in any
man, they might have been excused in Milton. But the
strength of his mind overcame every calamity. Neither
blindness, nor gout, nor age, nor penury, nor domestic
20 afflictions, nor political disappointments, nor abuse, nor
proscription, nor neglect, had power to disturb his sedate
and majestic patience. His spirits do not seem to have
been high, but they were singularly equable. His temper
was serious, perhaps stern; but it was a temper which no
sufferings could render sullen or fretful. Such as it was
when, on the eve of great events, he returned from his
travels, in the prime of health and manly beauty, loaded
with literary distinctions, and glowing with patriotic hopes,
such it continued to be when, after having experienced
30 every calamity which is incident to our nature, old, poor,
sightless and disgraced, he retired to his hovel to die.

Hence it was that, though he wrote the *Paradise Lost* at
a time of life when images of beauty and tenderness are in
general beginning to fade, even from those minds in which
they have not been effaced by anxiety and disappointment,

he adorned it with all that is most lovely and delightful in the physical and in the moral world. Neither Theocritus nor Ariosto had a finer or a more healthful sense of the pleasantness of external objects, or loved better to luxuriate amidst sunbeams and flowers, the songs of nightingales, the juice of summer fruits, and the coolness of shady fountains. His conception of love unites all the voluptuousness of the Oriental harem, and all the gallantry of the chivalric tournament, with all the pure and quiet affection of an English fireside. His poetry reminds us of the 10 miracles of Alpine scenery. Nooks and dells, beautiful as fairy-land, are embosomed in its most rugged and gigantic elevations. The roses and myrtles bloom unchilled on the verge of the avalanche.

Traces, indeed, of the peculiar character of Milton may be found in all his works; but it is most strongly displayed in the Sonnets. Those remarkable poems have been undervalued by critics who have not understood their nature. They have no epigrammatic point. There is none of the ingenuity of Filicaja in the thought, none of 20 the hard and brilliant enamel of Petrarch in the style. They are simple but majestic records of the feelings of the poet; as little tricked out for the public eye as his diary would have been. A victory, an unexpected attack upon the city, a momentary fit of depression or exultation, a jest thrown out against one of his books, a dream which for a short time restored to him that beautiful face over which the grave had closed for ever, led him to musings, which, without effort, shaped themselves into verse. The unity of sentiment and severity of style which characterize these 30 little pieces remind us of the Greek Anthology, or perhaps still more of the Collects of the English Liturgy. The noble poem on the Massacres of Piedmont is strictly a collect in verse.

The Sonnets are more or less striking, according as the

occasions which gave birth to them are more or less interesting. But they are, almost without exception, dignified
by a sobriety and greatness of mind to which we know not
where to look for a parallel. It would, indeed, be scarcely
safe to draw any decided inferences as to the character of
a writer from passages directly egotistical. But the qualities
which we have ascribed to Milton, though perhaps most
strongly marked in those parts of his works which treat of
his personal feelings, are distinguishable in every page, and
10 impart to all his writings, prose and poetry, English, Latin,
and Italian, a strong family likeness. . . .

It is to be regretted that the prose writings of Milton
should, in our time, be so little read. As compositions,
they deserve the attention of every man who wishes to
become acquainted with the full power of the English
language. They abound with passages compared with
which the finest declamations of Burke sink into insignifi-
cance. They are a perfect field of cloth of gold. The
style is stiff with gorgeous embroidery. Not even in the
20 earlier books of the *Paradise Lost* has the great poet ever
risen higher than in those parts of his controversial works
in which his feelings, excited by conflict, find a vent in
bursts of devotional and lyric rapture. It is, to borrow his
own majestic language, 'a sevenfold chorus of hallelujahs
and harping symphonies'.

Selections from

M I L T O N'S

POETRY and PROSE

ON THE MORNING OF CHRIST'S NATIVITY

Compos'd 1629

I

THIS is the month, and this the happy morn,
Wherein the Son of Heav'n's eternal King,
Of wedded maid and virgin mother born,
Our great redemption from above did bring;
For so the holy sages once did sing,   5
   That he our deadly forfeit should release,
And with his Father work us a perpetual peace.

II

That glorious Form, that Light unsufferable,
And that far-beaming blaze of Majesty,
Wherewith he wont at Heav'n's high council-table   10
To sit the midst of Trinal Unity,
He laid aside; and here with us to be,
   Forsook the courts of everlasting day,
And chose with us a darksome house of mortal clay.

III

Say Heav'nly Muse, shall not thy sacred vein   15
Afford a present to the Infant God?
Hast thou no verse, no hymn, or solemn strain,
To welcome him to this his new abode;
Now while the Heav'n by the sun's team untrod
   Hath took no print of the approaching light,   20
And all the spangled host keep watch in squadrons bright?

IV

See how from far upon the eastern road
The star-led wizards haste with odours sweet:
O run, prevent them with thy humble ode,
And lay it lowly at his blessed feet;   25
Have thou the honour first, thy Lord to greet,
   And join thy voice unto the Angel Quire,
From out his secret altar touch'd with hallow'd fire.

The Hymn

I

It was the winter wild,
While the Heav'n-born child,   30
   All meanly wrapp'd in the rude manger lies:
Nature in awe to him
Had doff'd her gaudy trim,
   With her great Master so to sympathize:
It was no season then for her   35
To wanton with the sun her lusty paramour.

II

Only with speeches fair
She woos the gentle Air
   To hide her guilty front with innocent snow,
And on her naked shame,   40
Pollute with sinful blame,
   The saintly veil of maiden white to throw;
Confounded, that her Maker's eyes
Should look so near upon her foul deformities.

III

But he, her fears to cease,   45
Sent down the meek-ey'd Peace;
   She crown'd with olive green, came softly sliding

Down through the turning sphere
His ready harbinger,
   With turtle wing the amorous clouds dividing,   50
And waving wide her myrtle wand,
She strikes a universal peace through sea and land.

IV

No war, or battle's sound
Was heard the world around:
   The idle spear and shield were high up hung;   55
The hooked chariot stood
Unstain'd with hostile blood,
   The trumpet spake not to the armed throng;
And kings sat still with awful eye,
As if they surely knew their sovran Lord was by.   60

V

But peaceful was the night
Wherein the Prince of light
   His reign of peace upon the earth began:
The winds with wonder whist
Smoothly the waters kist,   65
   Whispering new joys to the mild Ocean,
Who now hath quite forgot to rave,
While birds of calm sit brooding on the charmed wave.

VI

The stars with deep amaze
Stand fix'd in steadfast gaze,   70
   Bending one way their precious influence:
And will not take their flight,
For all the morning light,
   Or Lucifer that often warn'd them thence;
But in their glimmering orbs did glow,   75
Until their Lord himself bespake, and bid them go.

VII

And though the shady gloom
Had given day her room,
   The sun himself withheld his wonted speed;
And hid his head for shame,   80
As his inferior flame
   The new-enlightn'd world no more should need;
He saw a greater Sun appear
Than his bright throne, or burning axletree could bear.

VIII

The shepherds on the lawn,   85
Or ere the point of dawn,
   Sat simply chatting in a rustic row;
Full little thought they than
That the mighty Pan
   Was kindly come to live with them below;   90
Perhaps their loves, or else their sheep,
Was all that did their silly thoughts so busy keep.

IX

When such music sweet
Their hearts and ears did greet,
   As never was by mortal finger strook;   95
Divinely warbled voice
Answering the stringed noise,
   As all their souls in blissful rapture took:
The air such pleasure loth to lose,
With thousand echoes still prolongs each heav'nly close.

X

Nature that heard such sound   101
Beneath the hollow round
   Of Cynthia's seat, the airy region thrilling,

Now was almost won
To think her part was done, 105
  And that her reign had here its last fulfilling;
She knew such harmony alone
Could hold all Heav'n and Earth in happier union.

XI

At last surrounds their sight
A globe of circular light, 110
  That with long beams the shame-fac'd night array'd;
The helmed cherubim
And sworded seraphim
  Are seen in glittering ranks with wings display'd,
Harping in loud and solemn quire, 115
With unexpressive notes to Heav'n's new-born Heir.

XII

Such music (as 'tis said)
Before was never made,
  But when of old the sons of morning sung;
While the Creator Great 120
His constellations set,
  And the well-balanc'd world on hinges hung,
And cast the dark foundations deep,
And bid the welt'ring waves their oozy channel keep.

XIII

Ring out ye crystal spheres, 125
Once bless our human ears,
  (If ye have power to touch our senses so),
And let your silver chime
Move in melodious time;
  And let the base of Heav'n's deep organ blow; 130
And with your ninefold harmony
Make up full consort to th' angelic symphony.

F 2

XIV

For if such holy song
Enwrap our fancy long,
    Time will run back, and fetch the age of gold;   135
And speckl'd Vanity
Will sicken soon and die,
    And leprous Sin will melt from earthly mould;
And Hell itself will pass away,
And leave her dolorous mansions to the peering day.

XV

Yea Truth and Justice then   141
Will down return to men,
    Orb'd in a rainbow; and like glories wearing
Mercy will sit between,
Thron'd in celestial sheen,   145
    With radiant feet the tissu'd clouds down steering;
And Heav'n as at some festival
Will open wide the gates of her high palace hall.

XVI

But wisest Fate says no,
This must not yet be so,   150
    The Babe lies yet in smiling infancy,
That on the bitter cross
Must redeem our loss,
    So both himself and us to glorify:
Yet first to those ychain'd in sleep,   155
The wakeful trump of doom must thunder through the
    deep,

XVII

With such a horrid clang
As on mount Sinai rang
    While the red fire and smould'ring clouds out brake:

The aged Earth aghast   160
With terror of that blast,
   Shall from the surface to the centre shake ;
When at the world's last session,
The dreadful Judge in middle air shall spread his throne.

XVIII

And then at last our bliss   165
Full and perfect is,
   But now begins ; for from this happy day
Th' old Dragon under ground
In straiter limits bound,
   Not half so far casts his usurped sway ;   170
And wrath to see his kingdom fail,
Swinges the scaly horror of his folded tail.

XIX

The oracles are dumb,
No voice or hideous hum
   Runs through the arched roof in words deceiving. 175
Apollo from his shrine
Can no more divine,
   With hollow shriek the steep of Delphos leaving.
No nightly trance, or breathed spell,
Inspires the pale-ey'd priest from the prophetic cell.   180

XX

The lonely mountains o'er,
And the resounding shore,
   A voice of weeping heard, and loud lament ;
From haunted spring, and dale
Edg'd with poplar pale,   185
   The parting genius is with sighing sent.
With flower-inwov'n tresses torn
The nymphs in twilight shade of tangled thickets mourn.

XXI

In consecrated earth,
And on the holy hearth,   190
  The Lars and Lemures moan with midnight plaint;
In urns and altars round,
A drear and dying sound
  Affrights the Flamens at their service quaint;
And the chill marble seems to sweat,   195
While each peculiar power forgoes his wonted seat.

XXII

Peor and Baälim
Forsake their temples dim,
  With that twice-batter'd god of Palestine;
And mooned Ashtaroth,   200
Heav'n's queen and mother both,
  Now sits not girt with tapers' holy shine;
The Libyc Hammon shrinks his horn,
In vain the Tyrian maids their wounded Thammuz mourn.

XXIII

And sullen Moloch fled,   205
Hath left in shadows dread
  His burning idol all of blackest hue;
In vain with cymbals' ring,
They call the grisly king,
  In dismal dance about the furnace blue;   210
The brutish gods of Nile as fast,
Isis and Orus, and the dog Anubis haste.

XXIV

Nor is Osiris seen
In Memphian grove, or green,
  Trampling the unshowr'd grass with lowings loud; 215

Nor can he be at rest
Within his sacred chest,
  Naught but profoundest Hell can be his shroud;
In vain with timbrell'd anthems dark
The sable-stoled sorcerers bear his worshipp'd ark.   220

XXV

He feels from Juda's land
The dreaded Infant's hand,
  The rays of Bethlehem blind his dusky eyn;
Nor all the gods beside
Longer dare abide,   225
  Not Typhon huge ending in snaky twine:
Our Babe, to show his Godhead true,
Can in his swaddling bands control the damned crew.

XXVI

So when the sun in bed,
Curtain'd with cloudy red,   230
  Pillows his chin upon an orient wave;
The flocking shadows pale
Troop to th' infernal jail,
  Each fetter'd ghost slips to his several grave;
And the yellow-skirted fays   235
Fly after the night-steeds, leaving their moon-lov'd maze.

XXVII

But see the Virgin blest,
Hath laid her Babe to rest.
  Time is our tedious song should here have ending:
Heav'n's youngest teemed star,   240
Hath fix'd her polish'd car,
  Her sleeping Lord with handmaid lamp attending.
And all about the courtly stable,
Bright-harness'd angels sit in order serviceable.

ON SHAKESPEAR. 1630

WHAT needs my Shakespear for his honour'd bones,
The labour of an age in piled stones,
Or that his hallow'd relics should be hid
Under a star-ypointing pyramid?
Dear son of memory, great heir of fame,   5
What need'st thou such weak witness of thy name?
Thou in our wonder and astonishment
Hast built thyself a live-long monument:
For whilst to th' shame of slow-endeavouring art
Thy easy numbers flow; and that each heart   10
Hath from the leaves of thy unvalu'd book
Those Delphic lines with deep impression took;
Then thou our fancy of itself bereaving,
Dost make us marble with too much conceiving;
And so sepulcher'd in such pomp dost lie,   15
That kings for such a tomb would wish to die.

[ON HIS BEING ARRIVED TO THE AGE OF 23]

How soon hath Time, the subtle thief of youth,
    Stol'n on his wing my three-and-twentieth year!
    My hasting days fly on with full career,
    But my late spring no bud or blossom shew'th.
Perhaps my semblance might deceive the truth,   5
    That I to manhood am arriv'd so near;
    And inward ripeness doth much less appear,
    That some more timely-happy spirits endu'th.
Yet be it less or more, or soon or slow,
    It shall be still in strictest measure ev'n   10
    To that same lot, however mean, or high,
Toward which Time leads me, and the will of Heav'n;
    All is, if I have grace to use it so,
    As ever in my great Task-Master's eye.

[TO THE NIGHTINGALE]

O NIGHTINGALE, that on yon bloomy spray
  Warbl'st at eve, when all the woods are still,
  Thou with fresh hope the lover's heart dost fill,
  While the jolly hours lead on propitious May;
Thy liquid notes that close the eye of day,   5
  First heard before the shallow cuckoo's bill,
  Portend success in love; O if Jove's will
  Have link'd that amorous power to thy soft lay,
Now timely sing, ere the rude bird of hate
  Foretell my hopeless doom in some grove nigh: 10
  As thou from year to year hast sung too late
For my relief, yet hadst no reason why :
  Whether the Muse, or Love call thee his mate,
  Both them I serve, and of their train am I.

AT A SOLEMN MUSIC

BLEST pair of Sirens, pledges of Heav'n's joy,
Sphere-born harmonious sisters, Voice and Verse,
Wed your divine sounds; and mix'd power employ
Dead things with inbreath'd sense able to pierce;
And to our high-rais'd phantasy present   5
That undisturbed song of pure concent,
Aye sung before the sapphire-colour'd throne
To him that sits thereon
With saintly shout, and solemn jubilee;
Where the bright seraphim in burning row   10
Their loud up-lifted angel trumpets blow,
And the cherubic host in thousand quires
Touch their immortal harps of golden wires,

With those just spirits that wear victorious palms,
Hymns devout and holy psalms　　　　　　　15
Singing everlastingly:
That we on earth with undiscording voice
May rightly answer that melodious noise;
As once we did, till disproportion'd sin
Jarr'd against nature's chime, and with harsh din　　20
Broke the fair music that all creatures made
To their great Lord; whose love their motion sway'd
In perfect diapason, whilst they stood
In first obedience, and their state of good.
O may we soon again renew that song,　　　　25
And keep in tune with Heav'n, till God ere long
To his celestial consort us unite,
To live with him, and sing in endless morn of light.

SONG

ON MAY MORNING

Now the bright morning-star, day's harbinger,
Comes dancing from the east, and leads with her
The flow'ry May, who from her green lap throws
The yellow cowslip, and the pale primrose.
　　Hail bounteous May that dost inspire　　　5
　　Mirth and youth, and warm desire;
　　Woods and groves, are of thy dressing,
　　Hill and dale, doth boast thy blessing;
Thus we salute thee with our early song,
And welcome thee, and wish thee long.　　　10

L'ALLEGRO

HENCE loathed Melancholy,
  Of Cerberus, and blackest Midnight born,
In Stygian cave forlorn
  'Mongst horrid shapes, and shrieks, and sights unholy
Find out some uncouth cell,   5
  Where brooding Darkness spreads his jealous wings,
And the night-raven sings;
  There under ebon shades, and low-brow'd rocks,
As ragged as thy locks,
  In dark Cimmerian desert ever dwell.   10
But come thou goddess fair and free,
In Heav'n yclept Euphrosyne,
And by men, heart-easing Mirth;
Whom lovely Venus at a birth
With two sister Graces more   15
To ivy-crowned Bacchus bore;
Or whether (as some sager sing)
The frolic wind that breathes the spring,
Zephyr with Aurora playing,
As he met her once a-Maying,   20
There on beds of violets blue,
And fresh-blown roses washed in dew,
Fill'd her with thee, a daughter fair,
So buxom, blithe, and debonair.
  Haste thee nymph, and bring with thee   25
Jest and youthful Jollity,
Quips and cranks, and wanton wiles,
Nods, and becks, and wreathed smiles,
Such as hang on Hebe's cheek,
And love to live in dimple sleek;   30
Sport that wrinkled Care derides,

And Laughter holding both his sides.
Come, and trip it as ye go
On the light fantastic toe,
And in thy right hand lead with thee   35
The mountain nymph, sweet Liberty;
And if I give thee honour due,
Mirth, admit me of thy crew,
To live with her, and live with thee,
In unreproved pleasures free;   40
To hear the lark begin his flight,
And singing startle the dull night,
From his watch-tow'r in the skies,
Till the dappled dawn doth rise;
Then to come, in spite of sorrow,   45
And at my window bid good morrow,
Through the sweet-briar, or the vine,
Or the twisted eglantine.
While the cock with lively din,
Scatters the rear of darkness thin,   50
And to the stack, or the barn-door,
Stoutly struts his dames before:
Oft list'ning how the hounds and horn
Cheerly rouse the slumb'ring Morn,
From the side of some hoar hill,   55
Through the high wood echoing shrill.
Sometime walking not unseen,
By hedge-row elms, on hillocks green,
Right against the eastern gate
Where the great Sun begins his state,   60
Rob'd in flames, and amber light,
The clouds in thousand liveries dight.
While the ploughman near at hand,
Whistles o'er the furrow'd land,
And the milkmaid singeth blithe,   65
And the mower whets his scythe,

And every shepherd tells his tale
Under the hawthorn in the dale.
Straight mine eye hath caught new pleasures
Whilst the landscape round it measures;   70
Russet lawns, and fallows gray,
Where the nibbling flocks do stray,
Mountains on whose barren breast
The labouring clouds do often rest;
Meadows trim with daisies pied,   75
Shallow brooks, and rivers wide.
Towers, and battlements it sees
Bosom'd high in tufted trees,
Where perhaps some beauty lies,
The cynosure of neighbouring eyes.   80
Hard by, a cottage chimney smokes,
From betwixt two aged oaks;
Where Corydon and Thyrsis met,
Are at their savoury dinner set
Of herbs, and other country messes,   85
Which the neat-handed Phillis dresses;
And then in haste her bower she leaves,
With Thestylis to bind the sheaves;
Or if the earlier season lead
To the tann'd haycock in the mead.   90
Sometimes with secure delight
The upland hamlets will invite:
When the merry bells ring round,
And the jocund rebecks sound
To many a youth, and many a maid,   95
Dancing in the chequer'd shade;
And young and old come forth to play
On a sunshine holiday,
Till the live-long day-light fail;
Then to the spicy nut-brown ale,   100
With stories told of many a feat,

How faery Mab the junkets eat;
She was pinch'd and pull'd she said;
And he by friars' lantern led,
Tells how the drudging goblin sweat   105
To earn his cream-bowl duly set;
When in one night, ere glimpse of morn,
His shadowy flail hath thresh'd the corn
That ten day-labourers could not end.
Then lies him down the lubber fiend,   110
And stretch'd out all the chimney's length,
Basks at the fire his hairy strength;
And crop-full out of doors he flings,
Ere the first cock his matin rings.
Thus done the tales, to bed they creep,   115
By whispering winds soon lull'd asleep.
Tower'd cities please us then,
And the busy hum of men,
Where throngs of knights and barons bold,
In weeds of peace high triumphs hold,   120
With store of ladies, whose bright eyes
Rain influence, and judge the prize
Of wit, or arms, while both contend
To win her grace, whom all commend.
There let Hymen oft appear,   125
In saffron robe, with taper clear,
And pomp, and feast, and revelry,
With mask, and antique pageantry;
Such sights as youthful poets dream
On summer eves by haunted stream.   130
Then to the well-trod stage anon,
If Jonson's learned sock be on,
Or sweetest Shakespeare, Fancy's child,
Warble his native wood-notes wild.
     And ever against eating cares,   135
Lap me in soft Lydian airs,

Married to immortal verse;
Such as the meeting soul may pierce,
In notes with many a winding bout
Of linked sweetness long drawn out;   140
With wanton heed, and giddy cunning,
The melting voice through mazes running;
Untwisting all the chains that tie
The hidden soul of harmony.
That Orpheus' self may heave his head   145
From golden slumber on a bed
Of heap'd Elysian flow'rs; and hear
Such strains as would have won the ear
Of Pluto, to have quite set free
His half-regain'd Eurydice.   150
    These delights, if thou canst give,
Mirth, with thee I mean to live.

IL PENSEROSO

Hence vain deluding joys,
    The brood of Folly without father bred,
How little you bestead,
    Or fill the fixed mind with all your toys;
Dwell in some idle brain;   5
    And fancies fond with gaudy shapes possess,
As thick and numberless
    As the gay motes that people the sun-beams,
Or likest hovering dreams,
    The fickle pensioners of Morpheus' train.   10
But hail thou Goddess, sage and holy,
Hail divinest Melancholy,

Whose saintly visage is too bright
To hit the sense of human sight;
And therefore to our weaker view,   15
O'erlaid with black, staid Wisdom's hue;
Black, but such as in esteem
Prince Memnon's sister might beseem;
Or that starr'd Ethiop queen that strove
To set her beauty's praise above   20
The sea nymphs, and their powers offended. //
Yet thou art higher far descended;
Thee bright-hair'd Vesta long of yore,
To solitary Saturn bore;
His daughter she (in Saturn's reign,   25
Such mixture was not held a stain);
Oft in glimmering bow'rs, and glades
He met her; and in secret shades
Of woody Ida's inmost grove,
While yet there was no fear of Jove. //   30
Come pensive Nun, devout and pure,
Sober, steadfast, and demure,
All in a robe of darkest grain,
Flowing with majestic train,
And sable stole of cypress lawn,   35
Over thy decent shoulders drawn. //
    Come, but keep thy wonted state,
    With ev'n step, and musing gait,
    And looks commercing with the skies,
    Thy rapt soul sitting in thine eyes: 40
    There held in holy passion still,
    Forget thyself to marble, till
    With a sad leaden downward cast,
    Thou fix them on the earth as fast.
    And join with thee calm Peace, and Quiet,   45
    Spare Fast, that oft with gods doth diet,
    And hears the Muses in a ring,

Aye round about Jove's altar sing.
And add to these retired Leisure,
That in trim gardens takes his pleasure;   50
But first, and chiefest, with thee bring,
Him that soars on golden wing,
Guiding the fiery-wheeled throne,
The cherub Contemplation,
And the mute Silence hist along,   55
'Less Philomel will deign a song,
In her sweetest, saddest plight,
Smoothing the rugged brow of Night,
While Cynthia checks her dragon yoke,
Gently o'er th' accustomed oak: 60
Sweet bird that shunn'st the noise of folly,
Most musical, most melancholy!
Thee chantress oft the woods among,
I woo to hear thy even-song;
And missing thee, I walk unseen   65
On the dry smooth-shaven green,
To behold the wand'ring Moon,
Riding near her highest noon,
Like one that had been led astray
Through the Heav'n's wide pathless way;   70
And oft, as if her head she bow'd,
Stooping through a fleecy cloud.
Oft on a plat of rising ground,
I hear the far-off curfew sound,
Over some wide-water'd shore,   75
Swinging slow with sullen roar;
Or if the air will not permit,
Some still removed place will fit,
Where glowing embers through the room
Teach light to counterfeit a gloom,   80
Far from all resort of mirth,
Save the cricket on the hearth,

Or the bellman's drowsy charm,
To bless the doors from nightly harm:
Or let my lamp at midnight hour　　　　　85
Be seen in some high lonely tow'r,
Where I may oft outwatch the Bear,
With thrice-great Hermes; or unsphere
The spirit of Plato to unfold
What worlds, or what vast regions hold　　90
The immortal mind that hath forsook
Her mansion in this fleshly nook;
And of those demons that are found
In fire, air, flood, or under ground,
Whose power hath a true consent　　　　95
With planet, or with element.
Sometime let gorgeous Tragedy
In scepter'd pall come sweeping by,
Presenting Thebes, or Pelops' line,
Or the tale of Troy divine,　　　　　　100
Or what (though rare) of later age,
Ennobled hath the buskin'd stage.
　　But, O sad Virgin, that thy power
Might raise Musaeus from his bower,
Or bid the soul of Orpheus sing　　　　105
Such notes as warbled to the string
Drew iron tears down Pluto's cheek,
And made Hell grant what love did seek.
Or call up him that left half told
The story of Cambuscan bold,　　　　　110
Of Camball, and of Algarsife,
And who had Canace to wife,
That own'd the virtuous ring and glass,
And of the wondrous horse of brass
On which the Tartar king did ride;　　　115
And if aught else great bards beside
In sage and solemn tunes have sung,

Of tourneys and of trophies hung;
Of forests, and enchantments drear,
Where more is meant than meets the ear.   120
   Thus Night oft see me in thy pale career,
Till civil-suited Morn appear;
Not trick'd and frounc'd, as she was wont
With the Attic boy to hunt,
But kerchief'd in a comely cloud,   125
While rocking winds are piping loud:
Or usher'd with a shower still,
When the gust hath blown his fill,
Ending on the rustling leaves,
With minute drops from off the eaves.   130
And when the sun begins to fling
His flaring beams, me, Goddess, bring
To arched walks of twilight groves,
And shadows brown that Sylvan loves,
Of pine, or monumental oak,   135
Where the rude axe with heaved stroke,
Was never heard the nymphs to daunt,
Or fright them from their hallow'd haunt.
There in close covert by some brook,
Where no profaner eye may look,   140
Hide me from day's garish eye;
While the bee with honeyed thigh,
That at her flow'ry work doth sing,
And the waters murmuring
With such consort as they keep,   145
Entice the dewy-feather'd Sleep;
And let some strange mysterious dream
Wave at his wings in airy stream
Of lively portraiture display'd,
Softly on my eyelids laid.   150
And as I wake, sweet music breathe
Above, about, or underneath,

Sent by some spirit to mortals good,
Or th' unseen Genius of the wood.

But let my due feet never fail   155
To walk the studious cloister's pale,
And love the high embowed roof,
With antique pillars massy proof,
And storied windows richly dight,
Casting a dim religious light.   160
There let the pealing organ blow
To the full voic'd quire below,
In service high, and anthems clear,
As may with sweetness, through mine ear
Dissolve me into ecstasies,   165
And bring all Heav'n before mine eyes.

And may at last my weary age
Find out the peaceful hermitage,
The hairy gown and mossy cell,
Where I may sit, and rightly spell   170
Of every star that Heav'n doth show,
And every herb that sips the dew;
Till old experience do attain
To something like prophetic strain.

These pleasures Melancholy give,   175
And I with thee will choose to live.

A MASKE

PRESENTED

At Ludlow Castle,

1 6 3 4 :

On *Michaelmasse night*, before the

RIGHT HONORABLE,

IOHN *Earle of Bridgewater* , *Vicount* BRACKLY,
Lord *Præsident of* WALES , And one of
His MAIESTIES moſt honorable
Privie Counſell.

Eheu quid volui miſero mihi ! floribus auſtrum
Perditus ————

LONDON

Printed for HYMPHREY ROBINSON,
at the ſigne of the *Three Pidgeons* in
Pauls Church-yard. 1 6 3 7.

From COMUS

THE PERSONS

THE ATTENDANT SPIRIT, *afterwards in the habit of* Thyrsis.
COMUS, *with his crew.*   THE LADY.   FIRST BROTHER.
SECOND BROTHER.   SABRINA, *the Nymph.*

THE CHIEF PERSONS WHICH PRESENTED WERE
The Lord BRACKLEY.   *Mr.* THOMAS EGERTON, *his brother.*
The Lady ALICE EGERTON.

COMUS *enters, with a charming-rod in one hand, his glass in the other:
with him a rout of monsters, headed like sundry sorts of wild beasts,
but otherwise like men and women, their apparel glistering. They come
in making a riotous and unruly noise, with torches in their hands.*

COMUS

THE star that bids the shepherd fold,
Now the top of Heav'n doth hold;
And the gilded car of day   95
His glowing axle doth allay
In the steep Atlantic stream;
And the slope Sun his upward beam
Shoots against the dusky pole;
Pacing toward the other goal   100
Of his chamber in the East.
Meanwhile welcome joy, and feast,
Midnight shout, and revelry,
Tipsy dance, and jollity.
Braid your locks with rosy twine,   105
Dropping odours, dropping wine.
Rigour now is gone to bed,
And Advice with scrupulous head,
Strict Age, and sour Severity,
With their grave saws in slumber lie.   110

We that are of purer fire
Imitate the starry quire,
Who in their nightly watchful spheres
Lead in swift round the months and years.
The sounds, and seas with all their finny drove   115
Now to the moon in wavering morrice move;
And on the tawny sands and shelves,
Trip the pert fairies and the dapper elves.
By dimpled brook, and fountain brim,
The wood-nymphs deck'd with daisies trim,   120
Their merry wakes and pastimes keep:
What hath night to do with sleep?
Come, knit hands, and beat the ground,
In a light fantastic round.

THE MEASURE

Break off, break off, I feel the different pace   145
Of some chaste footing near about this ground.
Run to your shrouds, within these brakes and trees;
Our number may affright: some virgin sure
(For so I can distinguish by mine art)
Benighted in these woods. Now to my charms,   150
And to my wily trains; I shall ere long
Be well stock'd with as fair a herd as graz'd
About my mother Circe. Thus I hurl
My dazzling spells into the spungy air,
Of power to cheat the eye with blear illusion,   155
And give it false presentments; lest the place
And my quaint habits breed astonishment,
And put the damsel to suspicious flight,
Which must not be, for that's against my course;
I under fair pretence of friendly ends,   160
And well-plac'd words of glozing courtesy,
Baited with reasons not unplausible,
Wind me into the easy-hearted man,

And hug him into snares. When once her eye
Hath met the virtue of this magic dust,   165
I shall appear some harmless villager
Whom thrift keeps up about his country gear.
But here she comes; I fairly step aside
And hearken, if I may, her business here.

The LADY *enters*

Lady. This way the noise was, if mine ear be true,
My best guide now; methought it was the sound 171
Of riot, and ill-manag'd merriment;
Such as the jocund flute; or gamesome pipe
Stirs up among the loose unletter'd hinds,
When for their teeming flocks, and granges full, 175
In wanton dance they praise the bounteous Pan,
And thank the gods amiss. I should be loth
To meet the rudeness, and swill'd insolence
Of such late wassailers; yet O where else
Shall I inform my unacquainted feet   180
In the blind mazes of this tangl'd wood?
My brothers when they saw me wearied out
With this long way, resolving here to lodge
Under the spreading favour of these pines,
Stepp'd, as they said, to the next thicket side   185
To bring me berries, or such cooling fruit
As the kind hospitable woods provide.
They left me then, when the grey-hooded Ev'n,
Like a sad votarist in palmer's weed,
Rose from the hindmost wheels of Phoebus' wain.   190
But where they are, and why they came not back,
Is now the labour of my thoughts; 'tis likeliest
They had engag'd their wand'ring steps too far,
And envious Darkness, ere they could return,
Had stole them from me; else, O thievish Night,   195

Why shouldst thou, but for some felonious end,
In thy dark lantern thus close up the stars,
That Nature hung in Heav'n, and fill'd their lamps
With everlasting oil, to give due light
To the misled and lonely traveller?   200
This is the place, as well as I may guess,
Whence even now the tumult of loud mirth
Was rife, and perfect in my list'ning ear,
Yet nought but single darkness do I find.
What might this be? A thousand fantasies   205
Begin to throng into my memory
Of calling shapes, and beck'ning shadows dire,
And airy tongues, that syllable men's names
On sands, and shores, and desert wildernesses.
These thoughts may startle well, but not astound 210
The virtuous mind, that ever walks attended
By a strong siding champion, Conscience.—
O welcome pure-ey'd Faith, white-handed Hope,
Thou hovering angel girt with golden wings,
And thou unblemish'd form of Chastity!   215
I see ye visibly, and now believe
That he, the Supreme good, t' whom all things ill
Are but as slavish officers of vengeance,
Would send a glist'ring guardian, if need were,
To keep my life and honour unassail'd.   220
Was I deceiv'd, or did a sable cloud
Turn forth her silver lining on the night?
I did not err, there does a sable cloud
Turn forth her silver lining on the night,
And casts a gleam over this tufted grove.   225
I cannot hallo to my brothers, but
Such noise as I can make to be heard farthest
I'll venture, for my new enliv'n'd spirits
Prompt me; and they perhaps are not far off.

SONG

Sweet Echo, sweetest Nymph, that liv'st unseen 230
    Within thy airy shell
    By slow Meander's margent green;
And in the violet embroider'd vale,
    Where the love-lorn nightingale
Nightly to thee her sad song mourneth well: 235
Canst thou not tell me of a gentle pair
    That likest thy Narcissus are?
     O if thou have
    Hid them in some flow'ry cave,
     Tell me but where,   240
Sweet Queen of Parley, Daughter of the Sphere;
So may'st thou be translated to the skies,
And give resounding grace to all Heav'n's harmonies.

Comus. Can any mortal mixture of earth's mould
Breathe such divine enchanting ravishment?   245
Sure something holy lodges in that breast,
And with these raptures moves the vocal air
To testify his hidd'n residence;
How sweetly did they float upon the wings
Of silence, through the empty-vaulted night,   250
At every fall smoothing the raven down
Of Darkness till it smil'd: I have oft heard
My mother Circe with the Sirens three,
Amidst the flowery-kirtl'd Naiades
Culling their potent herbs, and baleful drugs;   255
Who as they sung, would take the prison'd soul
And lap it in Elysium; Scylla wept,
And chid her barking waves into attention;
And fell Charybdis murmur'd soft applause:
Yet they in pleasing slumber lull'd the sense,   260
And in sweet madness robb'd it of itself;

But such a sacred, and home-felt delight,
Such sober certainty of waking bliss
I never heard till now. I'll speak to her,
And she shall be my queen. Hail, foreign wonder,
Whom certain these rough shades did never breed ; 266
Unless the goddess that in rural shrine
Dwell'st here with Pan, or Sylvan, by blest song
Forbidding every bleak unkindly fog
To touch the prosperous growth of this tall wood.   270
   Lady. Nay, gentle shepherd, ill is lost that praise
That is address'd to unattending ears ;
Not any boast of skill, but extreme shift
How to regain my sever'd company,
Compell'd me to awake the courteous Echo   275
To give me answer from her mossy couch.
   Com. What chance, good lady, hath bereft you thus ?
   Lady. Dim darkness, and this leafy labyrinth.
   Com. Could that divide you from near-ushering guides ?
   Lady. They left me weary on a grassy turf.   280
   Com. By falsehood, or discourtesy, or why ?
   Lady. To seek i' th' valley some cool friendly spring.
   Com. And left your fair side all unguarded, lady ?
   Lady. They were but twain, and purpos'd quick return.
   Com. Perhaps forestalling night prevented them.   285
   Lady. How easy my misfortune is to hit !
   Com. Imports their loss, beside the present need ?
   Lady. No less than if I should my brothers lose.
   Com. Were they of manly prime, or youthful bloom ?
   Lady. As smooth as Hebe's their unrazor'd lips.   290
   Com. Two such I saw, what time the labour'd ox
In his loose traces from the furrow came,
And the swink'd hedger at his supper sat ;
I saw them under a green mantling vine
That crawls along the side of yon small hill,   295
Plucking ripe clusters from the tender shoots,
Their port was more than human, as they stood ;

I took it for a faëry vision
Of some gay creatures of the element
That in the colours of the rainbow live,   300
And play i' th' plighted clouds. I was awe-struck,
And as I pass'd, I worshipp'd ; if those you seek,
It were a journey like the path to Heav'n,
To help you find them.
    Lady.   Gentle villager,
What readiest way would bring me to that place ?   305
    Comus. Due west it rises from this shrubby point.
    Lady. To find out that, good shepherd, I suppose,
In such a scant allowance of star-light,
Would overtask the best land-pilot's art,
Without the sure guess of well-practis'd feet.   310
    Comus. I know each lane, and every alley green,
Dingle, or bushy dell of this wild wood,
And every bosky bourn from side to side,
My daily walks and ancient neighbourhood :
And if your stray attendance be yet lodg'd,   315
Or shroud within these limits, I shall know
Ere morrow wake, or the low-roosted lark
From her thatch'd pallet rouse ; if otherwise,
I can conduct you, Lady, to a low
But loyal cottage, where you may be safe   320
Till further quest.
    Lady.   Shepherd, I take thy word,
And trust thy honest offer'd courtesy,
Which oft is sooner found in lowly sheds
With smoky rafters, than in tap'stry halls
In courts of princes, where it first was nam'd,   325
And yet is most pretended : in a place
Less warranted than this, or less secure,
I cannot be, that I should fear to change it.
Eye me, blest Providence, and square my trial
To my proportion'd strength. Shepherd, lead on.— 330
                        [*Exeunt.*

The TWO BROTHERS *enter*

El. Br. Unmuffle, ye faint stars; and thou fair Moon
That wont'st to love the traveller's benison,
Stoop thy pale visage through an amber cloud,
And disinherit Chaos, that reigns here
In double night of darkness, and of shades;   335
Or if your influence be quite damm'd up
With black usurping mists, some gentle taper,
Though a rush-candle from the wicker hole
Of some clay habitation, visit us
With thy long levell'd rule of streaming light,   340
And thou shalt be our star of Arcady,
Or Tyrian Cynosure.
    Second Brother.   Or if our eyes
Be barr'd that happiness, might we but hear
The folded flocks penn'd in their wattled cotes,
Or sound of pastoral reed with oaten stops,   345
Or whistle from the lodge, or village cock
Count the night watches to his feathery dames,
'Twould be some solace yet, some little cheering
In this close dungeon of innumerous boughs.
But O that hapless virgin our lost sister,   350
Where may she wander now, whither betake her
From the chill dew, amongst rude burs and thistles?
Perhaps some cold bank is her bolster now,
Or 'gainst the rugged bark of some broad elm
Leans her unpillow'd head, fraught with sad fears.   355
What if in wild amazement, and affright,
Or, while we speak, within the direful grasp
Of savage hunger, or of savage heat?
    Elder Brother. Peace brother, be not over-exquisite
To cast the fashion of uncertain evils;   360
For grant they be so, while they rest unknown,
What need a man forestall his date of grief,

And run to meet what he would most avoid?
Or if they be but false alarms of fear,
How bitter is such self-delusion?   365
I do not think my sister so to seek,
Or so unprincipl'd in virtue's book,
And the sweet peace that goodness bosoms ever,
As that the single want of light and noise
(Not being in danger, as I trust she is not),   370
Could stir the constant mood of her calm thoughts,
And put them into misbecoming plight.
Virtue could see to do what Virtue would
By her own radiant light, though sun and moon
Were in the flat sea sunk.   And Wisdom's self   375
Oft seeks to sweet retired solitude;
Where with her best nurse Contemplation,
She plumes her feathers, and lets grow her wings,
That in the various bustle of resort
Were all to-ruffl'd and sometimes impair'd.   380
He that has light within his own clear breast
May sit i' th' centre, and enjoy bright day;
But he that hides a dark soul, and foul thoughts,
Benighted walks under the mid-day sun;
Himself is his own dungeon.
   Second Brother.   'Tis most true   385
That musing Meditation most affects
The pensive secrecy of desert cell,
Far from the cheerful haunt of men, and herds,
And sits as safe as in a senate-house;
For who would rob a hermit of his weeds,   390
His few books, or his beads, or maple dish,
Or do his grey hairs any violence?
But Beauty, like the fair Hesperian tree
Laden with blooming gold, had need the guard
Of dragon watch with unenchanted eye,   395
To save her blossoms, and defend her fruit

From the rash hand of bold Incontinence.
You may as well spread out the unsunn'd heaps
Of misers' treasure by an outlaw's den,
And tell me it is safe, as bid me hope   400
Danger will wink on Opportunity,
And let a single helpless maiden pass
Uninjur'd in this wild surrounding waste.
Of night, or loneliness it recks me not;
I fear the dread events that dog them both,   405
Lest some ill greeting touch attempt the person
Of our unowned sister.
   Elder Brother.   I do not, brother,
Infer, as if I thought my sister's state
Secure without all doubt, or controversy:
Yet where an equal poise of hope and fear   410
Does arbitrate th' event, my nature is
That I incline to hope, rather than fear,
And gladly banish squint suspicion.
My sister is not so defenceless left
As you imagine; she has a hidden strength   415
Which you remember not.
   Second Brother.   What hidden strength,
Unless the strength of Heav'n, if you mean that?
   El. Br. I mean that too, but yet a hidden strength
Which if Heav'n gave it, may be term'd her own:
'Tis chastity, my brother, chastity: 420
She that has that, is clad in complete steel,
And like a quiver'd nymph with arrows keen
May trace huge forests, and unharbour'd heaths,
Infamous hills, and sandy perilous wilds;
Where through the sacred rays of chastity,   425
No savage fierce, bandit, or mountaineer
Will dare to soil her virgin purity;
Yea there, where very desolation dwells
By grots, and caverns shagg'd with horrid shades,

She may pass on with unblench'd majesty;   430
Be it not done in pride, or in presumption.
Some say, no evil thing that walks by night
In fog, or fire, by lake, or moorish fen,
Blue meagre hag, or stubborn unlaid ghost
That breaks his magic chains at curfew time,   435
No goblin, or swart faëry of the mine,
Hath hurtful power o'er true virginity.
Do ye believe me yet, or shall I call
Antiquity from the old schools of Greece
To testify the arms of chastity?   440
Hence had the huntress Dian her dread bow,
Fair silver-shafted queen for ever chaste,
Wherewith she tam'd the brinded lioness
And spotted mountain pard, but set at naught
The frivolous bolt of Cupid; gods and men   445
Fear'd her stern frown, and she was queen o' th' woods.
What was that snaky-headed Gorgon shield
That wise Minerva wore, unconquer'd virgin,
Wherewith she freez'd her foes to congeal'd stone?
But rigid looks of chaste austerity,   450
And noble grace that dash'd brute violence
With sudden adoration, and blank awe.
So dear to Heav'n is saintly chastity,
That when a soul is found sincerely so,
A thousand liveried angels lackey her,   455
Driving far off each thing of sin and guilt;
And in clear dream, and solemn vision,
Tell her of things that no gross ear can hear,
Till oft converse with heav'nly habitants
Begin to cast a beam on th' outward shape,   460
The unpolluted temple of the mind,
And turns it by degrees to the soul's essence,
Till all be made immortal: but when lust
By unchaste looks, loose gestures, and foul talk,

But most by lewd and lavish act of sin   465
Lets in defilement to the inward parts
The soul grows clotted by contagion,
Imbodies, and imbrutes, till she quite lose
The divine property of her first being.
Such are those thick and gloomy shadows damp   470
Oft seen in charnel vaults and sepulchres
Lingering, and sitting by a new-made grave;
As loth to leave the body that it lov'd,
And link'd itself by carnal sensualty
To a degenerate and degraded state.   475
  Second Brother. How charming is divine philo-
    sophy!
Not harsh, and crabbed as dull fools suppose,
But musical as is Apollo's lute,
And a perpetual feast of nectar'd sweets,
Where no crude surfeit reigns.
  Elder Brother.   List, list, I hear   480
Some far off hallo break the silent air.
  Second Brother. Methought so too; what should
    it be?
  Elder Brother.   For certain
Either some one like us night-founder'd here,
Or else some neighbour woodman, or at worst,
Some roving robber calling to his fellows.   485
  Sec. Br. Heav'n keep my sister! Again, again, and
    near;
Best draw, and stand upon our guard.
  Elder Brother.   I'll hallo;
If he be friendly he comes well; if not,
Defence is a good cause, and Heav'n be for us.

  *   *   *   *   *   *   *

SONG

Sabrina fair,
  Listen where thou art sitting   860
Under the glassy, cool, translucent wave:
  In twisted braids of lilies knitting
The loose train of thy amber-dropping hair;
  Listen for dear honour's sake,
  Goddess of the silver lake,   865
      Listen and save.
Listen and appear to us
In name of great Oceanus,
By the earth-shaking Neptune's mace,
And Tethys' grave majestic pace,   870
By hoary Nereus' wrinkled look,
And the Carpathian wizard's hook,
By scaly Triton's winding shell,
And old sooth-saying Glaucus' spell,
By Leucothea's lovely hands,   875
And her son that rules the strands,
By Thetis' tinsel-slipper'd feet,
And the songs of Sirens sweet,
By dead Parthenope's dear tomb,
And fair Ligea's golden comb,   880
Wherewith she sits on diamond rocks,
Sleeking her soft alluring locks,
By all the nymphs that nightly dance
Upon thy streams with wily glance,
Rise, rise, and heave thy rosy head   885
From thy coral-pav'n bed,
And bridle in thy headlong wave,
Till thou our summons answered have.
      Listen and save.

SABRINA *rises, attended by Water-Nymphs, and sings.*

By the rushy-fringed bank,   890
Where grows the willow and the osier dank,
　My sliding chariot stays;
Thick set with agate, and the azurn sheen
Of turkis blue, and em'rald green
　That in the channel strays;   895
Whilst from off the waters fleet,
Thus I set my printless feet
O'er the cowslip's velvet head,
　That bends not as I tread;
Gentle swain, at thy request   900
　I am here.

　Spirit.　Goddess dear,
We implore thy powerful hand
To undo the charmed band
Of true Virgin here distress'd,   905
Through the force, and through the wile
Of umblest enchanter vile.

　Sabrina.　Shepherd, 'tis my office best
To help ensnared chastity;
Brightest Lady, look on me;   910
Thus I sprinkle on thy breast
Drops that from my fountain pure,
I have kept of precious cure,
Thrice upon thy finger's tip,
Thrice upon thy rubied lip;   915
Next this marble venom'd seat
Smear'd with gums of glutinous heat
I touch with chaste palms moist and cold;
Now the spell hath lost his hold;
And I must haste ere morning hour   920
To wait in Amphitrite's bow'r.

　　*　　　*　　　*　　　*　　　*　　　*　　　*

H 2

The SPIRIT *epiloguizes.*

Spirit. To the ocean now I fly,
And those happy climes that lie
Where day never shuts his eye,
Up in the broad fields of the sky:
There I suck the liquid air   980
All amidst the gardens fair
Of Hesperus, and his daughters three
That sing about the golden tree:
Along the crisped shades and bowers
Revels the spruce and jocund Spring;   985
The Graces, and the rosy-bosom'd Hours,
Thither all their bounties bring,
That there eternal summer dwells;
And west winds, with musky wing
About the cedarn alleys fling   990
Nard, and cassia's balmy smells.
Iris there with humid bow,
Waters the odorous banks that blow
Flowers of more mingled hue
Than her purfl'd scarf can show;   995
And drenches with Elysian dew
(List mortals, if your ears be true)
Beds of hyacinth and roses,
Where young Adonis oft reposes,
Waxing well of his deep wound   1000
In slumber soft; and on the ground
Sadly sits th' Assyrian queen:
But far above in spangled sheen
Celestial Cupid her fam'd son advanc'd,
Holds his dear Psyche sweet entranc'd,   1005
After her wand'ring labours long;
Till free consent the gods among
Make her his eternal bride;
And from her fair unspotted side

Two blissful twins are to be born,   1010
Youth and Joy; so Jove hath sworn.
  But now my task is smoothly done,
I can fly, or I can run
Quickly to the green earth's end,
Where the bow'd welkin slow doth bend;   1015
And from thence can soar as soon
To the corners of the moon.
  Mortals that would follow me,
Love Virtue; she alone is free:
She can teach ye how to climb   1020
Higher than the sphery chime;
Or if Virtue feeble were,
Heav'n itself would stoop to her.

Obsequies to the memorie of Mr EDWARD KING,

Anno Dom. 1638.

Printed by *Th. Buck*, and *R. Daniel*, printers to the *Universitie* of *Cambridge*. 1638.

LYCIDAS

In this MONODY *the Author bewails a learned friend,
unfortunately drowned in his passage from Chester on
the Irish seas,* 1637. *And by occasion foretells the ruin
of our corrupted clergy then in their height.*

YET once more, O ye laurels, and once more,
Ye myrtles brown, with ivy never-sere,
I come to pluck your berries harsh and crude,
And with forc'd fingers rude
Shatter your leaves before the mellowing year.   5
Bitter constraint, and sad occasion dear,
Compels me to disturb your season due:
For Lycidas is dead, dead ere his prime,
Young Lycidas, and hath not left his peer:
Who would not sing for Lycidas? he knew   10
Himself to sing, and build the lofty rhyme.
He must not float upon his wat'ry bier
Unwept, and welter to the parching wind,
Without the meed of some melodious tear.

   Begin then, Sisters of the sacred well,   15
That from beneath the seat of Jove doth spring;
Begin, and somewhat loudly sweep the string:
Hence with denial vain, and coy excuse,
So may some gentle Muse
With lucky words favour my destin'd urn;   20
And as he passes turn,
And bid fair peace be to my sable shroud.
For we were nurs'd upon the self-same hill,
Fed the same flock, by fountain, shade, and rill.

Together both, ere the high lawns appear'd   25
Under the opening eyelids of the Morn,
We drove afield; and both together heard
What time the gray-fly winds her sultry horn,
Batt'ning our flocks with the fresh dews of night,
Oft till the star that rose at ev'ning, bright,   30
Toward Heav'n's descent had slop'd his westering wheel.
Meanwhile the rural ditties were not mute,
Temper'd to th' oaten flute;
Rough Satyrs danc'd, and Fauns with clov'n heel
From the glad sound would not be absent long,   35
And old Damœtas lov'd to hear our song.

    But O the heavy change, now thou art gone,
Now thou art gone, and never must return!
Thee shepherd, thee the woods, and desert caves,
With wild thyme and the gadding vine o'ergrown,   40
And all their echoes mourn.
The willows, and the hazel copses green,
Shall now no more be seen,
Fanning their joyous leaves to thy soft lays:
As killing as the canker to the rose,   45
Or taint-worm to the weanling herds that graze,
Or frost to flowers, that their gay wardrobe wear,
When first the white-thorn blows;
Such, Lycidas, thy loss to shepherd's ear.

    Where were ye, Nymphs, when the remorseless deep
Clos'd o'er the head of your lov'd Lycidas?   51
For neither were ye playing on the steep,
Where your old bards, the famous Druids lie,
Nor on the shaggy top of Mona high,
Nor yet where Deva spreads her wizard stream: 55
Ay me, I fondly dream!
Had ye been there . . . for what could that have done?
What could the Muse herself that Orpheus bore,
The Muse herself, for her enchanting son

Whom universal nature did lament;   60
When by the rout that made the hideous roar,
His gory visage down the stream was sent,
Down the swift Hebrus to the Lesbian shore?
Alas! what boots it with incessant care
To tend the homely slighted shepherd's trade,   65
And strictly meditate the thankless Muse?
Were it not better done as others use,
To sport with Amaryllis in the shade,
Or with the tangles of Neæra's hair?
Fame is the spur that the clear spirit doth raise   70
(That last infirmity of noble mind),
To scorn delights, and live laborious days;
But the fair guerdon when we hope to find,
And think to burst out into sudden blaze,
Comes the blind Fury with th' abhorred shears,   75
And slits the thin-spun life. 'But not the praise,'
Phœbus repli'd, and touch'd my trembling ears;
'Fame is no plant that grows on mortal soil,
Nor in the glistering foil
Set off to th' world, nor in broad rumour lies;   80
But lives and spreads aloft by those pure eyes,
And perfect witness of all-judging Jove;
As he pronounces lastly on each deed,
Of so much fame in Heav'n expect thy meed.'

O fountain Arethuse, and thou honour'd flood,   85
Smooth-sliding Mincius, crown'd with vocal reeds,
That strain I heard was of a higher mood:
But now my oat proceeds,
And listens to the Herald of the sea
That came in Neptune's plea;   90
He ask'd the waves, and ask'd the felon winds,
What hard mishap hath doom'd this gentle swain?
And question'd every gust of rugged wings
That blows from off each beaked promontory;

They knew not of his story,   95
And sage Hippotades their answer brings;
That not a blast was from his dungeon stray'd,
The air was calm, and on the level brine
Sleek Panope with all her sisters play'd.
It was that fatal and perfidious bark,   100
Built in th' eclipse, and rigg'd with curses dark,
That sunk so low that sacred head of thine.
   Next Camus, reverend sire, went footing slow,
His mantle hairy, and his bonnet sedge,
Inwrought with figures dim, and on the edge   105
Like to that sanguine flower inscrib'd with woe.
'Ah! who hath reft (quoth he) my dearest pledge?'
Last came, and last did go,
The pilot of the Galilean lake;
Two massy keys he bore, of metals twain,   110
(The golden opes, the iron shuts amain)
He shook his mitr'd locks, and stern bespake:
'How well could I have spar'd for thee, young swain,
Enow of such as for their bellies' sake,
Creep and intrude, and climb into the fold?   115
Of other care they little reck'ning make,
Than how to scramble at the shearers' feast,
And shove away the worthy bidden guest.
Blind mouths! that scarce themselves know how to hold
A sheephook, or have learn'd aught else the least   120
That to the faithful herdsman's art belongs!
What recks it them? What need they? They are sped;
And when they list, their lean and flashy songs
Grate on their scrannel pipes of wretched straw:
The hungry sheep look up, and are not fed,   125
But swoll'n with wind, and the rank mist they draw,
Rot inwardly, and foul contagion spread:
Besides what the grim wolf with privy paw
Daily devours apace, and nothing said;

But that two-handed engine at the door 130
Stands ready to smite once, and smite no more.
  Return Alpheus, the dread voice is past,
That shrunk thy streams; return Sicilian Muse,
And call the vales, and bid them hither cast
Their bells, and flowrets of a thousand hues. 135
Ye valleys low, where the mild whispers use
Of shades and wanton winds, and gushing brooks,
On whose fresh lap the swart star sparely looks,
Throw hither all your quaint enamell'd eyes,
That on the green turf suck the honeyed show'rs, 140
And purple all the ground with vernal flow'rs.
Bring the rathe primrose that forsaken dies,
The tufted crow-toe, and pale jessamine,
The white pink, and the pansy freak'd with jet,
The glowing violet, 145
The musk-rose, and the well-attir'd woodbine;
With cowslips wan that hang the pensive head,
And every flower that sad embroidery wears:
Bid Amaranthus all his beauty shed,
And daffadillies fill their cups with tears, 150
To strew the laureat hearse where Lycid lies.
For so to interpose a little ease,
Let our frail thoughts dally with false surmise.
Ay me! whilst thee the shores, and sounding seas
Wash far away, where'er thy bones are hurl'd; 155
Whether beyond the stormy Hebrides,
Where thou perhaps under the whelming tide
Visit'st the bottom of the monstrous world;
Or whether thou to our moist vows deni'd,
Sleep'st by the fable of Bellerus old, 160
Where the great vision of the guarded mount
Looks toward Namancos, and Bayona's hold;
Look homeward Angel now, and melt with ruth:
And, O ye dolphins, waft the hapless youth.

Weep no more, woeful shepherds, weep no more;　165
For Lycidas your sorrow is not dead,
Sunk though he be beneath the wat'ry floor;
So sinks the day-star in the ocean bed;
And yet anon repairs his drooping head,
And tricks his beams, and with new-spangled ore　170
Flames in the forehead of the morning sky:
So Lycidas sunk low, but mounted high,
Through the dear might of him that walk'd the waves:
Where other groves and other streams along,
With nectar pure his oozy locks he laves,　175
And hears the unexpressive nuptial song,
In the blest kingdoms meek of joy and love.
There entertain him all the saints above,
In solemn troops, and sweet societies,
That sing, and singing in their glory move,　180
And wipe the tears for ever from his eyes.
Now, Lycidas, the shepherds weep no more;
Henceforth thou art the Genius of the shore,
In thy large recompense; and shalt be good
To all that wander in that perilous flood.　185
　Thus sang the uncouth swain to th' oaks and rills,
While the still morn went out with sandals gray;
He touch'd the tender stops of various quills,
With eager thought warbling his Doric lay:
And now the sun had stretch'd out all the hills,　190
And now was dropp'd into the western bay;
At last he rose, and twitch'd his mantle blue:
To-morrow to fresh woods, and pastures new.

WHEN THE ASSAULT WAS INTENDED TO THE CITY

CAPTAIN or Colonel, or Knight in arms,
  Whose chance on these defenceless doors may seize,
  If ever deed of honour did thee please,
  Guard them, and him within protect from harms:
He can requite thee, for he knows the charms   5
  That call fame on such gentle acts as these;
  And he can spread thy name o'er lands and seas,
  Whatever clime the sun's bright circle warms.
Lift not thy spear against the Muses' bow'r;
  The great Emathian conqueror bid spare   10
  The house of Pindarus, when temple and tow'r
Went to the ground; and the repeated air
  Of sad Electra's poet had the power
  To save th' Athenian walls from ruin bare.

TO THE LORD GENERAL CROMWELL

May, 1652

On the proposals of certain Ministers at the Committee for Propagation of the Gospel

CROMWELL, our chief of men, who through a cloud
  Not of war only, but detractions rude,
  Guided by faith and matchless fortitude,
  To peace and truth thy glorious way hast plough'd,
And on the neck of crowned Fortune proud   5
  Hast rear'd God's trophies, and his work pursu'd;
  While Darwen stream with blood of Scots imbru'd,
  And Dunbar field, resounds thy praises loud,
And Worcester's laureat wreath. Yet much remains
  To conquer still; peace hath her victories   10
  No less renown'd than war; new foes arise,
Threat'ning to bind our souls with secular chains:
  Help us to save free conscience from the paw
  Of hireling wolves, whose Gospel is their maw.

[ON HIS BLINDNESS]

When I consider how my light is spent,
  Ere half my days, in this dark world and wide,
  And that one talent which is death to hide
  Lodg'd with me useless, though my soul more bent
To serve therewith my Maker, and present   5
  My true account, lest he returning chide;
  'Doth God exact day-labour, light deni'd?'
  I fondly ask: but Patience, to prevent
That murmur, soon replies, 'God doth not need
  Either man's work, or his own gifts; who best   10
  Bear his mild yoke, they serve him best: his state
Is kingly; thousands at his bidding speed,
  And post o'er land and ocean without rest;
  They also serve who only stand and wait.'

ON THE LATE MASSACRE IN PIEDMONT

Avenge, O Lord, thy slaughter'd saints, whose bones
  Lie scatter'd on the Alpine mountains cold;
  Ev'n them who kept thy truth so pure of old
  When all our fathers worshipp'd stocks and stones
Forget not: in thy book record their groans   5
  Who were thy sheep, and in their ancient fold
  Slain by the bloody Piedmontese that roll'd
  Mother with infant down the rocks. Their moans
The vales redoubl'd to the hills, and they
  To Heav'n. Their martyr'd blood and ashes sow   10
  O'er all the Italian fields, where still doth sway
The triple tyrant; that from these may grow
  A hundredfold, who having learnt thy way,
  Early may fly the Babylonian woe.

Paradise Lost.

A

POEM

IN
TWELVE BOOKS.

The Author
JOHN MILTON.

𝕿𝖍𝖊 𝕾𝖊𝖈𝖔𝖓𝖉 𝕰𝖉𝖎𝖙𝖎𝖔𝖓
Revised and Augmented by the
same Author.

LONDON,
Printed by *S. Simmons* next door to the
Golden Lion in *Aldersgate-street,* 1674.

THE VERSE

THE measure is English heroic verse without rhyme, as that of Homer in Greek, and of Virgil in Latin ; rhyme being no necessary adjunct or true ornament of poem or good verse, in longer works especially, but the invention of a barbarous age to set off wretched matter and lame metre ; graced indeed since by the use of some famous modern poets, carried away by custom, but much to their own vexation, hindrance, and constraint to express many things otherwise, and for the most part worse, than else they would have expressed them. Not without cause therefore, some both Italian and Spanish poets of prime note have rejected rhyme both in longer and shorter works, as have long since our best English tragedies ; as a thing of itself, to all judicious ears, trivial and of no true musical delight ; which consists only in apt numbers, fit quantity of syllables, and the sense variously drawn out from one verse into another ; not in the jingling sound of like endings, a fault avoided by the learned ancients both in poetry and all good oratory. This neglect then of rhyme so little is to be taken for a defect, though it may seem so perhaps to vulgar readers, that it is rather to be esteemed an example set, the first in English, of ancient liberty recovered to heroic poem, from the troublesome and modern bondage of rhyming.

From PARADISE LOST

First published 1667; *Second Edition* 1674

From BOOK I

THE ARGUMENT.

THIS first Book proposes, first in brief, the whole subject; Man's disobedience, and the loss thereupon of Paradise wherein he was placed:
then touches the prime cause of his Fall, the Serpent, or rather Satan in
the serpent; who revolting from God, and drawing to his side many
legions of angels, was by the command of God driven out of Heaven
with all his crew into the great deep. Which action passed over, the
Poem hastes into the midst of things, presenting Satan with his angels
now fallen into Hell, described here, not in the centre (for heaven and
earth may be supposed as yet not made, certainly not yet accursed), but
in a place of utter darkness, fitliest called Chaos: here Satan with his
angels lying on the burning lake, thunder-struck and astonished, after
a certain space recovers, as from confusion; calls up him who next in
order and dignity lay by him; they confer of their miserable fall. Satan
awakens all his legions, who lay till then in the same manner confounded.
They rise; their numbers; array of battle; their chief leaders named,
according to the idols known afterwards in Canaan and the countries
adjoining. To these Satan directs his speech; comforts them with hope
yet of regaining Heaven; but tells them lastly of a new world and a new
kind of creature to be created, according to an ancient prophecy or
report in Heaven: for that angels were long before this visible creation,
was the opinion of many ancient Fathers. To find out the truth of this
prophecy, and what to determine thereon, he refers to a full council.
What his associates thence attempt. Pandemonium, the palace of Satan,
rises, suddenly built out of the deep. The infernal peers there sit
in council.

OF Man's first disobedience, and the fruit
Of that forbidden tree, whose mortal taste
Brought death into the world, and all our woe

With loss of Eden, till one greater Man
Restore us, and regain the blissful seat,   5
Sing Heav'nly Muse, that on the secret top
Of Oreb, or of Sinai, didst inspire
That shepherd, who first taught the chosen seed,
In the beginning how the Heav'ns and Earth
Rose out of Chaos: or if Sion hill   10
Delight thee more, and Siloa's brook that flow'd
Fast by the oracle of God; I thence
Invoke thy aid to my advent'rous song,
That with no middle flight intends to soar
Above th' Aonian mount, while it pursues   15
Things unattempted yet in prose or rhyme.
And chiefly Thou, O Spirit! that dost prefer
Before all temples th' upright heart and pure,
Instruct me, for thou know'st; Thou from the first
Wast present, and with mighty wings outspread   20
Dove-like sat'st brooding on the vast abyss
And mad'st it pregnant: what in me is dark
Illumine, what is low raise and support;
That to the height of this great argument
I may assert Eternal Providence,   25
And justify the ways of God to men.

  *   *   *   *   *   *   *   *   *   *

'If thou beest he; but O how fall'n! how chang'd
From him, who in the happy realms of light   85
Cloth'd with transcendent brightness didst outshine
Myriads though bright: if he whom mutual league,
United thoughts and counsels, equal hope
And hazard in the glorious enterprise,
Join'd with me once, now misery hath join'd   90
In equal ruin: into what pit thou seest
From what height fall'n; so much the stronger prov'd
He with his thunder: and till then who knew
The force of those dire arms? Yet not for those,

Nor what the potent Victor in his rage   95
Can else inflict, do I repent or change
(Though chang'd in outward lustre) that fix'd mind,
And high disdain from sense of injur'd merit,
That with the Mightiest rais'd me to contend,
And to the fierce contention brought along   100
Innumerable force of spirits arm'd
That durst dislike his reign, and me preferring,
His utmost power with adverse power oppos'd
In dubious battle on the plains of Heav'n,
And shook his throne.   What though the field be lost?   105
All is not lost; the unconquerable will,
And study of revenge, immortal hate,
And courage never to submit or yield,
And what is else not to be overcome;
That glory never shall his wrath or might   110
Extort from me.   To bow and sue for grace
With suppliant knee, and deify his power,
Who from the terror of this arm so late
Doubted his empire, that were low indeed,
That were an ignominy and shame beneath   115
This downfall; since by fate the strength of gods
And this empyreal substance cannot fail,
Since through experience of this great event
In arms not worse, in foresight much advanc'd,
We may with more successful hope resolve   120
To wage by force or guile eternal war,
Irreconcilable to our grand Foe
Who now triumphs, and in th' excess of joy
Sole reigning holds the tyranny of Heav'n.'

*   *   *   *   *   *   *   *   *   *

'Is this the region, this the soil, the clime,'
Said then the lost Archangel; 'this the seat
That we must change for Heav'n? this mournful gloom
For that celestial light?   Be it so, since he   245

I 2

Who now is Sovran can dispose and bid
What shall be right: farthest from him is best,
Whom reason hath equall'd, force hath made supreme
Above his equals.   Farewell happy fields
Where joy for ever dwells: hail horrors, hail   250
Infernal world, and thou profoundest Hell
Receive thy new possessor; one who brings
A mind not to be chang'd by place or time.
The mind is its own place, and in itself
Can make a Heav'n of Hell, a Hell of Heav'n.   255
What matter where, if I be still the same,
And what I should be, all but less than he
Whom thunder hath made greater?   Here at least
We shall be free: th' Almighty hath not built
Here for his envy, will not drive us hence: 260
Here we may reign secure, and in my choice
To reign is worth ambition though in Hell:
Better to reign in Hell, than serve in Heav'n.
But wherefore let we then our faithful friends,
Th' associates and co-partners of our loss,   265
Lie thus astonish'd on th' oblivious pool,
And call them not to share with us their part
In this unhappy mansion, or once more
With rallied arms to try what may be yet
Regain'd in Heav'n, or what more lost in Hell?'   270
    So Satan spake, and him Beëlzebub
Thus answer'd.   'Leader of those armies bright,
Which but th' Omnipotent none could have foil'd,
If once they hear that voice, their liveliest pledge
Of hope in fears and dangers, heard so oft   275
In worst extremes, and on the perilous edge
Of battle when it rag'd, in all assaults
Their surest signal, they will soon resume
New courage and revive, though now they lie
Groveling and prostrate on yon lake of fire,   280

As we erewhile, astounded and amaz'd;
No wonder, fall'n such a pernicious height.'
  He scarce had ceas'd when the superior Fiend
Was moving toward the shore; his ponderous shield,
Ethereal temper, massy, large and round,   285
Behind him cast; the broad circumference
Hung on his shoulders like the moon, whose orb
Through optic glass the Tuscan artist views
At ev'ning from the top of Fesole,
Or in Valdarno, to descry new lands,   290
Rivers or mountains in her spotty globe.
His spear, to equal which the tallest pine
Hewn on Norwegian hills, to be the mast
Of some great ammiral, were but a wand,
He walk'd with to support uneasy steps   295
Over the burning marl, not like those steps
On Heavens azure; and the torrid clime
Smote on him sore besides, vaulted with fire:
Nathless he so endur'd, till on the beach
Of that inflamed sea, he stood and call'd   300
His legions, angel forms, who lay entranc'd
Thick as autumnal leaves that strew the brooks
In Vallombrosa, where th' Etrurian shades
High over-arch'd embow'r; or scatter'd sedge
Afloat, when with fierce winds Orion arm'd   305
Hath vex'd the Red-Sea coast, whose waves o'erthrew
Busiris and his Memphian chivalry,
While with perfidious hatred they pursu'd
The sojourners of Goshen, who beheld
From the safe shore their floating carcases   310
And broken chariot-wheels; so thick bestrewn
Abject and lost lay these, covering the flood,
Under amazement of their hideous change.
He call'd so loud, that all the hollow deep
Of Hell resounded: 'Princes, Potentates,   315

Warriors, the flow'r of Heav'n, once yours, now lost,
If such astonishment as this can seize
Eternal spirits; or have ye chos'n this place
After the toil of battle to repose
Your wearied virtue, for the ease you find   320
To slumber here, as in the vales of Heav'n?
Or in this abject posture have ye sworn
To adore the Conqueror? who now beholds
Cherub and seraph rolling in the flood
With scatter'd arms and ensigns, till anon   325
His swift pursuers from Heav'n-gates discern
Th' advantage; and descending tread us down
Thus drooping, or with linked thunderbolts
Transfix us to the bottom of this gulf.
Awake, arise, or be for ever fall'n.'   330
    They heard, and were abash'd, and up they sprung
Upon the wing; as when men wont to watch
On duty, sleeping found by whom they dread,
Rouse and bestir themselves ere well awake.
Nor did they not perceive the evil plight   335
In which they were, or the fierce pains not feel;
Yet to their general's voice they soon obey'd
Innumerable. As when the potent rod
Of Amram's son in Egypt's evil day
Wav'd round the coast, up call'd a pitchy cloud   340
Of locusts, warping on the eastern wind,
That o'er the realm of impious Pharaoh hung
Like night, and darken'd all the land of Nile:
So numberless were those bad angels seen
Hovering on wing under the cope of Hell   345
'Twixt upper, nether, and surrounding fires;
Till, as a signal giv'n, th' uplifted spear
Of their great sultan waving to direct
Their course, in even balance down they light
On the firm brimstone, and fill all the plain;   350

A multitude, like which the populous North
Pour'd never from her frozen loins, to pass
Rhene or the Danaw; when her barbarous sons
Came like a deluge on the South, and spread
Beneath Gibraltar to the Libyan sands. 355
Forthwith from every squadron and each band
The heads and leaders thither haste where stood
Their great commander; godlike shapes and forms
Excelling human, princely Dignities,
And Powers that erst in Heaven sat on thrones; 360
Though of their names in Heav'nly records now
Be no memorial, blotted out and raz'd
By their rebellion from the books of life.

*   *   *   *   *   *   *   *   *   *

All these and more came flocking; but with looks
Downcast and damp, yet such wherein appear'd
Obscure some glimpse of joy, to have found their chief
Not in despair, to have found themselves not lost 525
In loss itself; which on his count'nance cast
Like doubtful hue: but he his wonted pride
Soon recollecting, with high words that bore
Semblance of worth, not substance, gently rais'd
Their fainted courage, and dispell'd their fears: 530
Then straight commands that at the warlike sound
Of trumpets loud and clarions be uprear'd
His mighty standard; that proud honour claim'd
Azazel as his right, a Cherub tall;
Who forthwith from the glittering staff unfurl'd 535
Th' imperial ensign, which full high advanc'd
Shone like a meteor streaming to the wind,
With gems and golden lustre rich emblaz'd,
Seraphic arms and trophies: all the while
Sonorous metal blowing martial sounds: 540
At which the universal host upsent
A shout that tore Hell's concave, and beyond

Frighted the reign of Chaos and old Night.
All in a moment through the gloom were seen
Ten thousand banners rise into the air   545
With orient colours waving; with them rose
A forest huge of spears; and thronging helms
Appear'd, and serried shields in thick array
Of depth immeasurable; anon they move
In perfect phalanx to the Dorian mood   550
Of flutes and soft recorders; such as rais'd
To height of noblest temper heroes old
Arming to battle, and instead of rage
Deliberate valour breath'd, firm and unmov'd
With dread of death to flight or foul retreat;   555
Nor wanting power to mitigate and swage
With solemn touches, troubl'd thoughts, and chase
Anguish and doubt and fear and sorrow and pain
From mortal or immortal minds. Thus they
Breathing united force with fixed thought   560
Mov'd on in silence, to soft pipes that charm'd
Their painful steps o'er the burnt soil; and now
Advanc'd in view, they stand, a horrid front
Of dreadful length and dazzling arms, in guise
Of warriors old with order'd spear and shield,   565
Awaiting what command their mighty chief
Had to impose: he through the armed files
Darts his experienc'd eye; and soon traverse
The whole battalion views, their order due,
Their visages and stature as of gods;   570
Their number last he sums. And now his heart
Distends with pride, and hard'ning in his strength
Glories: for never since created man,
Met such embodied force, as nam'd with these
Could merit more than that small infantry   575
Warr'd on by cranes; though all the giant brood
Of Phlegra with th' heroic race were join'd

That fought at Theb's and Ilium, on each side
Mix'd with auxiliar Gods; and what resounds
In fable or romance of Uther's son,   580
Begirt with British and Armoric knights.
And all who since, baptiz'd or infidel,
Jousted in Aspramont or Montalban,
Damasco, or Marocco, or Trebisond;
Or whom Biserta sent from Afric shore   585
When Charlemain with all his peerage fell
By Fontarabbia.   Thus far these beyond
Compare of mortal prowess, yet observ'd
Their dread commander: he above the rest
In shape and gesture proudly eminent   590
Stood like a tow'r; his form had not yet lost
All her original brightness, nor appear'd
Less than archangel ruin'd, and th' excess
Of glory obscur'd: as when the sun new ris'n
Looks through the horizontal misty air   595
Shorn of his beams, or from behind the moon
In dim eclipse disastrous twilight sheds
On half the nations, and with fear of change
Perplexes monarchs.   Dark'n'd so, yet shone
Above them all th' Archangel: but his face   600
Deep scars of thunder had entrench'd, and care
Sat on his faded cheek, but under brows
Of dauntless courage, and considerate pride
Waiting revenge: cruel his eye, but cast
Signs of remorse and passion to behold   605
The fellows of his crime, the followers rather,
(Far other once beheld in bliss) condemn'd
For ever now to have their lot in pain,
Millions of spirits for his fault amerc'd
Of Heav'n, and from eternal splendours flung   610
For his revolt, yet faithful how they stood,
Their glory wither'd.   As when Heaven's fire

Hath scath'd the forest oaks, or mountain pines,
With singed top their stately growth though bare
Stands on the blasted heath. He now prepar'd   615
To speak; whereat their doubl'd ranks they bend
From wing to wing, and half enclose him round
With all his peers: attention held them mute.
Thrice he essay'd, and thrice in spite of scorn,
Tears such as angels weep, burst forth: at last   620
Words interwove with sighs found out their way.
    'O myriads of immortal spirits, O powers
Matchless, but with th' Almighty; and that strife
Was not inglorious, though th' event was dire,
As this place testifies, and this dire change   625
Hateful to utter: but what power of mind
Foreseeing or presaging, from the depth
Of knowledge past or present, could have fear'd,
How such united force of gods, how such
As stood like these, could ever know repulse?   630
For who can yet believe, though after loss,
That all these puissant legions, whose exile
Hath emptied Heav'n, shall fail to reascend
Self-rais'd, and repossess their native seat?
For me be witness all the host of Heav'n,   635
If counsels different, or danger shunn'd
By me, have lost our hopes. But he who reigns
Monarch in Heav'n, till then as one secure
Sat on his throne, upheld by old repute,
Consent or custom, and his regal state   640
Put forth at full, but still his strength conceal'd;
Which tempted our attempt, and wrought our fall.
Henceforth his might we know, and know our own;
So as not either to provoke, or dread
New war, provok'd; our better part remains,   645
To work in close design by fraud or guile
What force effected not: that he no less

At length from us may find, who overcomes
By force, hath overcome but half his foe.
Space may produce new worlds; whereof so rife 650
There went a fame in Heav'n that he ere long
Intended to create, and therein plant
A generation, whom his choice regard
Should favour equal to the sons of Heaven:
Thither, if but to pry, shall be perhaps 655
Our first eruption, thither or elsewhere:
For this infernal pit shall never hold
Celestial spirits in bondage, nor th' abyss
Long under darkness cover. But these thoughts
Full counsel must mature: peace is despair'd, 660
For who can think submission? War, then, war
Open or understood must be resolv'd.'

He spake: and, to confirm his words, out flew
Millions of flaming swords, drawn from the thighs
Of mighty cherubim; the sudden blaze 665
Far round illumin'd Hell: highly they rag'd
Against the Highest; and fierce with grasped arms
Clash'd on their sounding shields the din of war,
Hurling defiance toward the vault of Heav'n.

From BOOK II

THE ARGUMENT.

THE consultation begun, Satan debates, whether another battle be to be hazarded for the recovery of Heaven: some advise it, others dissuade. A third proposal is preferred, mentioned before by Satan, to search the truth of that prophecy or tradition in Heaven concerning another world, and another kind of creature equal or not much inferior to themselves, about this time to be created: their doubt who should be sent on this difficult search. Satan, their chief, undertakes alone the voyage, is honoured and applauded. The council thus ended, the rest betake them several ways and to several employments, as their inclinations lead them, to entertain the time till Satan return. He passes on his journey to

Hell-gates; finds them shut, and who sat there to guard them, by whom
at length they are opened, and discover to him the great gulf between
Hell and Heaven; with what difficulty he passes through, directed by
Chaos, the Power of that place, to the sight of this new world which
he sought.

HIGH on a throne of royal state, which far
Outshone the wealth of Ormus and of Ind,
Or where the gorgeous East with richest hand
Show'rs on her kings barbaric pearl and gold,
Satan exalted sat, by merit rais'd   5
To that bad eminence; and from despair
Thus high uplifted beyond hope, aspires
Beyond thus high, insatiate to pursue
Vain war with Heav'n, and by success untaught
His proud imaginations thus display'd: 10
  'Powers and Dominions, Deities of Heav'n,
For since no deep within her gulf can hold
Immortal vigour, though oppress'd and fall'n,
I give not Heav'n for lost. From this descent
Celestial virtues rising, will appear   15
More glorious and more dread than from no fall,
And trust themselves to fear no second fate.
Me though just right, and the fix'd laws of Heav'n
Did first create your leader, next free choice,
With what besides, in counsel or in fight,   20
Hath been achiev'd of merit, yet this loss
Thus far at least recover'd, hath much more
Establish'd in a safe unenvied throne
Yielded with full consent. The happier state
In Heav'n which follows dignity, might draw   25
Envy from each inferior; but who here
Will envy whom the highest place exposes
Foremost to stand against the Thunderer's aim
Your bulwark, and condemns to greatest share
Of endless pain? where there is then no good   30

For which to strive, no strife can grow up there
From faction; for none sure will claim in Hell
Precedence; none, whose portion is so small
Of present pain, that with ambitious mind
Will covet more. With this advantage then   35
To union, and firm faith, and firm accord,
More than can be in Heav'n, we now return
To claim our just inheritance of old,
Surer to prosper than prosperity
Could have assur'd us; and by what best way,   40
Whether of open war or covert guile,
We now debate; who can advise, may speak.'
  He ceas'd; and next him Moloch, scepter'd king,
Stood up, the strongest and the fiercest spirit
That fought in Heav'n; now fiercer by despair: 45
His trust was with th' Eternal to be deem'd
Equal in strength, and rather than be less
Cared not to be at all; with that care lost
Went all his fear; of God, or Hell, or worse
He reck'd not, and these words thereafter spake.   50
  'My sentence is for open war: of wiles,
More unexpert, I boast not: them let those
Contrive who need, or when they need, not now.
For while they sit contriving, shall the rest,
Millions that stand in arms, and longing wait   55
The signal to ascend, sit ling'ring here
Heav'n's fugitives, and for their dwelling-place
Accept this dark opprobrious den of shame,
The prison of his tyranny who reigns
By our delay? No, let us rather choose   60
Arm'd with Hell-flames and fury all at once
O'er Heav'n's high tow'rs to force resistless way,
Turning our tortures into horrid arms
Against the Torturer; when to meet the noise
Of his almighty engine he shall hear   65

Infernal thunder; and for lightning see
Black fire and horror shot with equal rage
Among his angels; and his throne itself
Mix'd with Tartarean sulphur, and strange fire,
His own invented torments. But perhaps   70
The way seems difficult and steep to scale
With upright wing against a higher foe.
Let such bethink them, if the sleepy drench
Of that forgetful lake benumb not still,
That in our proper motion we ascend   75
Up to our native seat: descent and fall
To us is adverse. Who but felt of late
When the fierce foe hung on our brok'n rear
Insulting, and pursu'd us through the deep,
With what compulsion and laborious flight   80
We sunk thus low? Th' ascent is easy then;
Th' event is fear'd; should we again provoke
Our stronger, some worse way his wrath may find
To our destruction: if there be in Hell
Fear to be worse destroy'd: what can be worse   85
Than to dwell here, driv'n out from bliss, condemn'd
In this abhorred deep to utter woe ;
Where pain of unextinguishable fire
Must exercise us without hope of end
The vassals of his anger, when the scourge   90
Inexorably, and the torturing hour
Calls us to penance? More destroy'd than thus
We should be quite abolish'd and expire.
What fear we then? what doubt we to incense
His utmost ire? which to the height enrag'd,   95
Will either quite consume us, and reduce
To nothing this essential, happier far
Than miserable to have eternal being:
Or if our substance be indeed divine,
And cannot cease to be, we are at worst   100

On this side nothing ; and by proof we feel
Our power sufficient to disturb his Heav'n,
And with perpetual inroads to alarm,
Though inaccessible, his fatal throne :
Which if not victory is yet revenge.'   105
   He ended frowning, and his look denounc'd
Desperate revenge, and battle dangerous
To less than Gods. On th' other side uprose
Belial, in act more graceful and humane ;
A fairer person lost not Heav'n ; he seem'd   110
For dignity compos'd and high exploit ;
But all was false and hollow ; though his tongue
Dropp'd manna, and could make the worse appear
The better reason, to perplex and dash
Maturest counsels ; for his thoughts were low ;   115
To vice industrious, but to nobler deeds
Timorous and slothful : yet he pleas'd the ear ;
And with persuasive accent thus began.
   'I should be much for open war, O peers,
As not behind in hate ; if what was urg'd   120
Main reason to persuade immediate war,
Did not dissuade me most, and seem to cast
Ominous conjecture on the whole success :
When he who most excels in fact of arms,
In what he counsels and in what excels   125
Mistrustful, grounds his courage on despair
And utter dissolution, as the scope
Of all his aim, after some dire revenge.
First, what revenge ? The tow'rs of Heav'n are fill'd
With armed watch, that render all access   130
Impregnable : oft on the bordering deep
Encamp their legions, or with obscure wing
Scout far and wide into the realm of night,
Scorning surprise. Or could we break our way
By force, and at our heels all Hell should rise   135

With blackest insurrection, to confound
Heav'ns purest light, yet our great Enemy
All incorruptible would on his throne
Sit unpolluted; and th' ethereal mould
Incapable of stain would soon expel   140
Her mischief, and purge off the baser fire
Victorious.   Thus repuls'd, our final hope
Is flat despair: we must exasperate
Th' Almighty Victor to spend all his rage,
And that must end us, that must be our cure,   145
To be no more; sad cure; for who would lose,
Though full of pain, this intellectual being,
Those thoughts that wander through eternity,
To perish rather, swallow'd up and lost
In the wide womb of uncreated night,   150
Devoid of sense and motion? and who knows,
Let this be good, whether our angry Foe
Can give it, or will ever? how he can
Is doubtful; that he never will is sure.
Will he, so wise, let loose at once his ire,   155
Belike through impotence, or unaware,
To give his enemies their wish, and end
Them in his anger, whom his anger saves
To punish endless?   "Wherefore cease we then?"
Say they who counsel war; "we are decreed,   160
Reserv'd and destin'd to eternal woe;
Whatever doing, what can we suffer more?
What can we suffer worse?"   Is this then worst,
Thus sitting, thus consulting, thus in arms?
What when we fled amain, pursu'd and struck   165
With Heav'n's afflicting thunder, and besought
The deep to shelter us? this Hell then seem'd
A refuge from those wounds: or when we lay
Chain'd on the burning lake? that sure was worse.
What if the breath that kindl'd those grim fires,   170

Awak'd should blow them into seven-fold rage,
And plunge us in the flames? or from above
Should intermitted vengeance arm again
His red right hand to plague us? What if all
Her stores were open'd, and this firmament   175
Of Hell should spout her cataracts of fire,
Impendent horrors, threat'ning hideous fall
One day upon our heads; while we perhaps
Designing or exhorting glorious war,
Caught in a fiery tempest shall be hurl'd   180
Each on his rock transfix'd, the sport and prey
Of racking whirlwinds, or for ever sunk
Under yon boiling ocean, wrapp'd in chains;
There to converse with everlasting groans,
Unrespited, unpitied, unrepriev'd,   185
Ages of hopeless end? this would be worse.
War therefore, open or conceal'd, alike
My voice dissuades; for what can force or guile
With him, or who deceive his mind, whose eye
Views all things at one view? He from Heav'n's height
All these our motions vain, sees and derides;   191
Not more almighty to resist our might
Than wise to frustrate all our plots and wiles.
Shall we then live thus vile, the race of Heav'n
Thus trampl'd, thus expell'd to suffer here   195
Chains and these torments? better these than worse,
By my advice; since fate inevitable
Subdues us, and omnipotent decree,
The Victor's will. To suffer, as to do,
Our strength is equal; nor the law unjust   200
That so ordains: this was at first resolv'd,
If we were wise, against so great a foe
Contending, and so doubtful what might fall.
I laugh, when those who at the spear are bold
And vent'rous, if that fail them, shrink and fear   205

What yet they know must follow, to endure
Exile, or ignominy, or bonds, or pain,
The sentence of their conqueror: this is now
Our doom; which if we can sustain and bear,
Our supreme Foe in time may much remit   210
His anger, and perhaps thus far remov'd
Not mind us not offending, satisfi'd
With what is punish'd; whence these raging fires
Will slack'n, if his breath stir not their flames.
Our purer essence then will overcome   215
Their noxious vapour, or inur'd not feel,
Or chang'd at length, and to the place conform'd
In temper and in nature, will receive
Familiar the fierce heat, and void of pain;
This horror will grow mild, this darkness light,   220
Besides what hope the never-ending flight
Of future days may bring, what chance, what change;
Worth waiting, since our present lot appears
For happy though but ill, for ill not worst,
If we procure not to ourselves more woe.'   225
    Thus Belial with words cloth'd in reason's garb
Counsell'd ignoble ease, and peaceful sloth,
Not peace: and after him thus Mammon spake.
    'Either to disenthrone the King of Heav'n
We war, if war be best, or to regain   230
Our own right lost.   Him to enthrone we then
May hope, when everlasting Fate shall yield
To fickle Chance, and Chaos judge the strife:
The former vain to hope argues as vain
The latter: for what place can be for us   235
Within Heav'n's bound, unless Heav'n's Lord Supreme
We overpower?   Suppose he should relent
And publish grace to all, on promise made
Of new subjection; with what eyes could we
Stand in his presence humble, and receive   240

Strict laws impos'd, to celebrate his throne
With warbl'd hymns, and to his Godhead sing
Forc'd Hallelujahs; while he lordly sits
Our envied Sovran, and his altar breathes
Ambrosial odours and ambrosial flowers,   245
Our servile offerings? This must be our task
In Heav'n, this our delight; how wearisome
Eternity so spent in worship paid
To whom we hate! Let us not then pursue
By force impossible, by leave obtain'd   250
Unacceptable, though in Heav'n, our state
Of splendid vassalage, but rather seek
Our own good from ourselves, and from our own
Live to ourselves, though in this vast recess,
Free, and to none accountable, preferring   255
Hard liberty before the easy yoke
Of servile pomp. Our greatness will appear
Then most conspicuous, when great things of small,
Useful of hurtful, prosperous of adverse
We can create; and in what place soe'er   260
Thrive under evil, and work ease out of pain
Through labour and endurance. This deep world
Of darkness do we dread? How oft amidst
Thick clouds and dark doth Heav'n's all-ruling Sire
Choose to reside, his glory unobscur'd,   265
And with the majesty of darkness round
Covers his throne; from whence deep thunders roar
Must'ring their rage, and Heav'n resembles Hell!
As he our darkness, cannot we his light
Imitate when we please? This desert soil   270
Wants not her hidden lustre, gems and gold;
Nor want we skill or art, from whence to raise
Magnificence; and what can Heav'n show more?
Our torments also may in length of time
Become our elements, these piercing fires   275

As soft as now severe, our temper chang'd
Into their temper; which must needs remove
The sensible of pain. All things invite
To peaceful counsels, and the settl'd state
Of order, how in safety best we may   280
Compose our present evils, with regard
Of what we are and where, dismissing quite
All thoughts of war: ye have what I advise.'
  He scarce had finish'd, when such murmur fill'd
Th' assembly, as when hollow rocks retain   285
The sound of blust'ring winds, which all night long
Had rous'd the sea, now with hoarse cadence lull
Seafaring men o'er-watch'd, whose bark by chance
Or pinnace anchors in a craggy bay
After the tempest: such applause was heard   290
As Mammon ended, and his sentence pleas'd,
Advising peace: for such another field
They dreaded worse than Hell: so much the fear
Of thunder and the sword of Michael
Wrought still within them; and no less desire   295
To found this nether empire, which might rise
By policy, and long process of time,
In emulation opposite to Heav'n.
Which when Beëlzebub perceiv'd; than whom,
Satan except, none higher sat, with grave   300
Aspect he rose, and in his rising seem'd
A pillar of state; deep on his front engraven
Deliberation sat and public care;
And princely counsel in his face yet shone,
Majestic though in ruin: sage he stood   305
With Atlantean shoulders fit to bear
The weight of mightiest monarchies; his look
Drew audience and attention still as night
Or summer's noontide air, while thus he spake.
  'Thrones and Imperial Powers, offspring of Heav'n, 310

Ethereal Virtues; or these titles now
Must we renounce, and changing style be call'd
Princes of Hell? for so the popular vote
Inclines, here to continue, and build up here
A growing empire; doubtless! while we dream,   315
And know not that the King of Heav'n hath doom'd
This place our dungeon, not our safe retreat
Beyond his potent arm, to live exempt
From Heav'n's high jurisdiction, in new league
Banded against his throne; but to remain   320
In strictest bondage, though thus far remov'd,
Under th' inevitable curb, reserv'd
His captive multitude: for he, be sure,
In height or depth, still first and last will reign
Sole King, and of his kingdom lose no part   325
By our revolt; but over Hell extend
His empire, and with iron sceptre rule
Us here, as with his golden those in Heav'n.
What sit we then projecting peace and war?
War hath determin'd us, and foil'd with loss   330
Irreparable: terms of peace yet none
Vouchsaf'd or sought; for what peace will be giv'n
To us enslav'd, but custody severe,
And stripes, and arbitrary punishment
Inflicted? and what peace can we return,   335
But to our power hostility and hate,
Untam'd reluctance, and revenge though slow,
Yet ever plotting how the Conqueror least
May reap his conquest, and may least rejoice
In doing what we most in suffering feel?   340
Nor will occasion want, nor shall we need
With dangerous expedition to invade
Heav'n, whose high walls fear no assault or siege,
Or ambush from the deep. What if we find
Some easier enterprise? There is a place   345

(If ancient and prophetic fame in Heav'n
Err not) another world, the happy seat
Of some new race call'd Man, about this time
To be created like to us, though less
In power and excellence, but favour'd more   350
Of him who rules above; so was his will
Pronounc'd among the gods, and by an oath,
That shook Heav'n's whole circumference, confirm'd.
Thither let us bend all our thoughts, to learn
What creatures there inhabit, of what mould,   355
Or substance, how endu'd, and what their power,
And where their weakness, how attempted best,
By force or subtlety. Though Heav'n be shut,
And Heav'n's high Arbitrator sit secure
In his own strength, this place may lie expos'd   360
The utmost border of his kingdom, left
To their defence who hold it: here perhaps
Some advantageous act may be achiev'd
By sudden onset; either with Hell-fire
To waste his whole creation, or possess   365
All as our own, and drive as we were driven,
The puny habitants; or if not drive,
Seduce them to our party, that their God
May prove their foe, and with repenting hand
Abolish his own works. This would surpass   370
Common revenge, and interrupt his joy
In our confusion, and our joy upraise
In his disturbance; when his darling sons
Hurl'd headlong to partake with us, shall curse
Their frail originals, and faded bliss,   375
Faded so soon. Advise if this be worth
Attempting, or to sit in darkness here
Hatching vain empires.' Thus Beëlzebub
Pleaded his devilish counsel, first devis'd
By Satan, and in part propos'd: for whence,   380

But from the Author of all ill could spring
So deep a malice, to confound the race
Of mankind in one root, and Earth with Hell
To mingle and involve; done all to spite
The great Creator? But their spite still serves   385
His glory to augment. The bold design
Pleas'd highly those infernal States, and joy
Sparkl'd in all their eyes; with full assent
They vote: whereat his speech he thus renews.
    'Well have ye judg'd, well ended long debate,   390
Synod of gods; and like to what ye are,
Great things resolv'd: which from the lowest deep
Will once more lift us up, in spite of fate,
Nearer our ancient seat; perhaps in view
Of those bright confines, whence with neighbouring arms
And opportune excursion, we may chance   396
Re-enter Heav'n; or else in some mild zone
Dwell not unvisited of Heav'n's fair light
Secure, and at the bright'ning orient beam
Purge off this gloom; the soft delicious air,   400
To heal the scar of these corrosive fires,
Shall breathe her balm. But first whom shall we send
In search of this new world, whom shall we find
Sufficient? who shall tempt with wand'ring feet
The dark unbottom'd infinite abyss,   405
And through the palpable obscure find out
His uncouth way, or spread his airy flight
Upborne with indefatigable wings
Over the vast abrupt, ere he arrive
The happy isle? What strength, what art can then   410
Suffice, or what evasion bear him safe
Through the strict senteries and stations thick
Of angels watching round? Here he had need
All circumspection, and we now no less
Choice in our suffrage; for on whom we send,   415

The weight of all and our last hope relies.'
    This said, he sat; and expectation held
His look suspense, awaiting who appear'd
To second, or oppose, or undertake
The perilous attempt: but all sat mute,   420
Pondering the danger with deep thoughts; and each
In other's count'nance read his own dismay,
Astonish'd: none among the choice and prime
Of those Heav'n-warring champions could be found
So hardy as to proffer or accept   425
Alone the dreadful voyage; till at last
Satan, whom now transcendent glory rais'd
Above his fellows, with monarchal pride
Conscious of highest worth, unmov'd thus spake.
    'O progeny of Heav'n, empyreal Thrones,   430
With reason hath deep silence and demur
Seiz'd us, though undismay'd: long is the way
And hard, that out of Hell leads up to light;
Our prison strong, this huge convex of fire,
Outrageous to devour, immures us round   435
Ninefold, and gates of burning adamant
Barr'd over us prohibit all egress.
These pass'd, if any pass, the void profound
Of unessential Night receives him next
Wide gaping, and with utter loss of being   440
Threatens him, plung'd in that abortive gulf.
If thence he 'scape into whatever world,
Or unknown region, what remains him less
Than unknown dangers and as hard escape?
But I should ill become this throne, O peers,   445
And this imperial sov'ranty, adorn'd
With splendour, arm'd with power, if aught propos'd
And judg'd of public moment, in the shape
Of difficulty or danger could deter
Me from attempting. Wherefore do I assume   450

These royalties, and not refuse to reign,
Refusing to accept as great a share
Of hazard as of honour, due alike
To him who reigns, and so much to him due
Of hazard more, as he above the rest   455
High honour'd sits? Go therefore, mighty powers,
Terror of Heav'n, though fall'n; intend at home,
While here shall be our home, what best may ease
The present misery, and render Hell
More tolerable; if there be cure or charm   460
To respite or deceive, or slack the pain
Of this ill mansion: intermit no watch
Against a wakeful foe, while I abroad
Through all the coasts of dark destruction seek
Deliverance for us all: this enterprise   465
None shall partake with me.' Thus saying, rose
The Monarch, and prevented all reply;
Prudent, lest from his resolution rais'd,
Others among the chief might offer now
(Certain to be refus'd) what erst they fear'd;   470
And so refus'd might in opinion stand
His rivals, winning cheap the high repute
Which he through hazard huge must earn. But they
Dreaded not more th' adventure than his voice
Forbidding; and at once with him they rose;   475
Their rising all at once was as the sound
Of thunder heard remote. Towards him they bend
With awful reverence prone; and as a god
Extol him equal to the Highest in Heav'n:
Nor fail'd they to express how much they prais'd,   480
That for the general safety he despis'd
His own: for neither do the spirits damn'd
Lose all their virtue; lest bad men should boast
Their specious deeds on earth, which glory excites,
Or close ambition varnish'd o'er with zeal.   485

Thus they their doubtful consultations dark
Ended rejoicing in their matchless chief:
As when from mountain-tops the dusky clouds
Ascending, while the north-wind sleeps, o'erspread
Heav'ns cheerful face, the low'ring element   490
Scowls o'er the dark'n'd landscape snow, or show'r;
If chance the radiant sun with farewell sweet
Extend his ev'ning beam, the fields revive,
The birds their notes renew, and bleating herds
Attest their joy, that hill and valley rings.   495
O shame to men! devil with devil damn'd
Firm concord holds, men only disagree
Of creatures rational, though under hope
Of heavenly grace; and God proclaiming peace,
Yet live in hatred, enmity, and strife   500
Among themselves, and levy cruel wars,
Wasting the earth, each other to destroy;
As if (which might induce us to accord)
Man had not hellish foes enow besides,
That day and night for his destruction wait.   505

From BOOK III

THE ARGUMENT.

GOD sitting on his throne sees Satan flying towards this world, then
newly created; shows him to the Son, who sat at his right hand; foretells the success of Satan in perverting mankind; clears his own justice
and wisdom from all imputation, having created Man free and able
enough to have withstood his tempter; yet declares his purpose of grace
towards him, in regard he fell not of his own malice, as did Satan, but
by him seduced. The Son of God renders praises to his Father for the
manifestation of his gracious purpose towards Man: but God again
declares, that grace cannot be extended towards Man without the
satisfaction of divine justice; Man hath offended the majesty of God by
aspiring to Godhead, and therefore with all his progeny devoted to death
must die, unless some one can be found sufficient to answer for his
offence, and undergo his punishment. The Son of God freely offers

himself a ransom for Man: the Father accepts him, ordains his incarnation, pronounces his exaltation above all names in Heaven and Earth;
commands all the angels to adore him: they obey, and hymning to their
harps in full quire, celebrate the Father and the Son. Meanwhile
Satan alights upon the bare convex of this world's outermost orb; where
wandering he first finds a place since called the Limbo of Vanity; what
persons and things fly up thither; thence comes to the gate of Heaven,
described ascending by stairs, and the waters above the firmament that
flow about it: his passage thence to the orb of the sun; he finds there
Uriel the regent of that orb, but first changes himself into the shape of
a meaner angel; and pretending a zealous desire to behold the new
creation and Man whom God had placed here, inquires of him the place
of his habitation, and is directed: alights first on Mount Niphates.

HAIL, holy Light, offspring of Heav'n first-born,
Or of th' Eternal co-eternal beam
May I express thee unblam'd? since God is Light,
And never but in unapproached light
Dwelt from eternity, dwelt then in thee,   5
Bright effluence of bright essence increate.
Or hear'st thou rather pure ethereal stream,
Whose fountain who shall tell? before the sun,
Before the Heavens thou wert, and at the voice
Of God, as with a mantle didst invest   10
The rising world of waters dark and deep,
Won from the void and formless infinite.
Thee I revisit now with bolder wing,
Escap'd the Stygian pool, though long detain'd
In that obscure sojourn, while in my flight   15
Through utter and through middle darkness borne,
With other notes than to th' Orphean lyre
I sung of Chaos and eternal Night,
Taught by the heav'nly muse to venture down
The dark descent, and up to re-ascend,   20
Though hard and rare: thee I revisit safe,
And feel thy sovran vital lamp; but thou
Revisit'st not these eyes, that roll in vain

To find thy piercing ray, and find no dawn;
So thick a drop serene hath quench'd their orbs,   25
Or dim suffusion veil'd. Yet not the more
Cease I to wander where the muses haunt
Clear spring, or shady grove, or sunny hill,
Smit with the love of sacred song: but chief
Thee, Sion, and the flow'ry brooks beneath   30
That wash thy hallow'd feet, and warbling flow,
Nightly I visit: nor sometimes forget
Those other two equall'd with me in fate,
So were I equall'd with them in renown,
Blind Thamyris and blind Maeonides,   35
And Tiresias and Phineus, prophets old.
Then feed on thoughts, that voluntary move
Harmonious numbers; as the wakeful bird
Sings darkling, and in shadiest covert hid
Tunes her nocturnal note. Thus with the year   40
Seasons return; but not to me returns
Day, or the sweet approach of ev'n or morn,
Or sight of vernal bloom, or summer's rose,
Or flocks, or herds, or human face divine;
But cloud instead, and ever-during dark   45
Surrounds me, from the cheerful ways of men
Cut off, and for the book of knowledge fair
Presented with a universal blank
Of Nature's works to me expung'd and raz'd,
And wisdom at one entrance quite shut out.   50
So much the rather thou celestial Light
Shine inward, and the mind through all her powers
Irradiate, there plant eyes, all mist from thence
Purge and disperse, that I may see and tell
Of things invisible to mortal sight.   55

From BOOK IV

THE ARGUMENT.

SATAN now in prospect of Eden, and nigh the place where he must now attempt the bold enterprise which he undertook alone against God and Man, falls into many doubts with himself, and many passions; fear, envy, and despair; but at length confirms himself in evil, journeys on to Paradise, whose outward prospect and situation is described, overleaps the bounds, sits in the shape of a cormorant on the tree of Life, as highest in the garden, to look about him. The garden described; Satan's first sight of Adam and Eve; his wonder at their excellent form and happy state, but with resolution to work their fall; overhears their discourse, thence gathers that the tree of Knowledge was forbidden them to eat of, under penalty of death; and thereon intends to found his temptation by seducing them to transgress: then leaves them a while to know further of their state by some other means. Meanwhile Uriel descending on a sunbeam warns Gabriel, who had in charge the gate of Paradise, that some evil spirit had escaped the deep, and passed at noon by his sphere in the shape of a good angel down to Paradise, discovered after by his furious gestures on the mount. Gabriel promises to find him ere morning. Night coming on, Adam and Eve discourse of going to their rest; their bower described; their evening worship. Gabriel drawing forth his bands of night-watch to walk the round of Paradise, appoints two strong angels to Adam's bower, lest the evil spirit should be there doing some harm to Adam or Eve sleeping; there they find him at the ear of Eve, tempting her in a dream, and bring him, though unwilling, to Gabriel: by whom questioned, he scornfully answers, prepares resistance, but hindered by a sign from Heaven, flies out of Paradise.

O FOR that warning voice, which he who saw
Th' Apocalypse, heard cry in Heav'n aloud,
Then when the Dragon, put to second rout,
Came furious down to be reveng'd on men,
'Woe to the inhabitants on Earth!' that now,   5
While time was, our first parents had been warn'd
The coming of their secret foe, and scap'd,
Haply so scap'd his mortal snare; for now
Satan, now first inflam'd with rage, came down,
The tempter ere th' accuser of mankind,   10

To wreak on innocent frail Man his loss
Of that first battle, and his flight to Hell:
Yet not rejoicing in his speed, though bold,
Far off and fearless, nor with cause to boast,
Begins his dire attempt, which nigh the birth   15
Now rolling, boils in his tumultuous breast,
And like a devilish engine back recoils
Upon himself; horror and doubt distract
His troubl'd thoughts, and from the bottom stir
The Hell within him, for within him Hell   20
He brings, and round about him, nor from Hell
One step no more than from himself can fly
By change of place.   Now conscience wakes despair
That slumber'd, wakes the bitter memory
Of what he was, what is, and what must be   25
Worse; of worse deeds worse sufferings must ensue.
Sometimes towards Eden which now in his view
Lay pleasant, his griev'd look he fixes sad
Sometimes towards Heav'n and the full-blazing sun,
Which now sat high in his meridian tow'r: 30
Then much revolving, thus in sighs began.
    'O thou that with surpassing glory crown'd,
Look'st from thy sole dominion like the God
Of this new world; at whose sight all the stars
Hide their diminish'd heads; to thee I call,   35
But with no friendly voice, and add thy name,
O Sun, to tell thee how I hate thy beams
That bring to my remembrance from what state
I fell, how glorious once above thy sphere;
Till pride and worse ambition threw me down   40
Warring in Heav'n against Heav'n's matchless King:
Ah wherefore! he deserv'd no such return
From me, whom he created what I was
In that bright eminence, and with his good
Upbraided none; nor was his service hard.   45

What could be less than to afford him praise,
The easiest recompense, and pay him thanks,
How due! yet all his good prov'd ill iɳ me,
And wrought but malice; lifted up so high
I sdain'd subjection, and thought one step higher   50
Would set me highest, and in a moment quit
The debt immense of endless gratitude,
So burdensome still paying, still to owe;
Forgetful what from him I still receiv'd,
And understood not that a grateful mind   55
By owing owes not, but still pays, at once
Indebted and discharg'd; what burden then?
O had his powerful destiny ordain'd
Me some inferior angel, I had stood
Then happy; no unbounded hope had rais'd   60
Ambition. Yet why not? some other Power
As great might have aspir'd, and me though mean
Drawn to his part; but other Powers as great
Fell not, but stand unshak'n, from within
Or from without, to all temptations arm'd.   65
Hadst thou the same free will and power to stand?
Thou hadst: whom hast thou then, or what to accuse,
But Heav'n's free love dealt equally to all?
Be then his love accurs'd, since love or hate,
To me alike, it deals eternal woe.   70
Nay curs'd be thou; since against his thy will
Chose freely what it now so justly rues.
Me miserable! which way shall I fly
Infinite wrath, and infinite despair?
Which way I fly is Hell; myself am Hell;   75
And in the lowest deep a lower deep
Still threat'ning to devour me opens wide,
To which the Hell I suffer seems a Heav'n.
O then at last relent: is there no place
Left for repentance, none for pardon left?   80

None left but by submission; and that word
Disdain forbids me, and my dread of shame
Among the spirits beneath, whom I seduc'd
With other promises and other vaunts
Than to submit, boasting I could subdue   85
Th' Omnipotent. Ay me, they little know
How dearly I abide that boast so vain,
Under what torments inwardly I groan;
While they adore me on the throne of Hell,
With diadem and sceptre high advanc'd   90
The lower still I fall, only supreme
In misery; such joy ambition finds.
But say I could repent and could obtain
By act of grace my former state; how soon
Would height recall high thoughts, how soon unsay   95
What feign'd submission swore: ease would recant
Vows made in pain, as violent and void.
For never can true reconcilement grow
Where wounds of deadly hate have pierc'd so deep:
Which would but lead me to a worse relapse   100
And heavier fall: so should I purchase dear
Short intermission bought with double smart.
This knows my punisher; therefore as far
From granting he, as I from begging peace:
All hope excluded thus, behold instead   105
Of us outcast, exil'd, his new delight,
Mankind created, and for him this World.
So farewell hope, and with hope farewell fear,
Farewell remorse: all good to me is lost;
Evil be thou my good; by thee at least   110
Divided empire with Heav'n's King I hold;
By thee, and more than half perhaps will reign;
As Man ere long, and this new World shall know.'
    Thus while he spake, each passion dimm'd his face
Thrice chang'd with pale ire, envy and despair, 115

Which marr'd his borrow'd visage, and betray'd
Him counterfeit, if any eye beheld.
For heav'nly minds from such distempers foul
Are ever clear. Whereof he soon aware,
Each perturbation smooth'd with outward calm,   120
Artificer of fraud; and was the first
That practis'd falsehood under saintly show,
Deep malice to conceal, couch'd with revenge:
Yet not enough had practis'd to deceive
Uriel once warn'd; whose eye pursu'd him down   125
The way he went, and on th' Assyrian mount
Saw him disfigur'd, more than could befall
Spirit of happy sort: his gestures fierce
He mark'd and mad demeanour, then alone,
As he suppos'd, all unobserv'd, unseen.   130
So on he fares, and to the border comes
Of Eden, where delicious Paradise,
Now nearer, crowns with her enclosure green,
As with a rural mound the champaign head
Of a steep wilderness, whose hairy sides   135
With thicket overgrown, grotesque and wild,
Access deni'd; and overhead up-grew
Insuperable height of loftiest shade,
Cedar, and pine, and fir, and branching palm,
A sylvan scene; and as the ranks ascend   140
Shade above shade, a woody theatre
Of stateliest view. Yet higher than their tops
The verdurous wall of Paradise up-sprung;
Which to our general sire gave prospect large
Into his nether empire neighbouring round.   145
And higher than that wall a circling row
Of goodliest trees loaden with fairest fruit,
Blossoms and fruits at once of golden hue
Appear'd, with gay enamell'd colours mix'd:
On which the sun more glad impress'd his beams   150

Than in fair evening cloud, or humid bow,
When God hath show'r'd the earth; so lovely seem'd
That landscape: and of pure now purer air
Meets his approach, and to the heart inspires
Vernal delight and joy, able to drive   155
All sadness but despair: now gentle gales
Fanning their odoriferous wings dispense
Native perfumes, and whisper whence they stole
Those balmy spoils. As when to them who sail
Beyond the Cape of Hope, and now are past   160
Mozambic, off at sea north-east winds blow
Sabean odours from the spicy shore
Of Araby the blest; with such delay
Well pleas'd they slack their course, and many a league
Cheer'd with the grateful smell old Ocean smiles.   165
So entertain'd those odorous sweets the Fiend
Who came their bane; though with them better pleas'd
Than Asmodëus with the fishy fume,
That drove him, though enamour'd, from the spouse
Of Tobit's son, and with a vengeance sent   170
From Media post to Egypt, there fast bound.
   Now to th' ascent of that steep savage hill
Satan had journeyed on, pensive and slow;
But further way found none, so thick entwin'd,
As one continu'd brake, the undergrowth   175
Of shrubs and tangling bushes had perplex'd
All path of man or beast that pass'd that way;
One gate there only was, and that look'd east
On th' other side: which when th' Arch-felon saw,
Due entrance he disdain'd; and in contempt,   180
At one slight bound high overleap'd all bound
Of hill or highest wall, and sheer within
Lights on his feet. As when a prowling wolf,
Whom hunger drives to seek new haunt for prey,
Watching where shepherds pen their flocks at eve   185

In hurdl'd cotes amid the field secure,
Leaps o'er the fence with ease into the fold:
Or as a thief, bent to unhoard the cash
Of some rich burgher, whose substantial doors,
Cross-barr'd and bolted fast, fear no assault,   190
In at the window climbs, or o'er the tiles;
So clomb this first grand Thief into God's fold:
So since into his church lewd hirelings climb.
Thence up he flew, and on the tree of Life
The middle tree and highest there that grew,   195
Sat like a cormorant; yet not true life
Thereby regain'd, but sat devising death
To them who liv'd; nor on the virtue thought
Of that life-giving plant, but only us'd
For prospect, what well us'd had been the pledge   200
Of immortality. So little knows
Any, but God alone, to value right
The good before him, but perverts best things
To worst abuse, or to their meanest use.
Beneath him with new wonder now he views   205
To all delight of human sense expos'd
In narrow room nature's whole wealth; yea more,
A Heaven on Earth; for blissful Paradise
Of God the garden was, by him in the east
Of Eden planted; Eden stretch'd her line   210
From Auran eastward to the royal tow'rs
Of great Seleucia, built by Grecian kings,
Or where the sons of Eden long before
Dwelt in Telassar: in this pleasant soil
His far more pleasant garden God ordain'd.   215
Out of the fertile ground he caus'd to grow
All trees of noblest kind for sight, smell, taste;
And all amid them stood the tree of Life,
High eminent, blooming ambrosial fruit
Of vegetable gold; and next to life   220

Our death the tree of Knowledge grew fast by,
Knowledge of good bought dear by knowing ill.
Southward through Eden went a river large,
Nor chang'd his course, but through the shaggy hill
Pass'd underneath engulf'd, for God had thrown   225
That mountain as his garden mould high rais'd
Upon the rapid current; which through veins
Of porous earth with kindly thirst updrawn,
Rose a fresh fountain, and with many a rill
Water'd the garden; thence united fell   230
Down the steep glade, and met the nether flood,
Which from his darksome passage now appears,
And now divided into four main streams,
Runs diverse, wand'ring many a famous realm
And country, whereof here needs no account;   235
But rather to tell how, if art could tell,
How from that sapphire fount the crisped brooks,
Rolling on orient pearl and sands of gold,
With mazy error under pendent shades
Ran nectar, visiting each plant, and fed   240
Flow'rs worthy of Paradise, which not nice Art
In beds and curious knots, but Nature boon
Pour'd forth profuse on hill and dale and plain;
Both where the morning sun first warmly smote
The open field, and where the unpierc'd shade   245
Embrown'd the noontide bow'rs: thus was this place,
A happy rural seat of various view;
Groves whose rich trees wept odorous gums and balm,
Others whose fruit burnish'd with golden rind
Hung amiable, Hesperian fables true,   250
If true, here only, and of delicious taste:
Betwixt them lawns, or level downs, and flocks
Grazing the tender herb, were interpos'd,
Or palmy hillock, or the flow'ry lap
Of some irriguous valley spread her store,   255

Flow'rs of all hue, and without thorn the rose.
Another side, umbrageous grots and caves
Of cool recess, o'er which the mantling vine
Lays forth her purple grape, and gently creeps
Luxuriant; meanwhile murmuring waters fall   260
Down the slope hills, dispers'd, or in a lake,
That to the fringed bank with myrtle crown'd
Her crystal mirror holds, unite their streams.
The birds their quire apply; airs, vernal airs,
Breathing the smell of field and grove, attune   265
The trembling leaves, while universal Pan
Knit with the Graces and the Hours in dance
Led on th' eternal Spring.

    *   *   *   *   *   *   *   *   *   *

  So promis'd he; and Uriel to his charge
Return'd on that bright beam, whose point now rais'd   590
Bore him slope downward to the sun now fall'n
Beneath the Azores; whither the prime orb,
Incredible how swift, had thither roll'd
Diurnal, or this less volubil earth
By shorter flight to th' east, had left him there   595
Arraying with reflected purple and gold
The clouds that on his western throne attend:
Now came still ev'ning on, and twilight grey
Had in her sober livery all things clad;
Silence accompanied, for beast and bird,   600
They to their grassy couch, these to their nests
Were slunk, all but the wakeful nightingale;
She all night long her amorous descant sung;
Silence was pleas'd: now glow'd the firmament
With living sapphires: Hesperus that led   605
The starry host, rode brightest, till the moon,
Rising in clouded majesty, at length
Apparent queen unveil'd her peerless light,
And o'er the dark her silver mantle threw.

When Adam thus to Eve: 'Fair consort, th' hour 610
Of night, and all things now retir'd to rest
Mind us of like repose, since God hath set
Labour and rest, as day and night to men
Successive, and the timely dew of sleep
Now falling with soft slumb'rous weight inclines 615
Our eyelids; other creatures all day long
Rove idle unemploy'd, and less need rest;
Man hath his daily work of body or mind
Appointed, which declares his dignity,
And the regard of Heav'n on all his ways; 620
While other animals unactive range,
And of their doings God takes no account.
To-morrow ere fresh morning streak the east
With first approach of light, we must be ris'n,
And at our pleasant labour, to reform 625
Yon flow'ry arbours, yonder alleys green,
Our walk at noon, with branches overgrown,
That mock our scant manuring, and require
More hands than ours to lop their wanton growth:
Those blossoms also, and those dropping gums, 630
That lie bestrewn unsightly and unsmooth,
Ask riddance, if we mean to tread with ease;
Meanwhile, as Nature wills, Night bids us rest.'
    To whom thus Eve with perfect beauty adorn'd.
'My author and disposer, what thou bidd'st, 635
Unargu'd I obey; so God ordains,
God is thy law, thou mine: to know no more
Is woman's happiest knowledge and her praise.
With thee conversing I forget all time,
All seasons and their change; all please alike. 640
Sweet is the breath of Morn, her rising sweet,
With charm of earliest birds; pleasant the Sun
When first on this delightful land he spreads
His orient beams, on herb, tree, fruit, and flow'r,

Glist'ring with dew; fragrant the fertile earth   645
After soft showers; and sweet the coming on
Of grateful evening mild, then silent Night
With this her solemn bird and this fair moon.
And these the gems of Heav'n, her starry train:
But neither breath of Morn when she ascends   650
With charm of earliest birds, nor rising sun
On this delightful land, nor herb, fruit, flow'r,
Glist'ring with dew, nor fragrance after showers,
Nor grateful evening mild, nor silent Night
With this her solemn bird, nor walk by moon   655
Or glittering starlight without thee is sweet.

From BOOK V

THE ARGUMENT.

MORNING approached, Eve relates to Adam her troublesome dream; he
likes it not, yet comforts her: they come forth to their day labours:
their morning hymn at the door of their bower. God to render man
inexcusable sends Raphael to admonish him of his obedience, of his free
estate, of his enemy near at hand; who he is, and why his enemy, and
whatever else may avail Adam to know. Raphael comes down to
Paradise, his appearance described, his coming discerned by Adam afar
off sitting at the door of his bower; he goes out to meet him, brings him
to his lodge, entertains him with the choicest fruits of Paradise got
together by Eve; their discourse at table: Raphael performs his message,
minds Adam of his state and of his enemy; relates at Adam's request
who that enemy is, and how he came to be so, beginning from his first
revolt in Heaven, and the occasion thereof; how he drew his legions
after him to the parts of the north, and there incited them to rebel with
him, persuading all but only Abdiel a seraph, who in argument
dissuades and opposes him, then forsakes him.

*   *   *   *   *   *   *   *   *   *

So spake th' Eternal Father, and fulfill'd
All justice: nor delay'd the winged saint
After his charge receiv'd; but from among
Thousand celestial ardours, where he stood

Veil'd with his gorgeous wings, upspringing light   250
Flew through the midst of Heav'n; th' angelic quires
On each hand parting, to his speed gave way
Through all th' empyreal road; till at the gate
Of Heav'n arriv'd, the gate self-open'd wide
On golden hinges turning, as by work   255
Divine the sovran Architect had fram'd.
From hence, no cloud, or, to obstruct his sight,
Star interpos'd, however small he sees,
Not unconform to other shining globes,
Earth, and the gard'n of God, with cedars crown'd   260
Above all hills. As when by night the glass
Of Galileo, less assur'd, observes
Imagin'd lands and regions in the moon:
Or pilot, from amidst the Cyclades
Delos or Samos first appearing, kens   265
A cloudy spot. Down thither prone in flight
He speeds, and through the vast ethereal sky
Sails between worlds and worlds, with steady wing
Now on the polar winds, then with quick fan
Winnows the buxom air; till within soar   270
Of tow'ring eagles, to all the fowls he seems
A phoenix, gaz'd by all, as that sole bird
When to enshrine his relics in the sun's
Bright temple, to Egyptian Thebes he flies.
At once on th' eastern cliff of Paradise   275
He lights, and to his proper shape returns
A seraph wing'd; six wings he wore, to shade
His lineaments divine; the pair that clad
Each shoulder broad, came mantling o'er his breast,
With regal ornament; the middle pair   280
Girt like a starry zone his waist, and round
Skirted his loins and thighs with downy gold
And colours dipp'd in Heav'n; the third his feet
Shadow'd from either heel with feather'd mail,

Sky-tinctur'd grain. Like Maia's son he stood,   285
And shook his plumes, that Heav'nly fragrance fill'd
The circuit wide. Straight knew him all the bands
Of angels under watch; and to his state,
And to his message high in honour rise;
For on some message high they guess'd him bound.   290
Their glittering tents he pass'd, and now is come
Into the blissful field, through groves of myrrh,
And flow'ring odours, cassia, nard, and balm;
A wilderness of sweets; for Nature here
Wanton'd as in her prime, and play'd at will   295
Her virgin fancies, pouring forth more sweet,
Wild above rule or art, enormous bliss.

From BOOK IX

THE ARGUMENT.

SATAN having compassed the earth, with meditated guile returns as a
mist by night into Paradise, and enters into the serpent sleeping.
Adam and Eve in the morning go forth to their labours, which Eve
proposes to divide in several places, each labouring apart. Adam
consents not, alleging the danger, lest that Enemy, of whom they were
forewarned, should attempt her found alone. Eve, loth to be thought
not circumspect or firm enough, urges her going apart, the rather
desirous to make trial of her strength; Adam at last yields. The Serpent
finds her alone; his subtle approach, first gazing, then speaking, with
much flattery extolling Eve above all other creatures. Eve, wondering
to hear the Serpent speak, asks how he attained to human speech and
such understanding not till now; the Serpent answers, that by tasting of
a certain tree in the garden he attained both to speech and reason, till
then void of both. Eve requires him to bring her to that tree, and finds
it to be the tree of Knowledge forbidden. The Serpent, now grown
bolder, with many wiles and arguments induces her at length to eat; she,
pleased with the taste, deliberates awhile whether to impart thereof to
Adam or not; at last brings him of the fruit, relates what persuaded her
to eat thereof. Adam, at first amazed, but perceiving her lost, resolves
through vehemence of love to perish with her, and extenuating the
trespass, eats also of the fruit. The effects thereof in them both; they

seek to cover their nakedness ; then fall to variance and accusation of
one another.

No more of talk where God or angel guest
With Man, as with his friend, familiar us'd
To sit indulgent, and with him partake
Rural repast, permitting him the while
Venial discourse unblam'd : I now must change   5
These notes to tragic ; foul distrust, and breach
Disloyal on the part of Man, revolt,
And disobedience : on the part of Heav'n
Now alienated, distance and distaste,
Anger and just rebuke, and judgement giv'n,   10
That brought into this world a world of woe,
Sin and her shadow Death, and Misery,
Death's harbinger : sad task, yet argument
Not less but more heroic than the wrath
Of stern Achilles on his foe pursu'd   15
Thrice fugitive about Troy wall ; or rage
Of Turnus for Lavinia disespous'd,
Or Neptune's ire or Juno's, that so long
Perplex'd the Greek and Cytherea's son ;
If answerable style I can obtain   20
Of my celestial patroness, who deigns
Her nightly visitation unimplor'd,
And dictates to me slumb'ring, or inspires
Easy my unpremeditated verse :
Since first this subject for heroic song   25
Pleas'd me long choosing, and beginning late ;
Not sedulous by nature to indite
Wars, hitherto the only argument
Heroic deem'd, chief mast'ry to dissect
With long and tedious havoc fabl'd knights   30
In battles feign'd ; the better fortitude
Of patience and heroic martyrdom

Unsung; or to describe races and games,
Or tilting furniture, emblazon'd shields,
Impresses quaint, caparisons and steeds;   35
Bases and tinsel trappings, gorgeous knights
At joust and tournament; then marshall'd feast
Served up in hall with sewers, and seneschals:
The skill of artifice or office mean,
Not that which justly gives heroic name   40
To person or to poem. Me of these
Nor skill'd nor studious, higher argument
Remains, sufficient of itself to raise
That name, unless an age too late, or cold
Climate, or years damp my intended wing   45
Depress'd, and much they may, if all be mine,
Not hers who brings it nightly to my ear.

From BOOK XI

THE ARGUMENT.

The Son of God presents to his Father the prayers of our first parents
now repenting, and intercedes for them. God accepts them, but declares
that they must no longer abide in Paradise: sends Michael with a band
of cherubim to dispossess them; but first to reveal to Adam future things.
Michael's coming down. Adam shows to Eve certain ominous signs;
he discerns Michael's approach, goes out to meet him; the angel
denounces their departure. Eve's lamentation. Adam pleads, but
submits. The angel leads him up to a high hill, sets before him in vision
what shall happen till the Flood.

*   *   *   *   *   *   *   *   *   *

It was a hill
Of Paradise the highest, from whose top
The hemisphere of Earth in clearest ken
Stretch'd out to amplest reach of prospect lay.   380
Not higher that hill nor wider looking round,

Whereon for different cause the Tempter set
Our second Adam in the wilderness,
To show him all earth's kingdoms and their glory.
His eye might there command wherever stood   385
City of old or modern fame, the seat
Of mightiest empire, from the destin'd walls
Of Cambalu, seat of Cathaian Can,
And Samarchand by Oxus, Temir's throne,
To Paquin of Sinæan kings: and thence   390
To Agra and Lahor of great Mogul
Down to the golden Chersonese; or where
The Persian in Ecbatan sat, or since
In Hispahan; or where the Russian Ksar
In Mosco; or the Sultan in Bizance,   395
Turchestan-born; nor could his eye not ken
The empire of Negus to his utmost port
Ercoco, and the less maritime kings,
Mombaza, and Quiloa, and Melind,
And Sofala thought Ophir, to the realm   400
Of Congo, and Angola farthest south;
Or thence from Niger flood to Atlas mount
The kingdoms of Almansor, Fez, and Sus,
Marocco and Algiers, and Tremisen;
Or Europe thence, and where Rome was to sway
The world: in spirit perhaps he also saw   406
Rich Mexico the seat of Motezume,
And Cusco in Peru, the richer seat
Of Atabalipa; and yet unspoil'd
Guiana, whose great city Geryon's sons   410
Call El Dorado: but to nobler sights
Michael from Adam's eyes the film remov'd
Which that false fruit that promis'd clearer sight
Had bred; then purg'd with euphrasy and rue
The visual nerve, for he had much to see;   415
And from the well of Life three drops instill'd.

From BOOK XII

THE ARGUMENT.

THE angel Michael continues from the flood to relate what shall
succeed; then, in the mention of Abraham, comes by degrees to
explain, who that Seed of the Woman shall be, which was promised
Adam and Eve in the fall. His incarnation, death, resurrection, and
ascension; the state of the church till his second coming. Adam, greatly
satisfied and re-comforted by these relations and promises, descends the
hill with Michael: wakens Eve, who all this while had slept, but with
gentle dreams composed to quietness of mind and submission. Michael
in either hand leads them out of Paradise, the fiery sword waving
behind them, and the cherubim taking their stations to guard the place.

*   *   *   *   *   *   *   *   *   *

To whom thus also th' angel last repli'd:
'This having learnt, thou hast attain'd the sum   575
Of wisdom; hope no higher, though all the stars
Thou knew'st by name, and all th' ethereal powers,
All secrets of the deep, all Nature's works,
Or works of God in heav'n, air, earth, or sea,
And all the riches of this world enjoy'dst,   580
And all the rule, one empire; only add
Deeds to thy knowledge answerable, add faith,
Add virtue, patience, temperance; add love,
By name to come call'd charity, the soul
Of all the rest: then wilt thou not be loth   585
To leave this Paradise, but shalt possess
A Paradise within thee, happier far.
Let us descend now therefore from this top
Of speculation, for the hour precise
Exacts our parting hence; and see, the guards   590
By me encamp'd on yonder hill, expect
Their motion; at whose front a flaming sword,
In signal of remove, waves fiercely round;
We may no longer stay: go, waken Eve;
Her also I with gentle dreams have calm'd.   595

Portending good, and all her spirits compos'd
To meek submission: thou at season fit
Let her with thee partake what thou hast heard;
Chiefly what may concern her faith to know,
The great deliverance by her Seed to come   600
(For by the Woman's Seed) on all mankind;
That ye may live, which will be many days,
Both in one faith unanimous, though sad
With cause for evils past, yet much more cheer'd
With meditation on the happy end.'   605
　　He ended, and they both descend the hill;
Descended, Adam to the bow'r where Eve
Lay sleeping ran before, but found her wak'd;
And thus with words not sad she him receiv'd.
　　'Whence thou return'st, and whither went'st I know;
For God is also in sleep, and dreams advise,   611
Which he hath sent propitious, some great good
Presaging, since with sorrow and heart's distress
Wearied I fell asleep: but now lead on,
In me is no delay; with thee to go,   615
Is to stay here; without thee here to stay,
Is to go hence unwilling; thou to me
Art all things under Heav'n, all places thou,
Who for my wilful crime art banish'd hence.
This further consolation yet secure   620
I carry hence; though all by me is lost,
Such favour I unworthy am vouchsaf'd,
By me the promis'd Seed shall all restore.'
　　So spake our mother Eve; and Adam heard
Well pleas'd, but answer'd not; for now too nigh
Th' archangel stood; and from the other hill   626
To their fix'd station, all in bright array
The cherubim descended; on the ground
Gliding meteorous, as ev'ning mist
Ris'n from a river o'er the marish glides,   630

And gathers ground fast at the labourer's heel
Homeward returning. High in front advanc'd,
The brandish'd sword of God before them blaz'd
Fierce as a comet; which with torrid heat,
And vapour as the Libyan air adust,   635
Began to parch that temperate clime; whereat
In either hand the hast'ning angel caught
Our ling'ring parents, and to th' eastern gate
Led them direct, and down the cliff as fast
To the subjected plain; then disappear'd.   640
They looking back, all th' eastern side beheld
Of Paradise, so late their happy seat,
Wav'd over by that flaming brand; the gate
With dreadful faces throng'd and fiery arms: 644
Some natural tears they dropp'd, but wip'd them soon;
The world was all before them, where to choose
Their place of rest, and Providence their guide:
They hand in hand with wand'ring steps and slow,
Through Eden took their solitary way.

PARADISE
REGAIN'D.

A
POEM.

In IV BOOKS.

To which is added

SAMSON AGONISTES.

The Author
JOHN MILTON.

LONDON,

Printed by J. M for *John Starkey* at the
Mitre in *Fleetstreet*, near *Temple-Bar*.
MDCLXXI.

From PARADISE REGAINED

BOOK IV

'THE city which thou seest no other deem
Than great and glorious Rome, queen of the Earth, 45
So far renown'd, and with the spoils enrich'd
Of nations; there the Capitol thou seest,
Above the rest lifting his stately head
On the Tarpeian rock, her citadel
Impregnable; and there mount Palatine 50
The imperial palace, compass huge, and high
The structure, skill of noblest architects,
With gilded battlements conspicuous far,
Turrets and terraces, and glittering spires:
Many a fair edifice besides, more like 55
Houses of gods, (so well I have dispos'd
My aery microscope) thou may'st behold
Outside and inside both, pillars and roofs,
Carv'd work, the hand of fam'd artificers
In cedar, marble, ivory, or gold. 60
Thence to the gates cast round thine eye, and see
What conflux issuing forth, or ent'ring in;
Praetors, pro-consuls to their provinces
Hasting or on return, in robes of state;
Lictors and rods, the ensigns of their power, 65
Legions and cohorts, turms of horse and wings:
Or embassies from regions far remote,
In various habits, on the Appian road,
Or on the Æmilian; some from farthest south
Syene, and where the shadow both way falls, 70
Meroe, Nilotic isle; and more to west,
The realm of Bocchus to the Black-moor sea;

From the Asian kings, and Parthian among these;
From India and the golden Chersonese,
And utmost Indian isle Taprobane,   75
Dusk faces with white silken turbans wreath'd;
From Gallia, Gades, and the British west:
Germans and Scythians, and Sarmatians north
Beyond Danubius to the Tauric pool.
All nations now to Rome obedience pay,   80
To Rome's great emperor, whose wide domain,
In ample territory, wealth and power,
Civility of manners, arts, and arms,
And long renown, thou justly may'st prefer
Before the Parthian. These two thrones except,   85
The rest are barbarous, and scarce worth the sight,
Shar'd among petty kings too far remov'd;
These having shown thee, I have shown thee all
The kingdoms of the world, and all their glory.

*   *   *   *   *   *   *   *   *   *

To whom the Fiend, with fear abash'd, repli'd.   195
'Be not so sore offended, Son of God,
(Though sons of God both angels are and men)
If I to try whether in higher sort
Than these thou bear'st that title, have propos'd
Whet both from men and angels I receive,   200
Tetrarchs of fire, air, flood, and on the earth,
Nations beside from all the quarter'd winds,
God of this world invok'd, and world beneath;
Who then thou art, whose coming is foretold
To me most fatal, me it most concerns;   205
The trial hath endamag'd thee no way,
Rather more honour left and more esteem;
Me nought advantag'd, missing what I aim'd.
Therefore let pass, as they are transitory,
The kingdoms of this world; I shall no more   210
Advise thee; gain them as thou canst, or not.
And thou thyself seem'st otherwise inclin'd

Than to a worldly crown; addicted more
To contemplation and profound dispute,
As by that early action may be judg'd,   215
When slipping from thy mother's eye, thou went'st
Alone into the temple, there wast found
Among the gravest Rabbis, disputant
On points and questions fitting Moses' chair,
Teaching, not taught. The childhood shows the man,
As morning shows the day: be famous then   221
By wisdom; as thy empire must extend,
So let extend thy mind o'er all the world
In knowledge, all things in it comprehend.
All knowledge is not couch'd in Moses' law,   225
The Pentateuch, or what the Prophets wrote;
The Gentiles also know, and write, and teach
To admiration, led by Nature's light;
And with the Gentiles much thou must converse,
Ruling them by persuasion, as thou mean'st;   230
Without their learning how wilt thou with them,
Or they with thee hold conversation meet?
How wilt thou reason with them, how refute
Their idolisms, traditions, paradoxes?
Error by his own arms is best evinc'd.   235
Look once more, ere we leave this specular mount,
Westward, much nearer by south-west, behold;
Where on the Ægean shore a city stands
Built nobly, pure the air, and light the soil;
Athens, the eye of Greece, mother of arts   240
And eloquence, native to famous wits
Or hospitable, in her sweet recess,
City or suburban, studious walks and shades.
See there the olive grove of Academe,
Plato's retirement, where the Attic bird   245
Trills her thick-warbl'd notes the summer long;
There flow'ry hill Hymettus, with the sound
Of bees' industrious murmur, oft invites

To studious musing; there Ilissus rolls
His whispering stream: within the walls then view   250
The schools of ancient sages; his who bred
Great Alexander to subdue the world,
Lyceum there, and painted Stoa next:
There shalt thou hear and learn the secret power
Of harmony, in tones and numbers hit   255
By voice or hand; and various-measur'd verse,
Æolian charms and Dorian lyric odes,
And his, who gave them breath, but higher sung,
Blind Melesigenes thence Homer call'd,
Whose poem Phoebus challeng'd for his own.   260
Thence what the lofty grave tragedians taught
In chorus or Iambic, teachers best
Of moral prudence, with delight receiv'd
In brief sententious precepts, while they treat
Of fate, and chance, and change in human life,   265
High actions and high passions best describing:
Thence to the famous orators repair,
Those ancient, whose resistless eloquence
Wielded at will that fierce democracy,
Shook the Arsenal and fulmin'd over Greece   270
To Macedon, and Artaxerxes' throne:
To sage Philosophy next lend thine ear,
From Heaven descended to the low-roof'd house
Of Socrates; see there his tenement,
Whom well inspir'd the oracle pronounc'd   275
Wisest of men; from whose mouth issu'd forth
Mellifluous streams, that water'd all the schools
Of Academics old and new, with those
Surnam'd Peripatetics, and the sect
Epicurean, and the Stoic severe;   280
These here revolve, or, as thou lik'st, at home,
Till time mature thee to a kingdom's weight;
These rules will render thee a king complete
Within thyself, much more with empire join'd.'

SAMSON AGONISTES,

A

DRAMATIC POEM.

The Author

JOHN MILTON.

Aristot. Poet. Cap. 6.

Τραγωδία μίμησις πράξεως σπεδαίας, &c.

Tragædia est imitatio actionis seriæ, &c. Per misericordiam &
metum perficiens talium affectuum lustrationem.

LONDON,

Printed by *J. M.* for *John Starkey* at the
Mitre in *Fleetstreet,* near *Temple-Bar.*
MDCLXXI.

I

From SAMSON AGONISTES

THE PERSONS.

SAMSON.
MANOA, *the Father of Samson.*
DALILA, *his Wife.*
HARAPHA *of Gath.*
Public Officer.
Messenger.
Chorus of Danites.

The Scene before the Prison in Gaza.

Manoa. I know your friendly minds and—O what noise!
Mercy of Heav'n, what hideous noise was that!
Horribly loud, unlike the former shout.   1510

Chorus. Noise call you it, or universal groan
As if the whole inhabitation perish'd!
Blood, death, and deathful deeds are in that noise;
Ruin, destruction at the utmost point.

Manoa. Of ruin indeed methought I heard the noise:
Oh! it continues; they have slain my son.   1516

Chorus. Thy son is rather slaying them; that outcry
From slaughter of one foe could not ascend.

Manoa. Some dismal accident it needs must be;
What shall we do, stay here or run and see?   1520

Chorus. Best keep together here, lest running thither
We unawares run into danger's mouth.
This evil on the Philistines is fall'n;
From whom could else a general cry be heard?
The sufferers then will scarce molest us here;   1525
From other hands we need not much to fear.
What if his eyesight (for to Israel's God
Nothing is hard) by miracle restor'd,

He now be dealing dole among his foes,
And over heaps of slaughter'd walk his way?   1530
  Manoa. That were a joy presumptuous to be thought.
  Chorus. Yet God hath wrought things as incredible,
For his people of old; what hinders now?
  Manoa. He can, I know, but doubt to think he will;
Yet hope would fain subscribe, and tempts belief.   1535
A little stay will bring some notice hither.
  Chorus. Of good or bad so great, of bad the sooner;
For evil news rides post, while good news baits.
And to our wish I see one hither speeding,
A Hebrew, as I guess, and of our tribe.   1540
  Messenger. O whither shall I run, or which way fly
The sight of this so horrid spectacle
Which erst my eyes beheld, and yet behold?
For dire imagination still pursues me.
But providence or instinct of nature seems,   1545
Or reason though disturb'd, and scarce consulted,
To have guided me aright, I know not how,
To thee first, reverend Manoa, and to these
My countrymen, whom here I knew remaining,
As at some distance from the place of horror,   1550
So in the sad event too much concern'd.
  Manoa. The accident was loud, and here before thee
With rueful cry, yet what it was we hear not;
No preface needs, thou seest we long to know.
  Messenger. It would burst forth, but I recover breath
And sense distract, to know well what I utter.   1556
  Manoa. Tell us the sum, the circumstance defer.
  Messenger. Gaza yet stands, but all her sons are fall'n;
All in a moment overwhelm'd and fall'n.
  Manoa. Sad, but thou know'st to Israelites not saddest,
The desolation of a hostile city.   1561
  Messenger. Feed on that first; there may in grief be
    surfeit.

Manoa. Relate by whom.

Messenger.   By Samson.

Manoa.   That still lessens
The sorrow, and converts it nigh to joy.

Messenger. Ah! Manoa, I refrain too suddenly   1565
To utter what will come at last too soon;
Lest evil tidings, with too rude irruption
Hitting thy aged ear, should pierce too deep.

Manoa. Suspense in news is torture; speak them out.

Messenger. Take then the worst in brief, Samson is
         dead.   1570

Manoa. The worst indeed; O all my hopes defeated
To free him hence! but Death who sets all free
Hath paid his ransom now and full discharge.
What windy joy this day had I conceiv'd,
Hopeful of his delivery, which now proves   1575
Abortive as the first-born bloom of spring
Nipp'd with the lagging rear of winter's frost!
Yet ere I give the reins to grief, say first,
How died he? death to life is crown or shame.
All by him fell thou say'st; by whom fell he?   1580
What glorious hand gave Samson his death's wound?

Messenger. Unwounded of his enemies he fell.

Manoa. Wearied with slaughter, then, or how? explain.

Messenger. By his own hands.

Manoa.   Self-violence? what cause
Brought him so soon at variance with himself,   1585
Among his foes?

Messenger.   Inevitable cause,
At once both to destroy and be destroy'd:
The edifice, where all were met to see him,
Upon their heads and on his own he pull'd.

Manoa. O lastly over-strong against thyself!   1590
A dreadful way thou took'st to thy revenge.
More than enough we know; but while things yet

Are in confusion, give us if thou canst,
Eye-witness of what first or last was done,
Relation more particular and distinct.   1595
    Messenger. Occasions drew me early to this city;
And as the gates I enter'd with sunrise,
The morning trumpets festival proclaim'd
Through each high street: little I had dispatch'd,
When all abroad was rumour'd that this day   1600
Samson should be brought forth to show the people
Proof of his mighty strength in feats and games;
I sorrow'd at his captive state, but minded
Not to be absent at that spectacle.
The building was a spacious theatre   1605
Half round, on two main pillars vaulted high,
With seats where all the lords, and each degree
Of sort, might sit in order to behold;
The other side was op'n, where the throng
On banks and scaffolds under sky might stand;   1610
I among these aloof obscurely stood.
The feast and noon grew high, and sacrifice
Had fill'd their hearts with mirth, high cheer, and wine,
When to their sports they turn'd.   Immediately
Was Samson as a public servant brought,   1615
In their state livery clad; before him pipes
And timbrels, on each side went armed guards,
Both horse and foot before him and behind,
Archers, and slingers, cataphracts and spears.
At sight of him the people with a shout   1620
Rifted the air, clamouring their god with praise,
Who had made their dreadful enemy their thrall.
He patient but undaunted where they led him,
Came to the place, and what was set before him
Which without help of eye, might be essay'd,   1625
To heave, pull, draw, or break, he still perform'd
All with incredible, stupendious force,

None daring to appear antagonist.
At length for intermission sake they led him
Between the pillars; he his guide requested,　　　　1630
(For so from such as nearer stood we heard)
As over-tir'd, to let him lean awhile
With both his arms on those two massy pillars
That to the arched roof gave main support.
He unsuspicious led him; which when Samson　　　1635
Felt in his arms, with head awhile inclin'd,
And eyes fast fix'd he stood, as one who pray'd,
Or some great matter in his mind revolv'd.
At last with head erect thus cried aloud.
'Hitherto, lords, what your commands impos'd　　1640
I have perform'd, as reason was, obeying,
Not without wonder or delight beheld.
Now of my own accord such other trial
I mean to show you of my strength, yet greater,
As with amaze shall strike all who behold.'　　　1645
This utter'd, straining all his nerves he bow'd;
As with the force of winds and waters pent,
When mountains tremble, those two massy pillars
With horrible convulsion to and fro
He tugg'd, he shook, till down they came and drew
The whole roof after them, with burst of thunder　1651
Upon the heads of all who sat beneath,
Lords, ladies, captains, counsellors, or priests,
Their choice nobility and flower, not only
Of this, but each Philistian city round,　　　　　1655
Met from all parts to solemnize this feast.
Samson with these immix'd, inevitably,
Pull'd down the same destruction on himself;
The vulgar only scap'd who stood without.
　　Chorus.　O dearly bought revenge, yet glorious! 1660
Living or dying thou hast fulfill'd
The work for which thou wast foretold

To Israel ; and now li'st victorious
Among thy slain self-kill'd ;
Not willingly, but tangl'd in the fold   1665
Of dire necessity, whose law in death conjoin'd
Thee with thy slaughter'd foes, in number more
Than all thy life had slain before.
   1 *Semichorus.* While their hearts were jocund and
      sublime,
Drunk with idolatry, drunk with wine,   1670
And fat regorg'd of bulls and goats,
Chanting their idol, and preferring
Before our living Dread who dwells
In Silo his bright sanctuary :
Among them he a spirit of frenzy sent,   1675
Who hurt their minds,
And urg'd them on with mad desire
To call in haste for their destroyer :
They only set on sport and play
Unweetingly importun'd   1680
Their own destruction to come speedy upon them.
So fond are mortal men
Fall'n into wrath divine,
As their own ruin on themselves to invite ;
Insensate left, or to sense reprobate,   1685
And with blindness internal struck.
   2 *Semichorus.* But he, though blind of sight,
Despis'd and thought extinguish'd quite,
With inward eyes illuminated,
His fiery virtue rous'd   1690
From under ashes into sudden flame,
And as an ev'ning dragon came,
Assailant on the perched roosts,
And nests in order rang'd
Of tame villatic fowl ; but as an eagle   1695
His cloudless thunder bolted on their heads.

So virtue giv'n for lost,
Depress'd, and overthrown, as seem'd,
Like that self-begott'n bird
In the Arabian woods embost,   1700
That no second knows nor third,
And lay erewhile a holocaust,
From out her ashy womb now teem'd,
Revives, reflourishes, then vigorous most
When most unactive deem'd;   1705
And, though her body die, her fame survives,
A secular bird, ages of lives.

    Manoa. Come, come, no time for lamentation now,
Nor much more cause; Samson hath quit himself
Like Samson, and heroically hath finish'd   1710
A life heroic, on his enemies
Fully reveng'd, hath left them years of mourning,
And lamentation to the sons of Caphtor,
Through all Philistian bounds; to Israel
Honour hath left, and freedom, let but them   1715
Find courage to lay hold on this occasion;
To himself and father's house eternal fame;
And which is best and happiest yet, all this
With God not parted from him, as was fear'd,
But favouring and assisting to the end.   1720
Nothing is here for tears, nothing to wail
Or knock the breast, no weakness, no contempt,
Dispraise, or blame, nothing but well and fair,
And what may quiet us in a death so noble.
Let us go find the body where it lies   1725
Soak'd in his enemies' blood, and from the stream
With lavers pure and cleansing herbs wash off
The clotted gore. I with what speed the while
(Gaza is not in plight to say us nay)
Will send for all my kindred, all my friends   1730
To fetch him hence, and solemnly attend

With silent obsequy and funeral train
Home to his father's house: there will I build him
A monument, and plant it round with shade
Of laurel ever green, and branching palm,   1735
With all his trophies hung, and acts enroll'd
In copious legend, or sweet lyric song.
Thither shall all the valiant youth resort,
And from his memory inflame their breasts
To matchless valour, and adventures high: 1740
The virgins also shall on feastful days
Visit his tomb with flowers, only bewailing
His lot unfortunate in nuptial choice,
From whence captivity and loss of eyes.
   Chorus. All is best, though we oft doubt,   1745
What th' unsearchable dispose
Of highest Wisdom brings about,
And ever best found in the close.
Oft he seems to hide his face,
But unexpectedly returns;   1750
And to his faithful champion hath in place
Bore witness gloriously; whence Gaza mourns,
And all that band them to resist
His uncontrollable intent;
His servants he with new acquist   1755
Of true experience from this great event,
With peace and consolation hath dismiss'd,
And calm of mind, all passion spent.

AREOPAGITICA

A SPEECH
For the Liberty of
UNLICENC'D PRINTING

Published 1644

*   *   *   *   *   *   *   *   *   *

I deny not but that it is of greatest concernment in the Church and Commonwealth to have a vigilant eye how books demean themselves as well as men; and thereafter to confine, imprison, and do sharpest justice on them as malefactors: for books are not absolutely dead things, but do contain a potency of life in them to be as active as that soul was whose progeny they are; nay, they do preserve as in a vial the purest efficacy and extraction of that living intellect that bred them. I know they are as lively, 10 and as vigorously productive, as those fabulous dragon's teeth; and being sown up and down, may chance to spring up armed men. And yet on the other hand, unless wariness be used, as good almost kill a man as kill a good book; who kills a man kills a reasonable creature, God's image; but he who destroys a good book, kills reason itself, kills the image of God as it were in the eye. Many a man lives a burden to the earth; but a good book is the precious life-blood of a master spirit, embalmed and treasured up on purpose to a life beyond life. 'Tis true, no age can 20 restore a life, whereof perhaps there is no great loss; and revolutions of ages do not oft recover the loss of a rejected truth, for the want of which whole nations fare the worse. We should be wary therefore what persecution we raise against the living labours of public men, how we spill that seasoned life of man preserved and stored up in books;

since we see a kind of homicide may be thus committed, sometimes a martyrdom, and if it extend to the whole impression, a kind of massacre, whereof the execution ends not in the slaying of an elemental life, but strikes at that ethereal and fifth essence, the breath of reason itself, slays an immortality rather than a life.

* * * * * * * * * *

Good and evil we know in the field of this world grow up together almost inseparably; and the knowledge of good is so involved and interwoven with the knowledge of evil, and in so many cunning resemblances hardly to be 10 discerned, that those confused seeds, which were imposed on Psyche as an incessant labour to cull out and sort asunder, were not more intermixed. It was from out the rind of one apple tasted that the knowledge of good and evil as two twins cleaving together leapt forth into the world. And perhaps this is that doom which Adam fell into of knowing good and evil, that is to say, of knowing good by evil. As therefore the state of man now is, what wisdom can there be to choose, what continence to forbear without the knowledge of evil? He that can apprehend 20 and consider vice with all her baits and seeming pleasures, and yet abstain, and yet distinguish, and yet prefer that which is truly better, he is the true warfaring Christian. I cannot praise a fugitive and cloistered virtue, unexercised and unbreathed, that never sallies out and sees her adversary, but slinks out of the race, where that immortal garland is to be run for, not without dust and heat. Assuredly we bring not innocence into the world, we bring impurity much rather: that which purifies us is trial, and trial is by what is contrary. That virtue therefore which 30 is but a youngling in the contemplation of evil, and knows not the utmost that vice promises to her followers, and rejects it, is but a blank virtue, not a pure; her whiteness is but an excremental whiteness; which was the reason

why our sage and serious poet Spenser, whom I dare be
known to think a better teacher than Scotus or Aquinas,
describing true temperance under the person of Guyon
brings him in with his palmer through the cave of Mammon
and the bower of earthly bliss, that he might see and know,
and yet abstain. Since therefore the knowledge and survey
of vice is in this world so necessary to the constituting of
human virtue, and the scanning of error to the confirmation
of truth, how can we more safely and with less danger
10 scout into the regions of sin and falsity than by reading all
manner of tractates, and hearing all manner of reason?
And this is the benefit which may be had of books
promiscuously read.

*　　*　　*　　*　　*　　*　　*　　*　　*

And lest some should persuade ye, Lords and Commons,
that these arguments of learned men's discouragement at
this your order are mere flourishes and not real, I could
recount what I have seen and heard in other countries,
where this kind of inquisition tyrannizes; when I have
20 sat among their learned men, for that honour I had, and
been counted happy to be born in such a place of philo-
sophic freedom as they supposed England was, while
themselves did nothing but bemoan the servile condition
into which learning amongst them was brought; that this
was it which had damped the glory of Italian wits, that
nothing had been there written now these many years but
flattery and fustian. There it was that I found and visited
the famous Galileo grown old, a prisoner to the Inquisition,
for thinking in astronomy otherwise than the Franciscan
30 and Dominican licensers thought. And though I knew
that England then was groaning loudest under the prelatical yoke, nevertheless I took it as a pledge of future
happiness, that other nations were so persuaded of her
liberty. Yet was it beyond my hope that those worthies
were then breathing in her air, who should be her leaders

to such a deliverance as shall never be forgotten by any revolution of time that this world hath to finish.

* * * * * * * * * *

Lords and Commons of England, consider what nation it is whereof ye are and whereof ye are the governors : a nation not slow and dull, but of a quick, ingenious, and piercing spirit, acute to invent, subtle and sinewy to discourse, not beneath the reach of any point the highest that human capacity can soar to. Therefore the studies of learning in her deepest sciences have been so ancient and so eminent among us, that writers of good antiquity and 10 ablest judgement have been persuaded that even the school of Pythagoras and the Persian wisdom took beginning from the old philosophy of this island. And that wise and civil Roman, Julius Agricola, who governed once here for Caesar, preferred the natural wits of Britain before the laboured studies of the French. Nor is it for nothing that the grave and frugal Transylvanian sends out yearly from as far as the mountainous borders of Russia and beyond the Hercynian wilderness, not their youth, but their staid men, to learn our language and our theologic arts. Yet 20 that which is above all this, the favour and the love of heaven, we have great argument to think in a peculiar manner propitious and propending towards us. Why else was this nation chosen before any other, that out of her as out of Sion should be proclaimed and sounded forth the first tidings and trumpet of Reformation to all Europe? And had it not been the obstinate perverseness of our prelates against the divine and admirable spirit of Wicklif, to suppress him as a schismatic and innovator, perhaps neither the Bohemian Huss and Jerome, no, nor the 30 name of Luther or of Calvin, had been ever known ; the glory of reforming all our neighbours had been completely ours. But now, as our obdurate clergy have with violence demeaned the matter, we are become hitherto the latest

and the backwardest scholars, of whom God offered to have made us the teachers. Now once again by all concurrence of signs and by the general instinct of holy and devout men, as they daily and solemnly express their thoughts, God is decreeing to begin some new and great period in his Church, even to the reforming of Reformation itself. What does he then but reveal himself to his servants, and as his manner is, first to his Englishmen; I say as his manner is, first to us, though we mark not the
10 method of his counsels and are unworthy. Behold now this vast city: a city of refuge, the mansion house of liberty, encompassed and surrounded with his protection; the shop of war hath not there more anvils and hammers waking, to fashion out the plates and instruments of armed justice in defence of beleaguered truth, than there be pens and heads there, sitting by their studious lamps, musing, searching, revolving new notions and ideas wherewith to present, as with their homage and their fealty, the approaching Reformation; others as fast reading, trying all things,
20 assenting to the force of reason and convincement. What could a man require more from a nation so pliant and so prone to seek after knowledge? What wants there to such a towardly and pregnant soil but wise and faithful labourers, to make a knowing people, a nation of prophets, of sages, and of worthies? We reckon more than five months yet to harvest; there need not be five weeks; had we but eyes to lift up, the fields are white already. Where there is much desire to learn, there of necessity will be much arguing, much writing, many opinions; for opinion
30 in good men is but knowledge in the making. Under these fantastic terrors of sect and schism, we wrong the earnest and zealous thirst after knowledge and understanding which God hath stirred up in this city. What some lament of, we rather should rejoice at, should rather praise this pious forwardness among men, to reassume the

ill-deputed care of their religion into their own hands
again. A little generous prudence, a little forbearance of
one another, and some grain of charity might win all these
diligences to join and unite in one general and brotherly
search after truth, could we but forgo this prelatical
tradition of crowding free consciences and Christian liberties into canons and precepts of men. I doubt not, if some
great and worthy stranger should come among us, wise to
discern the mould and temper of a people and how to
govern it, observing the high hopes and aims, the diligent 10
alacrity of our extended thoughts and reasonings in the
pursuance of truth and freedom, but that he would cry out
as Pyrrhus did, admiring the Roman docility and courage:
If such were my Epirots, I would not despair the greatest
design that could be attempted to make a church or kingdom happy. Yet these are the men cried out against for
schismatics and sectaries; as if, while the Temple of the
Lord was building, some cutting, some squaring the
marble, others hewing the cedars, there should be a sort
of irrational men who could not consider there must be 20
many schisms and many dissections made in the quarry
and in the timber, ere the house of God can be built. And
when every stone is laid artfully together, it cannot be
united into a continuity, it can but be contiguous in this
world; neither can every piece of the building be of one
form; nay, rather the perfection consists in this: that out
of many moderate varieties and brotherly dissimilitudes
that are not vastly disproportional arises the goodly and
the graceful symmetry that commends the whole pile and
structure. Let us therefore be more considerate builders, 30
more wise in spiritual architecture, when great reformation
is expected. For now the time seems come, wherein
Moses the great prophet may sit in heaven rejoicing to
see that memorable and glorious wish of his fulfilled, when
not only our seventy elders but all the Lord's people are

become prophets. No marvel then though some men, and some good men too perhaps, but young in goodness, as Joshua then was, envy them. They fret, and out of their own weakness are in agony, lest those divisions and sub-divisions will undo us. The adversary again applauds, and waits the hour ; when they have branched themselves out, saith he, small enough into parties and partitions, then will be our time. Fool! he sees not the firm root, out of which we all grow though into branches ; nor will 10 beware until he see our small divided maniples cutting through at every angle of his ill-united and unwieldy brigade. And that we are to hope better of all these supposed sects and schisms, and that we shall not need that solicitude, honest perhaps though over-timorous of them that vex in this behalf, but shall laugh in the end at those malicious applauders of our differences, I have these reasons to persuade me :

First, when a city shall be as it were besieged and blocked about, her navigable river infested, inroads and 20 incursions round, defiance and battle oft rumoured to be marching up even to her walls and suburb trenches, that then the people, or the greater part, more than at other times, wholly taken up with the study of highest and most important matters to be reformed, should be disputing, reasoning, reading, inventing, discoursing, even to a rarity, and admiration, things not before discoursed or written of, argues first a singular goodwill, contentedness and confi-dence in your prudent foresight and safe government, Lords and Commons ; and from thence derives itself to 30 a gallant bravery and well-grounded contempt of their enemies, as if there were no small number of as great spirits among us, as his was, who when Rome was nigh besieged by Hannibal, being in the city, bought that piece of ground at no cheap rate, whereon Hannibal himself encamped his own regiment. Next it is a lively and

cheerful presage of our happy success and victory. For
as in a body, when the blood is fresh, the spirits pure and
vigorous not only to vital but to rational faculties, and those
in the acutest and the pertest operations of wit and subtlety,
it argues in what good plight and constitution the body is,
so when the cheerfulness of the people is so sprightly up,
as that it has not only wherewith to guard well its own
freedom and safety but to spare, and to bestow upon the
solidest and sublimest points of controversy and new invention, it betokens us not degenerated, nor drooping to a 10
fatal decay, but casting off the old and wrinkled skin of
corruption to outlive these pangs and wax young again,
entering the glorious ways of truth and prosperous virtue
destined to become great and honourable in these latter
ages. Methinks I see in my mind a noble and puissant
nation rousing herself like a strong man after sleep, and
shaking her invincible locks. Methinks I see her as an
eagle muing her mighty youth, and kindling her undazzled
eyes at the full midday beam, purging and unscaling her
long-abused sight at the fountain itself of heavenly radiance, 20
while the whole noise of timorous and flocking birds, with
those also that love the twilight, flutter about, amazed at
what she means, and in their envious gabble would
prognosticate a year of sects and schisms.

What should ye do then, should ye suppress all this
flowery crop of knowledge and new light sprung up and
yet springing daily in this city, should ye set an oligarchy
of twenty engrossers over it, to bring a famine upon our
minds again, when we shall know nothing but what is
measured to us by their bushel? Believe it, Lords and 30
Commons, they who counsel ye to such a suppressing do
as good as bid ye suppress yourselves; and I will soon
show how. If it be desired to know the immediate cause
of all this free writing and free speaking, there cannot be
assigned a truer than your own mild and free and human

government; it is the liberty, Lords and Commons, which your own valorous and happy counsels have purchased us, liberty which is the nurse of all great wits; this is that which hath rarefied and enlightened our spirits like the influence of heaven; this is that which hath enfranchised, enlarged and lifted up our apprehensions degrees above themselves. Ye cannot make us now less capable, less knowing, less eagerly pursuing of the truth, unless ye first make yourselves, that made us so, less the lovers, less the founders of our true liberty. We can grow ignorant again, brutish, formal, and slavish, as ye found us; but you then must first become that which ye cannot be, oppressive, arbitrary, and tyrannous, as they were from whom ye have freed us. That our hearts are now more capacious, our thoughts more erected to the search and expectation of greatest and exactest things, is the issue of your own virtue propagated in us; ye cannot suppress that unless ye reinforce an abrogated and merciless law, that fathers may dispatch at will their own children. And who shall then stick closest to ye, and excite others? Not he who takes up arms for coat and conduct and his four nobles of Danegelt. Although I dispraise not the defence of just immunities, yet love my peace better, if that were all. Give me the liberty to know, to utter, and to argue freely according to conscience, above all liberties.

THE REASON OF CHURCH-GOVERNMENT

BOOK II, INTRODUCTION
Published 1641

CONCERNING therefore this wayward subject against prelaty, the touching whereof is so distasteful and disquietous to a number of men, as by what hath been said I may deserve of charitable readers to be credited, that neither envy nor gall hath entered me upon this controversy, but the enforcement of conscience only, and a preventive fear lest the omitting of this duty should be against me when I would store up to myself the good provision of peaceful hours: so lest it should be still imputed to me, as I have found it hath been, that some self-pleasing humour of vain-glory 10 hath incited me to contest with men of high estimation, now while green years are upon my head, from this needless surmisal I shall hope to dissuade the intelligent and equal auditor, if I can but say successfully that which in this exigent behoves me, although I would be heard only, if it might be, by the elegant and learned reader, to whom principally for a while I shall beg leave I may address myself. To him it will be no new thing though I tell him that if I hunted after praise by the ostentation of wit and learning, I should not write thus out of mine own season, 20 when I have neither yet completed to my mind the full circle of my private studies, although I complain not of any insufficiency to the matter in hand; or were I ready to my wishes, it were a folly to commit anything elaborately composed to the careless and interrupted listening of these tumultuous times. Next, if I were wise only to mine own ends, I would certainly take such a subject as of itself might catch applause, whereas this hath all the disadvantages on the contrary, and such a subject as the publishing

whereof might be delayed at pleasure, and time enough to pencil it over with all the curious touches of art, even to the perfection of a faultless picture, whenas in this argument the not deferring is of great moment to the good speeding, that if solidity have leisure to do her office, art cannot have much. Lastly, I should not choose this manner of writing, wherein knowing myself inferior to myself, led by the genial power of nature to another task, I have the use, as I may account it, but of my left hand. And though I shall
10 be foolish in saying more to this purpose, yet since it will be such a folly as wisest men going about to commit, have only confessed and so committed, I may trust with more reason, because with more folly, to have courteous pardon. For although a Poet soaring in the high region of his fancies, with his garland and singing robes about him, might without apology speak more of himself than I mean to do, yet for me sitting here below in the cool element of prose, a mortal thing among many readers of no empyreal conceit, to venture and divulge unusual things of myself, I shall
20 petition to the gentler sort, it may not be envy to me. I must say therefore that after I had from my first years by the ceaseless diligence and care of my father, whom God recompense, been exercised to the tongues, and some sciences, as my age would suffer, by sundry masters and teachers both at home and at the schools, it was found that whether aught was imposed me by them that had the overlooking, or betaken to of mine own choice in English, or other tongue, prosing or versing, but chiefly this latter, the style, by certain vital signs it had, was likely to
30 live. But much latelier in the private academies of Italy, whither I was favoured to resort, perceiving that some trifles which I had in memory, composed at under twenty or thereabout (for the manner is that every one must give some proof of his wit and reading there) met with acceptance above what was looked for, and other things which

I had shifted in scarcity of books and conveniences to patch
up amongst them, were received with written encomiums,
which the Italian is not forward to bestow on men of this
side the Alps, I began thus far to assent both to them and
divers of my friends here at home, and not less to an
inward prompting which now grew daily upon me, that by
labour and intent study (which I take to be my portion
in this life) joined with the strong propensity of nature,
I might perhaps leave something so written to aftertimes,
as they should not willingly let it die.   These thoughts at 10
once possessed me, and these other : That if I were certain
to write as men buy leases, for three lives and downward,
there ought no regard be sooner had than to God's glory
by the honour and instruction of my country.   For which
cause, and not only for that I knew it would be hard to
arrive at the second rank among the Latins, I applied
myself to that resolution which Ariosto followed against
the persuasions of Bembo, to fix all the industry and art
I could unite to the adorning of my native tongue ; not to
make verbal curiosities the end, that were a toilsome 20
vanity, but to be an interpreter and relater of the best and
sagest things among mine own citizens throughout this
island in the mother dialect.   That what the greatest and
choicest wits of Athens, Rome, or modern Italy, and those
Hebrews of old did for their country, I in my proportion,
with this over and above of being a Christian, might do
for mine : not caring to be once named abroad, though
perhaps I could attain to that, but content with these
British Islands as my world, whose fortune hath hitherto
been, that if the Athenians, as some say, made their small 30
deeds great and renowned by their eloquent writers,
England hath had her noble achievements made small by
the unskilful handling of monks and mechanics.

Time serves not now, and perhaps I might seem too
profuse to give any certain account of what the mind at

home in the spacious circuits of her musing hath liberty to propose to herself, though of highest hope, and hardest attempting, whether that epic form whereof the two poems of Homer, and those other two of Virgil and Tasso are a diffuse, and the book of Job a brief model: or whether the rules of Aristotle herein are strictly to be kept, or nature to be followed, which in them that know art, and use judgement, is no transgression, but an enriching of art: and lastly what king or knight before the conquest
10 might be chosen in whom to lay the pattern of a Christian hero. And as Tasso gave to a prince of Italy his choice whether he would command him to write of Godfrey's expedition against the Infidels, or Belisarius against the Goths, or Charlemain against the Lombards; if to the instinct of nature and the emboldening of art aught may be trusted, and that there be nothing adverse in our climate, or the fate of this age, it haply would be no rashness from an equal diligence and inclination to present the like offer in our own ancient stories. Or whether those
20 dramatic constitutions, wherein Sophocles and Euripides reign, shall be found more doctrinal and exemplary to a nation, the Scripture also affords us a divine pastoral drama in the Song of Salomon consisting of two persons and a double chorus, as Origen rightly judges. And the Apocalypse of St. John is the majestic image of a high and stately tragedy, shutting up and intermingling her solemn scenes and acts with a sevenfold chorus of hallelujahs and harping symphonies: and this my opinion the grave authority of Pareus commenting that book is sufficient
30 to confirm. Or if occasion shall lead to imitate those magnific odes and hymns wherein Pindarus and Callimachus are in most things worthy, some others in their frame judicious, in their matter most and end faulty: But those frequent songs throughout the law and prophets beyond all these, not in their divine argument alone, but

in the very critical art of composition, may be easily made
appear over all the kinds of lyric poesy to be incomparable.
These abilities, wheresoever they be found, are the inspired
gift of God, rarely bestowed, but yet to some (though most
abuse) in every nation : and are of power beside the office
of a pulpit, to inbreed and cherish in a great people the
seeds of virtue and public civility, to allay the perturbations
of the mind, and set the affections in right tune, to celebrate in glorious and lofty hymns the throne and equipage
of God's almightiness, and what He works, and what He 10
suffers to be wrought with high providence in His church, to
sing the victorious agonies of martyrs and saints, the deeds
and triumphs of just and pious nations doing valiantly
through faith against the enemies of Christ, to deplore
the general relapses of kingdoms and states from justice
and God's true worship.   Lastly, whatsoever in religion is
holy and sublime, in virtue amiable or grave, whatsoever
hath passion or admiration in all the changes of that which
is called fortune from without, or the wily subtleties and
refluxes of man's thoughts from within ; all these things 20
with a solid and treatable smoothness to paint out and
describe, teaching over the whole book of sanctity and
virtue, through all the instances of example, with such
delight to those especially of soft and delicious temper,
who will not so much as look upon Truth herself, unless
they see her elegantly dressed, that whereas the paths of
honesty and good life appear now rugged and difficult,
though they be indeed easy and pleasant, they would then
appear to all men both easy and pleasant though they
were rugged and difficult indeed. . . . The thing which 30
I had to say, and those intentions which have lived within
me ever since I could conceive myself anything worth to
my country, I return to crave excuse that urgent reason
hath plucked from me by an abortive and foredated discovery. And the accomplishment of them lies not but

in a power above man's to promise; but that none hath by more studious ways endeavoured, and with more un-wearied spirit that none shall, that I dare almost aver of myself, as far as life and free leisure will extend, and that the land had once enfranchised herself from this imper-tinent yoke of prelaty, under whose inquisitorious and tyrannical duncery no free and splendid wit can flourish. Neither do I think it shame to covenant with any knowing reader, that for some few years yet I may go on trust with
10 him toward the payment of what I am now indebted, as being a work not to be raised from the heat of youth, or the vapours of wine, like that which flows at waste from the pen of some vulgar amourist, or the trencher fury of a rhyming parasite, nor to be obtained by the invocation of Dame Memory and her Siren daughters, but by devout prayer to that eternal Spirit who can enrich with all utterance and knowledge, and sends out his Seraphim with the hallowed fire of his altar to touch and purify the lips of whom he pleases: to this must be added industrious and
20 select reading, steady observation, insight into all seemly and generous arts and affairs; till which in some measure be compassed, at mine own peril and cost I refuse not to sustain this expectation from as many as are not loth to hazard so much credulity upon the best pledges that I can give them. Although it nothing content me to have dis-closed thus much beforehand, but that I trust hereby to make it manifest with what small willingness I endure to interrupt the pursuit of no less hopes than these, and leave a calm and pleasing solitariness fed with cheerful and
30 confident thoughts, to embark in a troubled sea of noises and hoarse disputes, put from beholding the bright coun-tenance of truth in the quiet and still air of delightful studies. . . .

NOTES

JOHNSON'S LIFE OF MILTON

PAGE 1, l. 6. *an unfinished poem.* Johnson refers to 'The Passion', at the end of the eighth stanza of which Milton adds: 'This subject the author finding to be Above the years he had when he wrote it, and nothing satisfied with what was begun, left it unfinished.'

PAGE 2, l. 1. *preserved at Cambridge.* The library of Trinity College, Cambridge, contains the manuscripts of 'Arcades', 'Lycidas', 'Comus', fourteen sonnets, and three of the minor poems.

l. 14. *a lion,* &c. Paradise Lost, iv. 343. Hannah More notes in her diary a conversation with Johnson in 1781: 'I praised Lycidas, which he absolutely abused, adding "if Milton had not written the Paradise Lost, he would have only ranked among the minor poets: he was a Phidias that could cut a Colossus out of a rock, but could not cut heads out of cherry stones"' (Memoirs, ed. 1834, i. 212).

l. 28. *a pastoral.* Johnson disliked pastorals in general. In his Life of Shenstone he writes: 'The four parts of his "Pastoral Ballad" demand particular notice. I cannot but regret that it is pastoral; an intelligent reader acquainted with the scenes of real life, sickens at the mention of the crook, the pipe, the sheep, and the kids, which it is not necessary to bring forward to notice.'

l. 31. Cowley's poem 'On the Death of Mr. William Hervey'.

PAGE 3, l. 24. Johnson's censure is too indiscriminate. Pastoral imagery and phraseology are throughout transparent poetical fictions. The shepherd is never a real feeder of sheep. In the first part of Lycidas he is a poet, as King was: in lines 113-31 he is a religious teacher, as King was destined to be. The defect lies not in the blending of truths and fictions, real shepherds and ecclesiastical pastors, but in the use of the figure of the shepherd, first in its classical, afterwards in its scriptural sense.

PAGE 5, l. 6. L'Allegro, ll. 131-4.

l. 8. Il Penseroso, ll. 155-66.

l. 13. L'Allegro, l. 148; Il Penseroso, ll. 105-8.

PAGE 7, l. 8. *a short fit of rhyming*: Comus, ll. 495-512.

l. 21. *not very musical in their numbers.* Contrast Sir Henry Wotton's letter quoted in Macaulay's Essay, p. 49.

l. 25. The great defect of Johnson's criticism of 'Comus' is that he judges a masque as if it were an acting drama.

l. 30. *the eighth and twenty-first.* The sonnets Johnson excepts from his general condemnation are the one headed 'When the Assault was intended to the City', and the first of those addressed to Cyriack Skinner.

PAGE 9, l. 28. See Paradise Lost, Bk. ix, ll. 782, 1000.

l. 34. *of which the least could wield.* Paradise Lost, vi. 221–3.

PAGE 10, l. 22. *the most exalted and most depraved being.* 'His sentiments are every way answerable to his character, and suitable to a created being of the most exalted and most depraved nature' (Addison, Spectator, No. 303).

l. 23. John Clarke, master of the Grammar School in Hull. His 'Essay upon Study' was published in 1731.

PAGE 11, l. 14. Paradise Lost, v. 152–208.

l. 19. Paradise Lost, ix. 1067–1189; x. 867–1096.

l. 23. *the probable and the marvellous.* 'Aristotle observes that the fable of an epic poem should abound in circumstances that are both credible and astonishing. . . . If the fable is only probable, it differs nothing from a true history; if it is only marvellous, it is no better than a romance. The great secret, therefore, of heroic poetry is to relate such circumstances as may produce in the reader at the same time both belief and astonishment' (Addison, Spectator, No. 315).

PAGE 13, l. 4. 'Spenser has a better plea for his Fairy Queen, had his action been finished, or had been one. And Milton, if the Devil had not been his hero, instead of Adam; if the giant had not foiled the knight, and driven him out of his stronghold, to wander through the world with his lady errant' (Dryden, Dedication of the Æneis, ed. W. P. Ker, ii, p. 165).

l. 29. Paradise Lost, v. 805–907; viii. 64–216.

PAGE 15, l. 4. Dryden says of Shakespeare, 'Those who accuse him to have wanted learning give him the greater commendation: he was naturally learned; he needed not the spectacles of books to read nature; he looked inwards, and found her there' (Essay of Dramatic Poesy).

l. 7. Paradise Lost, iv. 268.

l. 10. Paradise Lost, ii. 1017.

l. 23. Paradise Lost, i. 284.

PAGE 16, l. 1. *Pravity*: immorality, a moral perversity.

l. 28. *the port of mean suitors*: Paradise Lost, xi. 8.

PAGE 17, l. 21. Richard Bentley published his edition of Paradise Lost in 1732. In Book I, lines 287, 351, 355, are, with many others, assumed to be interpolated by the reviser; but there is no ground for the statement that Bentley privately owned the falsity of his supposition.

PAGE 19, l. 30. *burning marl*: Paradise Lost, i. 296.

l. 33. Paradise Lost, ii. 932.

l. 34. Paradise Lost, iv. 800.

l. 35. *starts up in his own shape*: Paradise Lost, iv. 819.

PAGE 20, l. 2. *a spear and a shield*: Paradise Lost, iv. 990.

l. 6. *incorporeal spirits*, &c.: Paradise Lost, i. 789.

l. 9. *crushed in upon their substance*, &c.: Paradise Lost, vi. 656, 661.

l. 12. *sooner for their arms*, &c.: Paradise Lost, vi. 595-7.

l. 17. Paradise Lost, iv. 556.

l. 18. Paradise Lost, ix. 484.

PAGE 21, l. 19. *aggregated soil*: Paradise Lost, x. 293-324.

l. 26. Paradise Lost, iv. 820-1015.

l. 29. *rife in Heaven*: Paradise Lost, i. 650.

l. 34. Paradise Lost, v. 95-116.

PAGE 22, l. 2. Paradise Lost, viii. 179-202.

l. 5. Paradise Lost, vi. 857.

l. 8. ''Tis true he runs into a flat of thought sometimes for a hundred lines together, but 'tis when he has got into a track of Scripture' (Dedication to Juvenal, ed. W. P. Ker, ii, p. 29). 'Milton's Paradise Lost is admirable: but am I therefore bound to maintain that there are no flats amongst his elevations, when 'tis evident he creeps along sometimes for above an hundred lines together?' (Preface to Sylvæ, 1685, ed. W. P. Ker, i, p. 268).

l. 24. Paradise Lost, iii. 496.   Orlando Furioso, Bk. xxxiv.

PAGE 24, l. 7. 'The language of this great poet . . . is often too much laboured and sometimes obscured by old words, transpositions and foreign idioms. . . . Milton's sentiments and ideas were so wonderfully sublime, that it would have been impossible for him to have represented them in their full strength and beauty, without having recourse to these foreign assistances.   Our language sunk under him, and was unequal to that greatness of soul, which furnished him with such glorious conceptions' (Addison, Spectator, No. 297).

l. 23. 'Spenser in affecting the ancients writ no language' (Jonson, Discoveries).

l. 24. *a Babylonish Dialect*.   Butler says of the language of Sir Hudibras:

> 'When he pleased to shew't, his speech
> In loftiness of sound was rich,
> A Babylonish dialect,
> Which learned pedants much affect.
> It was a particoloured dress
> Of patch'd and piebald languages,
> 'Twas English cut on Greek and Latin,
> Like fustian heretofore on satin.'

> (Hudibras, Part I, Canto i, l. 89.)

l. 35. *The measure*, &c. See the preface on ' The Verse' prefixed to Paradise Lost. Milton quotes as precedents : ' Italian and Spanish poets of prime note ', and ' our best English tragedies '. The Earl of Surrey translated the second and fourth books of the Aeneid into blank verse ; the fourth book was printed separately about 1548, the second did not appear till 1557 when both were printed together. The first tragedy written in blank verse was ' Gorboduc ', by Thomas Sackville, Lord Buckhurst, and Thomas Norton. It was acted in 1562 and printed in 1565. The earliest original poems in blank verse are those by Nicholas Grimoald in Tottel's Miscellany (1557), and Gascoigne's ' Steel Glass ' (1576). The poem on Guiana referred to by Johnson is probably George Chapman's ' De Guiana, Carmen epicum ', published in 1596, prefixed to ' A relation of the Second Voyage to Guiana ', by Lawrence Keymis. Giovanni Trissino, who is termed by Hallam ' the father of blank verse ', published his ' Italia Liberata ' in 1548.

PAGE **25**, l. 12. Voltaire remarks : ' Je me souviendrai toujours que je demandai au célèbre Pope, pourquoi Milton n'avait pas rimé son Paradis Perdu, et qu'il me répondit, Because he could not, parcequ'il ne le pouvait pas ' (Voltaire, Works, xxxv. 435, ed. 1819).

l. 32. *an ingenious critic.* ' The gentleman whom he thus characterizes is (as he told Mr. Seward) Mr. Lock, of Norbury Park, in Surrey, whose knowledge and taste in the fine arts is universally celebrated ' (Boswell, Life of Johnson).

PAGE **26**, l. 2. *lapidary style.* By a ' lapidary style ' Johnson means the style usually adopted in monumental inscriptions. In this passage he compares the measured periods of such inscriptions with the rhythm of blank verse. In the present case he seems to be thinking of the habitual exaggerations of inscriptions. Elsewhere he says, ' the writer of an epitaph must not be considered as saying nothing but what is true. Allowance must be made for some degree of exaggerated praise. In lapidary inscriptions a man is not upon oath ' (Boswell's Life of Johnson, ed. Hill, ii. 407).

l. 8. Johnson devotes four papers of the ' Rambler ' to an examination of Milton's versification. He concludes : ' If the poetry of Milton be examined, with regard to the pauses and flow of his verses into each other, it will appear, that he has performed all that our language would admit ; and the comparison of his numbers with those who have cultivated the same manner of writing, will show that he excelled as much in the lower as the higher parts of his art, and that his skill in harmony was not less than his invention or his learning ' (Rambler, No. 90).

HAZLITT'S LECTURE ON MILTON

PAGE 27, l. 19. *Blind Thamyris*, &c.: Paradise Lost, iii. 35, 36.

PAGE 28, l. 2. *With darkness*, &c.: Paradise Lost, vii. 27.

l. 5. *piling up every stone*, &c.: Paradise Lost, xi. 324, 325.

l. 8. *For after I had from my first years*, &c. The Reason of Church-Government, Book II, Introduction. See p. 184.

PAGE 29, l. 19. *The noble heart*, &c.: Faerie Queene, I. v. 1.

l. 34. *makes Ossa like a wart*: Hamlet, v. i. 271.

PAGE 30, l. 18. *Him followed Rimmon*, &c.: Paradise Lost, i. 467-9.

l. 24. *As when a vulture*, &c.: Paradise Lost, iii. 431-9.

PAGE 31, l. 6. *the great vision of the guarded mount*: Lycidas, l. 161.

l. 9. *the pilot*, &c.: Paradise Lost, i. 204.

l. 10. *the wandering moon*, &c.: Il Penseroso, ll. 67-70.

l. 28. *like a steam*, &c.: Comus, l. 556.

PAGE 32, l. 8. *He soon Saw within ken*, &c.: Paradise Lost, iii. 621-44.

l. 38. *With Atlantean shoulders*, &c.: Paradise Lost, ii. 306, 307.

PAGE 33, l. 1. *lay floating many a rood*: Paradise Lost, i. 196.

l. 2. *that sea beast Leviathan*, &c.: Paradise Lost, i. 200-2.

l. 17. See Johnson's Essay, p. 24, ll. 25-8.

PAGE 34, l. 2. *His hand was known*, &c.: Paradise Lost, i. 732-47.

l. 14. *But chief*, &c.: Paradise Lost, i. 762, 767-88.

l. 39. *Round he surveys*, &c.: Paradise Lost, iii. 555-67.

PAGE 35, l. 15. *Such as the meeting soul*, &c.: L'Allegro, ll. 138-40.

l. 22. *the hidden soul of harmony*: L'Allegro, l. 144.

l. 30. *God the Father turns a school-divine*: Pope, Epistle to Augustus, l. 102.

PAGE 36, l. 24. *stood like a tower*: Paradise Lost, i. 591.

l. 25. *As when Heaven's fire*, &c.: Paradise Lost, i. 612, 613.

PAGE 37, l. 1. *All is not lost*, &c.: Paradise Lost, i. 106-9.

l. 20. *that intellectual being*, &c.: Paradise Lost, ii. 147, 148.

l. 22. *swallowed up and lost*, &c.: Paradise Lost, ii. 149, 150.

l. 24. *Fallen cherub*, &c.: Paradise Lost, i. 157, 158.

PAGE 38, l. 3. *aloft incumbent on the dusky air*: Paradise Lost, i. 226.

l. 31. *Is this the region*, &c.: Paradise Lost, i. 242-63.

PAGE 39, l. 34. *Salmasius* (Claude de Saumaise), an eminent professor of Leyden, wrote in 1649, at the request of Charles II, his *Defensio Regia pro Carolo I*. Milton replied in 1651 in his *Pro Populo Anglicano Defensio*.

l. 35. *with hideous ruin and combustion dire* : see Paradise Lost, i. 46.

PAGE 40, l. 2. *retreated in a silent valley*, &c.: Paradise Lost, ii. 547-50.

l. 15. *a character* : Napoleon.

l. 30. 'For the same cause, I think, writing the Iliad in the heyday of his spirit, he made the whole structure dramatic and combative ; that of the Odyssey is in the main narrative, which is the special mark of age. So it is that in the Odyssey one might liken Homer to a setting sun ; the intensity is gone, but there remains the greatness. Here the tone of those great lays of Ilium is no longer maintained—the passages on one level of sublimity with no sinking anywhere, the same stream of passion poured upon passion, the readiness of turn, the closeness to life, the throng of images all drawn from the truth : as when Ocean retires into himself, and is left lonely around his proper bounds, only the ebbings of his greatness are left to our view, and a wandering among the shallows of the fabulous and the incredible' (Longinus, On the Sublime, trans. A. O. Prickard).

PAGE 41, l. 3. *no kind of traffic*, &c.: see Tempest, II. i. 142-55.

l. 10. *The generations were prepared*, &c.: Wordsworth, Excursion, vi. 554-7.

l. 18. *the unapparent deep* : Paradise Lost, vii. 103.

l. 29. *where no crude surfeit reigned* : Comus, l. 480.

l. 34. *know to know no more* : see Cowper, Truth, l. 327.

They toiled not : St. Matthew vi. 28, 29.

PAGE 42, l. 5. *In them the burthen*, &c.: Wordsworth, Lines composed a few miles above Tintern Abbey, ll. 38-41.

l. 11. *such as angels weep* : Paradise Lost, i. 620.

l. 24. *In either hand*, &c.: Paradise Lost, xii. 637-47.

MACAULAY'S ESSAY ON MILTON

PAGE 43, l. 4. *numbers* : metre. Cf. Pope :

'As yet a child, nor yet a fool to fame,
I lisped in numbers, for the numbers came.'

PAGE 44, l. 18. *the Arabian tale* : of 'The Forty Thieves'. Sesame is a seed-bearing plant which grows in the East. The seeds, from which an oil is first crushed out, are made into cakes. Hence Cassim's confusion of it with wheat and barley.

l. 23. In 1674 Dryden, then Poet Laureate, having first obtained Milton's permission, turned Paradise Lost into 'an Opera, written in Heroic Verse', under the title The State of Innocence.

l. 27. *muster-rolls of names* : e. g. Paradise Lost, i. 576-87 ; and xi. 385-411.

PAGE 45, l. 5. *housings*: a horse's trappings.

l. 32. *Mr. Newbery* : a London publisher of the eighteenth century, whose firm was famous for its children's books and for toys of the kind here described.

PAGE 46, l. 2. *Harold*: i. e. Childe Harold, the central figure of Byron's poem Childe Harold's Pilgrimage, a character beneath whose experiences and reflections are thinly veiled those of Byron himself.

l. 14. *Aeschylus*, 'the father of Greek Tragedy'. His lifetime covered the years of the great struggle between the Greeks and the Persians first under Darius and then under his son Xerxes, a struggle which saved Greece and so Europe from Oriental conquest. Aeschylus himself fought at the battle of Marathon (490 B.C.) and perhaps also at Salamis ten years later.

l. 20. *Herodotus* (? 484-? 425 B.C.), 'the father of History', as Cicero calls him, wrote a record of the conflict between the Greeks and their Eastern enemies, in the course of which he digresses very freely into the history and legends of Egypt and the East.

l. 25. *Pindar* (522-448 B.C.) was a contemporary of Aeschylus, and the greatest of the Greek lyric poets. Of his poems all that remain are some collections of odes written in praise of victors in the Olympic Games and other like contests.

l. 31. *Agamemnon*: one of the leaders of the Greeks in the Trojan war. Aeschylus' play *Agamemnon* treats of his return from that war, and in it his unfaithful wife Clytaemnestra, welcoming him home after his ten years' absence, makes a long speech describing the sorrow she pretends to have felt during their long separation.

l. 32. In another play of Aeschylus, *The Seven against Thebes*, Polynices, who has been wrongfully driven from that city by his brother, is preparing along with six Argive chieftains to attack it. There is a long description (some 300 lines in all) of the seven warriors as they stand at the head of their troops, each ready to attack one of the city's seven gates.

PAGE 47, l. 1. Whereas with Aeschylus tragedy had been mainly represented as the operation of Fate or Destiny, of the inexorable will of the gods, in Sophocles it is set forth rather as the working of human weakness and passion ; 'Sophocles is ', says Professor Jebb, ' pre-eminently the dramatist of human character; he excels in delineating the great primary emotions of our nature '.

l. 7. Euripides has been charged with undue realism and sensationalism at the expense of art. Apart from that disputed question, it is generally admitted that a great defect in his plays from the artistic point of view is his tendency to put into the mouths of his characters long philosophical or rhetorical speeches.

o 2

l. 14. '*sad Electra's poet*': see Milton's Sonnet 'When the Assault was intended to the City': p. 109 and note.

PAGE 48, l. 1. *the Italian Masque.* The Masque was introduced into this country from Italy during the sixteenth century.

l. 5. *The Faithful Shepherdess* (1610), by John Fletcher, was to some extent based on Guarini's Pastor Fido, produced in Italy in 1590, and this in its turn owed much to Tasso's Aminta, produced in 1573. See p. 55, l. 23 note.

l. 35. *Sir Henry Wotton* (1568-1639), a distinguished scholar who, besides acting as English ambassador at various foreign courts, was also a great patron of men of letters.

PAGE 49, l. 2. *Dorique*: the Dorians, one of the branches of the Greek race, had great colonies in Sicily. The earliest pastoral poets belonged to Sicily, and their poetry was therefore written in the Doric dialect of Greek.

l. 18. *the Hesperides*: the daughters of Night who lived in the extreme West on an island of the Ocean; their duty was to guard the golden apples that grew in their island home. Cf. Comus, l. 393, note.

l. 25. Macaulay is here alluding to the statement that Milton himself preferred Paradise Regained to Paradise Lost; the words of Milton's nephew, however, on which the statement is based, are that the poet 'could not hear with patience' the Paradise Regained 'censured to be much inferior to the other'.

PAGE 50, l. 27. *from the sixth to the seventh circle of hell.* Dante's Divina Commedia consists of three parts, the Inferno, the Purgatorio, and the Paradiso. In it he describes the journey which he in imagination made, with Virgil as his guide, through Hell, and then up the Mount of Purgatory.

l. 28. *Trent*: a town on the northern frontier of Italy.

l. 29. *Phlegethon*, or the River of Fire, was in Greek mythology one of the rivers of Hades.

Aqua Cheta: i. e. the Quiet Stream, the name given to the upper waters of the river Montone, which rises in the Apennines, and flows into the Adriatic a little south of Ravenna.

l. 32. *Arles*: a town on the Rhone, at the head of its delta. Outside it is an ancient Roman cemetery, afterwards consecrated for Christian burial also, and very famous in the Middle Ages.

PAGE 51, l. 2. *In one passage*: Paradise Lost, i. 192-210.

l. 3. *earth-born enemies*: v. notes on p. 56, l. 4.

l. 7. *Atlas*: in legend a solitary mountain in Libya, which bore up the heavens. It can hardly be identified with any peak in the range of the same name in Morocco.

l. 9. *Nimrod*: the 'mighty hunter' of Genesis x. 8-10. The quotation is from the Inferno (xxxi. 58-64), but Macaulay has made one blunder in his version: the words which he translates 'the ball' ('la pina di San Pietro') really mean 'the pine', and refer to a bronze pine-cone some $7\frac{1}{2}$ feet in height. This, 'which once ornamented the top of the mole of Adrian, was afterwards employed to decorate the top of the belfry of St. Peter.

l. 16. *Mr. Cary*: Henry Francis Cary (1772–1844). His translation of the Inferno appeared in 1805, and of the Purgatorio and Paradiso in 1812.

l. 19. *lazar-house*: home or hospital for the sick, especially for lepers. The name 'lazar' is derived from the Lazarus of the parable, St. Luke xvi. 19 ff. See Bk. xi, ll. 477–95.

l. 20. *the last ward of Malebolge* ('Evil Pits'). In the eighth circle of the Inferno were ten separate wards or pits in which the various classes of the Fraudulent or Treacherous were undergoing terrible torments.

l. 28. *Valdichiana*: i. e. the valley of the Chiana, in Tuscany; its marshes made it in Dante's time a hotbed of malaria.

PAGE 52, l. 6. *the portal*: of Hell, above which Dante saw an inscription of which the last line ran

Lasciate ogni speranza, voi ch'entrate.

i. e.   'All hope abandon, ye who enter here.'
(Inferno, iii. 9.)

l. 9. *Barbariccia and Draghignazzo*: two winged demons who with their hooks and pitchforks drove those guilty of fraud into the lake of boiling pitch in the Malebolge, and prevented their escape from it (Inf. xxii).

l. 12. *the purifying angel* stood at the gate of Purgatory and marked on Dante's forehead seven P's (representing the seven *peccata* or deadly sins) ; these were removed one at a time as the poet passed up the seven terraces of the mountain.

l. 18. *Amadis* of Gaul, the knight-errant hero of a famous group of romances very widely known in western Europe in the fifteenth and sixteenth centuries.

l. 28. *Gulliver*: Swift's Gulliver's Travels, published in 1726.

l. 30. *philosophizing horses*: the Houyhnhnms, the visit to whose land was the fourth and last of Gulliver's travels.

PAGE 54, l. 7. The quotation is from Johnson's Life of Milton, but 'seducing' should be 'enticing'. See p. 19, ll. 24–6.

PAGE 55, l. 6. *Don Juan*: according to legend, a nobleman of Seville, who, after a life of great profligacy, one day invited to supper the statue of a man whom he had murdered. The statue was animated by a fiend, who in the midst of the meal seized the Don and carried him off to Hell.

l. 11. *Farinata*, a leader of the Ghibelline party in Florence, is, in the Inferno, punished as a heretic by being placed in a red-hot tomb; from this he rises and converses with Dante about Florence and its affairs (Inf. x).

l. 12. *auto-da-fe* : i. e. 'act of faith', the title used for the condemnation of heretics by the Inquisition, and then for their punishment.

l. 23. *Tasso,* Torquato (1544–95), chiefly famous for his epic La Gerusalemme Liberata, which deals with the First Crusade and the taking of Jerusalem by Godfrey de Bouillon. In the course of it he describes the assembly of demons who aim at frustrating the crusade.

l. 24. *Klopstock* : a German poet (1724–1803) who, in imitation of Milton, wrote an epic called Messias.

l. 29. *demons* : in the Greek sense of 'divine powers', 'supernatural beings', as Eris or Strife, Dike or Justice.

PAGE 56, l. 4. *Titans* : the twelve children of Heaven and Earth, who existed even before the gods and were the first inhabitants of this world. According to the Greek legend a fierce war was waged between them and the gods of Olympus for the supreme power in the world.

PAGE 57, l. 17. *that noxious Sardinian soil.* It would seem that at one time there grew in Sardinia some plants of specially bitter flavour, and these too in such quantity as seriously to affect the flavour of its honey (see Horace, Ars Poetica, l. 375).

l. 20. *the Hebrew poet* : Job x. 22.

PAGE 58, l. 26. *on the eve of great events* : in 1639.

l. 31. *his hovel* : a typical exaggeration.

PAGE 59, l. 2. *Theocritus* : a Sicilian Greek of the third century B.C. He was the most famous of the pastoral poets spoken of in the note on p. 49, l. 2.

l. 3. *Ariosto,* Ludovico (1474–1533), author of Orlando Furioso.

l. 20. *Filicaja,* Vincenzo da (1642–1707) : a Florentine poet.

l. 27. *that beautiful face* : of his second wife, Sonnet XXIII.

l. 33. See p. 110 and note.

PAGE 60, l. 17. *Burke* : the great statesman and orator of the reign of George III, best known by his speeches on England's relations with America, his impeachment of Warren Hastings, and his Reflections on the French Revolution (1790). Macaulay's estimate of the relative merit of Burke's and Milton's prose is perhaps influenced by political feeling. Burke had entered Parliament as a Whig, but left the Whig party at the time of the French Revolution.

l. 25. '*a sevenfold chorus* . . .' : from The Reason of Church-Government. Book ii, Introduction. See p. 186, ll. 27, 28.

ON THE MORNING OF CHRIST'S NATIVITY

l. 6. *forfeit*: the penalty of misdoing.

l. 10. *wont*, ' was wont '.

l. 23. *wizards*: magicians, referring to the ' three Magi' (St. Matthew ii. 1).

l. 24. *prevent* : anticipate, forestall.

l. 33. *gaudy* (from Lat. *gaudium*): holiday. 'A gaudy day' Dr. Johnson gives as a ' University phrase ', and as such it is still used.

l. 56. The Soldan's chariot in Spenser (Faerie Queene, v. viii. 28) is

'With yron wheeles and hookes armed dreadfully.'

l. 60. *sovran*: sovereign (Ital. *sovrano*).

l. 64. *whist* : hushed ; participle of the verb *to whist* or *hist*. Cf. Il Penseroso, l. 55.

l. 66. *Ocean* is trisyllabic.

l. 68. Halcyone was the daughter of Aeolus. She and her husband, having called themselves Hera and Zeus, were for their presumption transformed into kingfishers. It was fabled that for seven days before and after the shortest day, while the kingfishers were breeding, the sea was calm. The halcyon days were in midwinter.

l. 71. *influence.* Whenever this word occurs in our poetry, down to comparatively a modern day, it refers to invisible illapses of power, skyey planetary effects, supposed to be exercised by the heavenly luminaries upon the lives of men (Trench).

l. 75. *orb* : here for *orbit*.

l. 81. *as*: for ' as if', a frequent usage in Shakespeare.

l. 85. *lawn* : a later form of *launde* (French *lande*). In the sixteenth century it meant 'shrubbery, heath '; here it has the sense 'grassy plain ', of which the modern sense is a specific application.

l. 88. *than* : old form for *then*, retained for rhyme's sake.

l. 89. In Spenser's Shepherd's Calendar (May and July), God and our Lord are called Pan, a poetical rendering of St. John x. 11.

l. 98. *took*: charmed, captivated.

l. 100. The *close* or cadence at the end of a piece of music is here meant.

l. 108. *happier union*: i. e. than that of Nature.

l. 116. Cf. Lycidas, l. 176, where *unexpressive* = inexpressible.

l. 119. Job xxxviii. 7.

l. 127. The spheres in their revolutions were supposed to produce the most ravishing harmony, consisting of eight melodies, of which the music of the ninth sphere was the diapason or concentus. Milton held that we should hear the music of the spheres, were our hearts pure, and our minds not bowed down to earth—an idea continually recurring in the poetry of the time. Cf. The Merchant of Venice, v. 1. 60-5.

l. 132. *consort*: cf. Solemn Music, l. 27.

l. 155. *y-chain'd*. Here *y-* is a survival of the old prefix of the past participle, *ge-* in Anglo-Saxon and then *i-* or *y-* in Middle English. Milton prefixes it wrongly to a present participle (ypointing) in the lines on Shakespeare.

l. 164. 1 Thessalonians iv. 17.

l. 172. *Swinges*: lashes.

l. 173. Stanzas 19 and 20 of this Ode are founded on a tradition that at the time of the Passion (the time is here changed to the Nativity), the pilot of a ship sailing from Italy to Cyprus was bidden by a supernatural voice to proclaim, when he came to a certain island, that Pan was dead. On arriving at the place named, the ship was suddenly becalmed, until he cried out that Pan was dead ; 'wherewithal was heard such piteous outcries and dreadful shrieking, as hath not been the like.' This is quoted in the Gloss to Spenser's Shepherd's Calendar (May), and is said to have been understood 'of the great Sathanas', for at that time 'all oracles surceased, and enchanted spirites that were wont to delude the people held their peace'.

l. 186. The genii were the guardian spirits of persons and of places. Cf. Lycidas, l. 183.

l. 191. *Lars*: the household Gods (*lares*) of Roman mythology; Milton uses the English plural form of *lar*.

Lemures: the spirits of the departed (pronounced as two syllables).

l. 194. *flamen*: priest.

quaint: from French *cointe*, and this again from Lat. *cognitus*, known, familiar, and therefore agreeable.

l. 197. Numbers xxv. 3. Baalim were Phoenician deities : Peor was one of these.

l. 200. *Ashtaroth*: Hebrew name for Astarte, the Syrian Aphrodite. She loved Adonis (*Thammuz*), the son of a Syrian king. He, dying of a wound received from a boar, was revived for six months of every year, a symbol of the revival of nature in summer. The worship of Adonis, of Phoenician origin, spread over nearly all the countries round the Mediterranean.

l. 203. *Hammon* (Amun) was an Egyptian deity. He was protector of flocks, and was represented with the horns of a ram.

l. 205. Sandys in his Travels, a book popular in Milton's time, says of the valley of Tophet: 'Therein the Hebrews sacrificed their children to *Moloch*, an idol of brass, having the head of a calf, the rest of a kingly figure with arms extended to receive the miserable sacrifice seared to death with his burning embracements. For the idol was hollow within, and filled with fire ; and lest their lamentable shrieks should sad the heart of their parents, the priests of

Moloch did deaf their ears with the continual clang of trumpets and timbrels.'

ll. 212, 3. *Osiris* was the Nile-god. *Isis*, his wife, was the goddess of earth. *Orus* was the sun-god, also the god of silence and mystery. *Anubis* was the dog-god. In l. 215 Milton gives Osiris the form of Apis, the bull-god.

l. 214. *Memphian . . . green* : the fields of the Egyptian city Memphis.

l. 215. *unshowr'd* : there is little or no rain in Egypt, which is fertilized by the overflowing of the Nile.

l. 217. Osiris was shut up in a chest, and thus destroyed, by his brother Set, whom the Greeks called *Typhon* (l. 226).

l. 223. *eyn* : old plural of *eye*, archaic in Milton's time.

l. 240. *youngest teemèd* : last born ; the star of Bethlehem.

l. 244. *bright-harness'd* : in bright armour.

EPITAPH ON SHAKESPEAR

'On Shakespear. 1630'—edition 1645. The title in the Second Folio of Shakespeare's plays, 1632, where these lines were first printed, is 'An Epitaph on the admirable Dramaticke Poet, W. Shakespeare'.

l. 11. *unvalu'd* : invaluable. Cf. note on L'Allegro, l. 40.

l. 12. *Delphic* : for 'oracular'.

l. 15. *sepúlchre* is so accented in Shakespeare (Lear, II. iv. 128).

SONNET I

l. 13. *All is*, i.e. all that matters is. He submits to the will of Heaven ; but will he make proper use of his talents?

SONNET II

l. 3. A fifteenth-century poem called The Cuckoo and the Nightingale, wrongly supposed in Milton's time to be by Chaucer, deals with the belief among lovers that it was a good omen to hear the nightingale earlier in the year than the cuckoo, and a bad omen to hear the cuckoo first.

AT A SOLEMN MUSIC

l. 4. In Milton's time *verse* and *pierce* formed a better rhyme than they do in our present pronunciation. An older spelling was *perse*.

l. 6. *concent* : so in the Cambridge MS. in the sense of harmony (Lat. *concentus*). Ed. 1645 has *content*.

l. 23. *diapason* : the concord of the octave. Bacon calls it the sweetest concord ' inasmuch as it is in effect a unison '.

l. 27. *consort* : symphony. Cf. Christ's Nativity, l. 132, and Il Penseroso, l. 145.

L'ALLEGRO

l. 3. Styx, 'the hateful', was one of the four rivers of Hades in classical mythology.

l. 10. The Cimmerians (Odyssey, xi. 14) were a mythical people who lived in perpetual mist, and on whom the sun never shone.

l. 14. This parentage of the Graces occurs in Servius on Aeneid i. 720 (Keightley). Aglaia (the bright) and Thalia (the blooming) are the other two sisters. Euphrosyne (the cheerful) presides over festivities.

l. 24. *Buxom*: connected with A.S. *būgan*, to bow, bend. Before the end of the sixteenth century the prevailing senses are 'obedient, tractable', 'gracious, amiable'; the Elizabethan writers also used the word to mean 'gladsome, lively' (as Milton uses it here).

l. 40. *unreproved*: that cannot be reproved. Cf. Paradise Lost, iii. 3, ix. 5, and note to Shakespear Epitaph, l. 11.

l. 45. *To come*: following in sense after 'admit me'.

l. 62. *dight*: decked, arranged.

l. 67. The *tale* here is the tale (number) of sheep counted by the shepherd as he turns them forth to pasture.

l. 79. *lies*: resides.

l. 80. Cynosure is the constellation of the Little Bear, by which the Phoenician mariners steered their course, as the Greeks did by the Great Bear. In Hacket's Life of Archbishop Williams (1693) the Countess of Buckingham is described as 'the Cynosura that all the Papists steered by'. Cf. note on Comus, l. 342.

l. 83. Milton's classic fancy plays round the sights and sounds of English rural life and gives to English peasants the names of Virgilian swains and shepherdesses.

l. 91. *secure*, not 'safe', but 'void of care' (Lat. *securus*).

l. 94. The *rebeck* was an early form of the fiddle with three strings.

l. 103. *she*, i. e. a girl who tells a story of how she was 'pinched and pulled' by the fairies; *he* (l. 104), a man who then tells his story.

l. 104. *Friar's lantern*: the Will-o'-the-Wisp, *ignis fatuus*.

l. 105. *drudging goblin*: Robin Goodfellow.

l. 120. *Weeds*: garments, dress (surviving in 'widow's weeds').

l. 122. *influence*: one of the words ('disastrous', 'ill-starred', 'ascendancy') which still testify to the once prevalent belief in astrology. See note on Christ's Nativity, l. 71.

l. 132. *sock* (Lat. *soccus*), or light shoe worn by ancient comic actors, was used allusively for comedy. The buskin (Il Penseroso, l. 102), or thick-soled boot worn by tragedians, was the symbol of tragedy.

Ben Jonson (1573–1637), the most learned of the Elizabethan dramatists, was regularly spoken of as 'the poet of art' in comparison with Shakespeare, 'the poet of nature'.

l. 133. *Fancy* had a wider range of meaning in Milton's time than now. Cf. Solemn Music, l. 5.

l. 136. The three (supposed) original ancient modes were the Dorian, the Phrygian, and the Lydian. The principal note of the last is F, its scale being the scale of F with B natural substituted for B flat. The tender character ascribed by the ancients to this mode results from the ascent by a semitone to the keynote, the form of cadence most conclusive and agreeable to us moderns.

IL PENSEROSO

l. 6. *fond* in its old meaning of 'foolish'. Cf. Lycidas, l. 56.

l. 10. Queen Elizabeth had for her guard a select band of tall and handsome gentlemen, called Pensioners. The word became common for 'train', 'retinue'.

> 'The cowslips tall her pensioners be.'
> (Midsummer Night's Dream, II. i. 10.)

l. 14. *to hit*: to meet, touch.

l. 18. Memnon, King of Ethiopia, was an auxiliary to the Trojans, and was slain by Achilles. As Memnon was the fairest of warriors (Odyssey xi. 522) his sister might be presumed to be no less beautiful.

l. 19. Cassiope was wife to Cepheus, King of Ethiopia. To appease the Nereids, she exposed her daughter Andromeda to the sea-monster which they had prevailed upon Poseidon to send into Ethiopia with an inundation. She was afterwards placed among the stars.

l. 23. *Vesta*, or Hestia, was the goddess of the hearth. She was daughter of Saturn or Cronos. According to classic legends, she swore by the head of Zeus to remain a virgin. To her father is attributed the origin of civilization. Milton's Melancholy is therefore the offspring of Retirement and Culture.

l. 33. *grain* (Lat. granum), purple colour. *Granum* means seed or kernel, and was early applied to objects resembling seeds. A species of oak common on all Mediterranean coasts, and especially in Spain, is frequented by an insect of the genus *Coccus*, the dried body, or rather ovarium, of which furnishes a variety of scarlet dyes. From its origin the name *granum* was given to the colour. Milton and other English poets often use *grain* as equivalent to Tyrian purple. Here the epithet 'darkest', and the character and attributes of the wearer of the robe, show that the poet meant the violet shade. In Paradise Lost, v. 285, 'sky-tinctured' need not mean azure; the sky in old writers includes the clouds which may be of various hues, and 'regal ornament' suggests the imperial purple. Though we commonly restrict purple to the violet shade, it is employed in poetry to express as wide a range of colour as its Greek and Latin equivalents—that is, all shades from scarlet to dark violet.

l. 35. *cypress lawn*: a light transparent material or crape, commonly black and used as mourning: cf. Winter's Tale, IV. iv. 220, I.

The name is from the island of Cyprus, which was famous for its textile fabrics.

l. 59. 'Night's swift dragons cut the clouds full fast.'
(Midsummer Night's Dream, III. ii. 379.)

l. 83. Keightley quotes Stow : 'The bell-man at every lane's end, and at the ward's end, gave warning of fire and candle, and to help the poor, and to pray for the dead.'

l. 87. 'As the Bear never sets, he could only out-watch him by sitting up till day-break' (Keightley).

l. 88. Hermes Trismegistus, 'thrice great'—a fabled king of Egypt, supposed contemporary with Moses. To him many books on politics, physics, and theology were ascribed. Chemistry, or rather alchemy, was called the hermetical art, from his supposed invention of it. Bacon speaks (Advancement of Learning, i) of the 'triplicity which in great veneration was ascribed to the ancient Hermes ; the power and fortune of a king, the knowledge and illumination of a priest, and the learning and universality of a philosopher'.

unsphere : call down from the sphere assigned to him.

l. 90. This is treated in the Phaedo of Plato. But the doctrine of the spirits or demons of the four elements (Fire, Air, Water, Earth) was developed by the later Platonists and especially in the Middle Ages.

l. 93. *of those demons*, i.e. tell of those demons.

l. 98. The *pall* is Lat. *palla*, the outer garment, usually of wool or cloth, often richly dyed or embroidered.

l. 99. *Presenting* : the technical word for producing or acting a masque or play.

Thebes, the capital of Boeotia. Aeschylus made it the scene of his Seven against Thebes, Sophocles of his Oedipus Tyrannus and Antigone, and Euripides of his Bacchae.

Pelops' line : allusion to the trilogy of Aeschylus on the subject of the murder of Agamemnon, a descendant of Pelops, King of Pisa in Elis, who has given his name to Peloponnesus.

l. 100. *Troy divine.* Its story is dramatically treated, at least in selected episodes, by Sophocles in his Ajax and his Philoctetes, and by Euripides in his Hecuba and his Andromache.

ll. 101, 102. This couplet is probably intended to include the tragedies of Shakespeare.

l. 104. *Musæus* : a mythical bard of Thrace, according to some legends the son of Orpheus.

l. 110. The Squire's Tale in Chaucer, which is incomplete. In this tale Cambuscan, 'the Tartar king', has two sons, Algarsyf and Cambalo, and a daughter, Canacee.

l. 116. *And if aught else*, &c. : referring to Spenser, in whose Faerie Queene all the enumerated circumstances may be found.

l. 123. *trick'd* : adorned.

frounc'd : curled, referring to the dressing of the hair.

l. 124. *The Attic boy* is Cephalus. His mother was daughter of Cecrops, King of Attica. He was beloved by Eos, the dawn.

l. 127. *still*: gentle, as in the stage-direction in Midsummer Night's Dream, IV. i, ' still music '.

l. 130. *minute-drops*: cf. ' minute-guns '.

l. 145. *consort*: cf. Solemn Music, l. 27.

l. 148. *Wave at his wings*: move gently to and fro at Sleep's wings. Cf. Spenser, Faerie Queene, I. i. 44 : 'And on his little winges the dreame he bore '.

l. 156. *Pale*: enclosure.

l. 158. *massy-proof*: able to resist the incumbent weight.

COMUS

l. 97. *steep*: deep ; like ' altus ' and our ' high ' sea.

l. 105. *rosy twine*: wreaths of roses.

l. 108. *Advice*: consideration, deliberation. Cf. note on Paradise Lost, ii. 376.

l. 110. *saws*: things said, proverbs.

l. 112. Allusion to the music of the spheres, line 1021.

l. 116. *morrice*: i.e. Moorish, a dance brought by the Moors into Spain, and thence said to have been introduced into England by John of Gaunt.

l. 121. *wake*: the vigil before a holyday ; applied to the festivities on the anniversary of the consecration of a church, &c.

l. 147. *shrouds*: hiding-places.

l. 151. *trains*: snares.

l. 155. *blear*, ' dim, indistinct in outline ', a transferred usage of the strict sense ' dim-sighted ' (said of the eyes).

l. 157. *quaint*: see note on Nativity, l. 194.

l. 167. *gear*: business.

l. 189. *votarist*: one bound by religious vows. *Sad*: serious.

palmer: strictly a pilgrim who carried a palm branch or leaf on his return from the Holy Land ; an itinerant monk who had taken a vow of poverty. *Weed*, see L'Allegro, l. 120.

l. 204. *single darkness*: darkness only.

l. 212. *side*, ' accompany', take the side of.

l. 215. *Chastity*: instead of Charity, the usual companion of Faith and Hope.

l. 231. *shell*. The MS. reading is ' cell '. The ' airy shell ' is the hemisphere, the ' hollow round of Cynthia's seat ', Nativity, l. 102.

l. 232. *Meander*: a Phrygian river. In its lower course it forms the boundary of ancient Lycia and Caria, and flows in those windings that have made its name a descriptive verb.

l. 241. *Echo* is supposed here to have her origin from the reverberation of the music of the spheres (Solemn Music, l. 2).

l. 248. *his hidd'n residence*: *his* refers to ' something holy '.

We should now use *its*. *Its* is of comparatively late use. Milton generally avoids the word.

l. 253. In this passage Milton has followed the poetic traditions of his own time.

l. 254. *flow'ry-kirtl'd*. A 'kirtle' was in Shakespeare's and in Milton's time a woman's garment, though anciently a man's also, worn by bishops and by Knights of the Garter at their installation.

l. 267. ' Unless [thou be] the goddess,' &c.

l. 277. The following passage is an imitation of those scenes of Greek tragedy wherein the dialogue runs in alternate lines.

l. 293. *swink'd*: tired with work (A.S. *swincan*, to labour).

l. 297. *port*: bearing, deportment.

l. 299. *element*: sky.

l. 301. *plighted*: folded, pleated.

l. 313. *bosky*: shaded by bushes, from *bosk*, originally the same word as *bush*.

l. 327. *warranted*: secured.

l. 342. Calisto, daughter of Lycaon, King of Arcadia, was changed into the Greater Bear (called also Helice) and her son Arcas into the Lesser (called also Cynosura). Cf. note on L'Allegro, l. 80.

l. 345. *stops*: the holes in a pipe or flute. Cf. Lycidas, l. 188.

l. 349. *Innumerous* is the Latin *innumerus*, unnumbered, innumerable.

l. 359. *exquisite*: curious.

l. 360. *cast*: predict.

l. 366. *to seek*: at a loss.

l. 367. *unprincipl'd*: ignorant of the principia, the beginnings of Virtue's lore.

l. 376. To *seek to* is a common construction in our authorized translation (Isaiah xi. 10).

l. 380. *all to-ruffl'd*: there is no hyphen in ed. 1645. The 'to' augments the force of the verb, and 'all' is an additional intensive. Cf. Judges ix. 53, 'all to brake his skull'.

l. 382. *the centre*: sc. of the earth, by an ellipse common in older writers. Cf. Hamlet, II. ii. 159.

l. 393. The Hesperian apples were those presented by Ge to Hera at her wedding with Zeus. Hera committed them to the charge of the nymphs, the Hesperides, and the dragon Ladon. To obtain this fruit was one of the labours of Hercules.

l. 395. *unenchanted*: not to be enchanted.

l. 401. *wink on* is used by Shakespeare as 'give a signal to a confederate', or 'shut the eye', 'refuse to see'.

l. 404. *It recks me not*: I take no account.

l. 423. *to trace*: to track.
unharbour'd: unsheltered.

l. 430. *unblench'd*. To *blench* is to cause to flinch or swerve, to cause to turn away the eyes through fear. The intransitive use = to flinch, swerve, start aside, is more common.

l. 455. *lackey*: accompany as a servant.

l. 459. *oft*: frequent (used as an adj.).

l. 483. *night-founder'd*: benighted.

l. 859. *Sabrina*: goddess of the Severn.

l. 868 et sqq. The epithets of *Oceanus* and *Neptune* are those assigned to them by Hesiod and Homer. *Tethys* is the wife of Oceanus, and the mother of the gods. Proteus had a cave at *Carpathus*, an island of the Mediterranean. He was a prophet, and Neptune's shepherd, therefore bearing a *hook* or crook (Georgics, iv. 395). *Triton* is described by Pliny as scaly, and his horn is mentioned in Ovid (Metamorphoses, i. 333). Aristotle writes that *Glaucus*, the sea-deity, prophesied to the Gods. Ino, flying from the rage of her husband Athamas, threw herself (with her son Melicerta in her arms) into the sea. Neptune, at the prayer of Venus, made them sea-deities, giving her the name of *Leucothea* (the white goddess), and him that of Palaemon. He was called by the Romans, Portumnus, the ruler of the ports (Ovid, Metamorphoses, iv. 541 ; Fasti, vi. 545).

l. 879. *Parthenope* and *Ligea* were Sirens. Ligea is the name of a sea-nymph in Virgil (Georgics, iv. 336). Parthenope was buried at Naples, which is called by her name in Virgil and Ovid. In his lines to Leonora, Milton asks Naples why it boasts the tomb of the dead Siren, when she is living and singing at Rome.

l. 880. The comb belongs to the mermaids of Northern, not to the Sirens of Greek mythology.

l. 893. *azurn* is perhaps from Ital. *azzurino*, as *cedarn* (l. 990) from *cedrino*. This conjecture seems probable as the words are only found in Milton. But the old Engl. adjectival termination was *n* as in *golden*, *leathern*.

l. 984. *crisped*, 'rippled' by the wind; cf. 'crisp channels', Tempest, IV. i. 130.

l. 993. *blow* is here used actively = make the flowers blow.

l. 995. *purfl'd*: fringed (Fr. *pourfiler*, to work on the edge).

l. 1002. Venus was worshipped by the Assyrians under the names of Astarte and Ashtoreth.

l. 1010. The legend of Cupid and Psyche. See Areopagitica, p. 175 and note.

l. 1017. *corner*: horn (Lat. *cornu*).

l. 1021. *sphery chime*: the music of the spheres.

LYCIDAS

Edward King was the son of Sir John King, Secretary to the Government of Ireland under Elizabeth, James I, and Charles I. In June 1626 he was admitted to Christ's College, Cambridge, to which Milton had been admitted in February 1625. He took his M.A. in 1633 and became a fellow and tutor of his college. When

Milton left Cambridge in 1632 he had been in residence with, King for six years.

On August 10, 1637, King was drowned off the Welsh coast when crossing from Chester to Ireland. In accordance with a fashion of the time, and from a keen sense of their loss, his Cambridge friends dedicated a collection of poems to his memory. The volume consists of two parts which were so printed that they might be issued separately. The first (entitled 'Justa Edouardo King naufrago', i.e. Rites to Edward King drowned at sea) contains twenty-three poems in Latin and Greek; the second (see the reproduction of the title) contains thirteen poems in English. The last of these is Lycidas, signed 'J. M.' It was written in November 1637, but the volume was not published till early in 1638.

The note 'In this monody . . . height' was added in ed. 1645.

l. 1. *Yet once more.* Milton had been compelled to forgo the resolution to wait till time should ripen his powers and enable him to enter on that great poetic work which he thought himself destined to achieve.

l. 15. *sisters of the sacred well*: the Muses; the 'sacred well' is the Pierian spring under Mount Olympus, where the Muses were born.

l. 19. *Muse*: here used for a poet inspired by her.

l. 28. The gray-fly is also called the trumpet-fly, and its 'sultry horn' is its hum heard in the noon-tide heat.

l. 29. *batten*: feed or fatten.

l. 33. *Temper'd*: modulated.

l. 36. *old Damœtas*: probably some fellow, or the Master, of Christ's College.

l. 45. *canker*: for 'cankerworm'.

l. 46. A small red spider called 'taint' is 'by the country people accounted a deadly poison to cows and horses' (Sir Thomas Browne).

l. 52. The *steep* is perhaps Penmaenmawr, opposite Anglesea.

l. 53. The places named are near where King was lost. Drayton (Polyolbion, ix) personifies Mona as boasting of the ancient worship of the Druids there celebrated, and commemorating their doctrines of the immortality and transmigration of the soul.

l. 54. *Mona*: Anglesea. *Deva*: the Dee.

l. 58. *the Muse herself*: Calliope. Orpheus was torn to pieces by the Thracian women, and his head, which was thrown into the river Hebrus, floated to the isle of Lesbos.

l. 70. *clear*: illustrious, noble (*clarus*).

l. 75. Milton, enraged against Atropos, calls her a Fury.

l. 85. Alpheus, a river in Arcadia, runs underground for some distance; whence arose the legend that the nymph Arethusa was pursued by Alpheus, who followed her under land and sea to Sicily, where she was changed by Artemis into the fountain bearing her name in the island of Ortygia at Syracuse. Arethusa and Mincius are here named in allusion to Theocritus, the Sicilian poet, and to Virgil, born near the Mincius.

l. 89. *the Herald of the Sea* : Triton, sent by Neptune to inquire into the drowning of Lycidas.

l. 96. *Hippotades* : Æolus, son of Hippotes.

l. 99. Panope's sisters are the Nereids.

l. 103. *Camus* : the god of the Cam, the river at Cambridge.

l. 105. *figures dim* : alluding to the fabulous traditions of the high antiquity of Cambridge.

l. 106. A commentator remarks, 'On sedge leaves when dried, or even when beginning to wither, there are not only certain indistinct or dusky streaks, but also a variety of dotted marks on the edge "scrawled over" (as Milton first wrote) which withers before the rest of the flag'. *That sanguine flower* is the hyacinth. The legend is that Hyacinth was the son of a king of Sparta. He was accidentally slain by Apollo with a quoit. On the leaves of the flower which bears his name are certain marks, said to be AI, AI, (alas!) or Υ the Greek initial of Hyacinth.

l. 107. *pledge* : child. Cf. Solemn Music, l. 1.

l. 109. *The pilot of the Galilean lake* : St. Peter.

l. 110. Cp. St. Matthew xvi. 19.

l. 111. *amain* : with force; from A.S. *mægen*, strength.

l. 122. *are sped* : are provided for.

l. 124. *Scrannel* : thin, meagre. The line, in its harshness, imitates the shrill, discordant notes of the false shepherds.

l. 128. The *wolf* may allude to the legendary origin of Rome.

l. 130. A double reference has been supposed to the axe of the Gospel (Matt. iii. 10, and Luke iii. 9) and to the axe of the headsman. But perhaps Laud's execution gave this after-significance. Another interpretation is that the *engine* is the sword of Michael (Paradise Lost, vi. 251) which is to smite off the head of Satan. Masson suggests that Milton refers to the coming Parliament, the two Houses that must deliver England from the episcopal tyranny.

l. 132. See note on l. 85.

l. 136. *use* : frequent, inhabit.

l. 138. *swart star* : either from its heat causing plants to become swart, or black, or in the meaning of black, injurious.

    sparely : sparingly.

l. 142. *rathe* : the old word for 'early', whence *rather*, sooner.

l. 158. *monstrous world* : world of monsters.

l. 160. *Bellerus* : probably coined by Milton from 'Bellerium', the Roman name for Land's End. He had previously written 'Corineus', the name of a Trojan who was said in the fabulous history of early Britain to have come with Brute and to have been made lord of Cornwall.

l. 161. The *guarded Mount* is St. Michael's Mount, near Land's End. The Archangel Michael is related to have appeared there, seated on a crag and looking seaward. Milton supposes the Archangel still seated (as in the vision) looking to Namancos near

Cape Finisterre, marked in Mercator's Atlas of 1623 and 1636 in the map of Galicia, where the Castle of Bayona is also conspicuous.

l. 164. *dolphins.* The allusion is to Arion and to the dolphins

'which him bore
Through the Ægaean seas from Pirates' view.'
(Faerie Queene, IV. xi. 23.)

l. 186. *uncouth* : unknown. Milton thus speaks in implied contrast with the future fame of which he justly felt assured.

l. 188. *stops* : see Comus, l. 345. *Quills* are pipes or flutes; *various quills* alludes to the changes of mood in the poem.

l. 189. *Doric lay* : pastoral poem. Theocritus and Moschus respectively wrote a pastoral on the deaths of Daphnis and Bion. Both poets were natives of Syracuse in Sicily, a Dorian colony. See p. 49, l. 2 note.

SONNET III

After the battle of Edgehill (Oct. 23, 1642) attempts were made by the Parliament to negotiate with the king, who continued to advance on London. A messenger had been dispatched to treat for an armistice, when Charles attempted to surprise a detachment of Parliamentary troops at Brentford. They were quickly reinforced: and though the king succeeded in occupying Brentford, his progress towards London was effectually barred.

l. 1. *colonel* : here a trisyllable.

l. 5. *Charms* : Lat. *carmina*, magic verses.

l. 10. The poets give the name of Emathia to the whole of Macedonia. Emathia is properly a province, and the original seat of the Macedonian monarchy. Pliny is the authority for the story thus told by the old commentator on Spenser: ' Alexander destroying Thebes, when he was informed that the famous lyric poet Pindarus was born in that city, commanded straitly that no man should under pain of death do any violence to that house.'

l. 13. *Sad* is an epithet often given to Electra in Euripides, and even put into her own mouth by that dramatist. The Chorus from the Electra of Euripides (v. 167, &c.), recited by a Phocian minstrel at the banquet of the conquerors of Athens, so wrought upon them that the city was saved from utter destruction—' ruin bare '.

SONNET XIII

l. 7. *Darwen* : a small stream that flows from east and south into the Ribble, falling therein near Preston.

l. 14. The same charges are here brought against the Presbyterian ministers, as in Lycidas against the Episcopal clergy.

SONNET XVI

The Duke of Savoy, urged by Capuchin propagandists, gave to the Vaudois, his Protestant subjects in Piedmont, the alternative of attending Mass or of leaving their country in twenty days. Savoyard troops were sent to enforce the edict, and carried fire and sword into the valleys of Piedmont. All England was indignant at this crime, and Cromwell loudly remonstrated with the Duke of Savoy and Louis XIV. A collection of £80,000 was made for the sufferers. A treaty was concluded between the Duke and his subjects by French mediation (August, 1655), and was ratified before the arrival of Cromwell's protest against the unfairness of its terms. Even this arrangement was violated three years afterwards, and Cromwell again employed Milton to write to Louis XIV. The Vaudois had peace thenceforward till the Restoration.

l. 10. Alluding to the proverb that 'the blood of the martyrs is the seed of the Church'.

l. 14. *Babylonian woe*: i.e. the woe denounced against Babylon. Milton, in his Latin verses on November 5, calls the Pope the Babylonian high-priest.

PARADISE LOST

The Verse. The first edition of Paradise Lost, in 1667, was without this preface. In 1668, when a new title-page was prefixed to the edition, it was added, with the following Address of the printer to the reader: '*Courteous Reader*, there was no Argument at first intended to the Book, but for the satisfaction of many that have desired it, I have procur'd it, and withal a reason of that which stumbled many others, why the Poem rimes not.'

Book I

l. 6. *Secret* is here used for 'separate', 'apart'.

l. 7. Horeb and Sinai are two peaks of the same mountain range, on which Moses had been a shepherd for forty years. The Law is said in Deuteronomy to have been given from Horeb, and in the other books of the Pentateuch Sinai is named as the 'mount' of its promulgation.

l. 10. Sion was the hill opposite to Moriah, on which latter the Temple was built. In the valley beside them was the Pool (not brook) of Siloam—an intermittent well, ebbing and flowing at irregular intervals.

l. 15. Aonia was the name of part of Boeotia, near Phocis, in which were the mountain Helicon and the fountain Aganippe, the favourite haunts of the Muses. The *Aonian mount* is here used for the productions of the Greek poets, which Milton intends to surpass in boldness of conception.

l. 21. *brooded* is the strict translation of the Hebrew word rendered in our version by 'moved' (Genesis i. 2).

l. 24. *argument*: subject.

l. 107. *Study*: here = Lat. *studium*, 'endeavour'.

l. 117. *empyreal substance*: fiery essence.

l. 266. *astonish'd*: here 'stunned, paralysed' (by a mental shock). The literal sense is 'thunderstruck', from the Old French *estonner* (modern French *étonner*), representing a popular Latin form *extonare*, synonymous with the classical Latin *attonare*. Cf. *astounded* (another form of the same word) in l. 281; also *astonishment* in l. 317.

oblivious pool: pool that causes oblivion, like 'forgetful lake' (Paradise Lost, ii. 74).

l. 288. *the Tuscan artist*, Galileo, applied the telescope (which he greatly improved, if not invented) to the observation of the heavenly bodies, and so discovered the moon to be a body of uneven surface.

l. 289. *Fesole* or Fiesole, is the hill three miles to the north-east of Florence. On it are the remains of the ancient city of Faesulae.

l. 290. *Valdarno*: the Val d'Arno is the valley in which Florence lies.

l. 294. *ammiral*: the principal vessel in a fleet (Ital. *ammiraglio*).

l. 303. *Vallombrosa* is eighteen miles from Florence.

l. 305. *Orion*, the mighty Boeotian hunter, was at his death placed among the stars, where he appears as a giant with a girdle and lion's skin, and *armed* with a sword and club. His setting, at the beginning of November, was attended by storms.

l. 306. The Hebrew name of the Red Sea is Sea of Sedge, from the abundance of seaweed therein.

l. 307. Pharaoh being a mere title, Milton gives to the oppressor of the Israelites an individual name. The *Busiris* of Greek legend was an Egyptian king who sacrificed all strangers that visited Egypt. Hercules, on his arrival, was bound and led to the altar, but he burst his bonds and slew Busiris. Memphis was on the west bank of the Nile. It contained the palace of the Pharaohs, and the temples of Apis and Serapis.

chivalry for 'cavalry'. *Cavalleria* in Italian has this double sense.

l. 309. Exodus xiv. 30.

l. 312. *abject*: thrown down, cast away.

l. 320. *virtue*: valour, manhood (*virtus*).

l. 341. *warping*: proceeding in an undulatory manner.

l. 345. *cope*: cap or dome, the 'concave' of l. 542.

l. 353. *Rhene* is the Latin name (Rhenus) of the Rhine, *Donau* the German name of the Danube.

l. 355. *Beneath*: to the south of, *infra*. The Vandals passed over from Spain and settled in northern Africa.

l. 534. *Azazel*: mentioned as an evil spirit in Leviticus xvi. 20, where 'for Azazel' is mistranslated 'for the scapegoat'.

l. 538. *emblaz'd*: blazoned. The *trophies* probably refer to the armorial bearings displayed upon banners.

l. 546. *Orient* in Milton's poems has three meanings : (1) 'rising', Paradise Lost, iv. 644; (2) 'eastern', Nativity Ode, l. 231; (3) 'bright', as here and at Paradise Lost, iv. 238.

l. 551. *recorder*: a kind of flute.

l. 554. *unmov'd*: immovable. Cf. L'Allegro, l. 40.

l. 563. *horrid* : bristling (Lat. *horridus*).

l. 573. *since created man* : Latinism, 'post hominem creatum'.

l. 575. The Pygmies (men of the height of a πυγμή, 13½ inches) were a fabulous people, first mentioned by Homer as dwelling on the shores of Ocean and attacked by the cranes in spring-time. They are variously placed by different writers in India, Ethiopia, or in the extreme north. Aristotle mentions the descent of the cranes from Scythia to the marshes at the sources of the Nile, where they are said to fight with the Pygmies.

l. 577. Phlegra was a name given to volcanic plains in Thrace and in Campania ; the former (mentioned by Pindar as the scene of the contest of the giants with the gods) was subsequently known as Pallene.

l. 579. Gods fought on both sides at Thebes and at Troy.

l. 580. *Uther's son* : Arthur, son of Uther Pendragon.

l. 581. *Armoric* : of Brittany (Armorica).

l. 582. The allusion is to the romances of Charlemagne. *Aspramont* is a town of Limburg ; *Montalban*, or Montauban, on the borders of Languedoc ; *Trebisond*, a city of Cappadocia, all famous in romance for jousting.

l. 585. *Biserta* : a town of Tunis, the ancient Utica.

l. 603. *considerate* : considering.

l. 609. *amerc'd* : punished by fine. This word is derived from *à merci*. 'Mercy' (either contracted from *misericordia*, or from Lat. *merx*) was the sum exacted in commutation for life forfeited by law or in battle. To 'cry mercy' was to beg for life, to 'grant mercy' was to spare it. As the forbearance was attributed to courtesy and not to covetousness, the word 'mercy' took the general sense of kindness.

l. 662. *understood*: not openly declared.

Book II

l. 2. *Ormus* : an island in the Persian Gulf, a mart for diamonds.

l. 4. An eastern coronation ceremony was the sprinkling of the monarch with gold-dust and seed-pearl.

l. 9. *success* is used by Shakespeare for 'event', either good or bad, and for *bad* success here.

l. 51. *sentence* : opinion, like Lat. *sententia*.

l. 73. *drench*: anything drunk (A.S. *drenc*, from *drincan*, to drink).

l. 89. *exercise*: discipline, chastise, like Lat. *exerceo*.

l. 97. *this essential*: adjective for substantive, a frequent Miltonic usage; cp. l. 278, 'the sensible of pain'.

l. 124. *In fact of arms*: literal translation of the Fr. 'en fait d'armes'.

l. 132. *obscure*: accented on the first syllable.

l. 301. *aspéct*: always thus accented in Milton and Shakespeare.

l. 306. *Atlantéan*: referring to Atlas, who bore up the columns that keep asunder earth and heaven (Odyssey, i. 52).

l. 330. *determin'd*: ended (our hopes).

l. 367. *puny* is from Fr. *puis né*, younger. It is here used in its primary sense.

l. 376. *advise*: consider (Fr. *aviser*).

l. 379. *first devis'd*. See i. 650.

l. 409. *arrive*: used absolutely, but elsewhere in Milton 'arrive at'. The word is from Lat. *adripare*, to come to shore.

l. 439. *unessential*: void of being, having no substance.

l. 441. *abortive*: i. e. rendering so, like 'forgetful' in l. 74.

l. 457. *intend*: attend to. So the Latin phrase 'intendere animum', to bend, apply the mind.

Book III

l. 7. *hear'st thou?*: a Latinism, meaning, 'art thou called?'

l. 16. *middle darkness* is the great gulf between Hell and Heaven.

l. 17. Alluding to the Hymn to Night, attributed to Orpheus, who was inspired by his mother Calliope, and sung '*with other notes*' than these sacred strains of Milton.

l. 25. Alluding to two kinds of blindness arising from *gutta serena* and *suffusio*. '*Gutta serena = amaurosis*, a disease of the optic nerve, and *suffusio* = cataract.'

l. 30. *brooks*: Kedron and Siloa, which last was, however, a pool.

l. 35. *Thamyris* was a Thracian, who, according to Pliny, invented the Dorian mode. He is mentioned by Homer, who relates his presumption in challenging the Muses to a singing contest, and his punishment in being deprived by them of sight, voice, and skill in music. Plutarch, in his treatise of Music, says that he had the finest voice of any of his time, and wrote a poem of the War of the Titans with the Gods. Suidas mentions his poem on the Generation of the World. *Maeonides*: Homer, so called, either from being the son of Maeon, or from being a native of Maeonia, a name of ancient Lydia.

l. 39. *darkling*: in the dark, an adverb.

Book IV

l. 3. *second rout* : the first was that recorded in Bk. i.

l. 50. *sdain'd* : disdained, from Ital. *sdegnare.*

l. 126. Niphates divides Armenia from Assyria.

l. 151. '*In* fair evening cloud' : so in the early editions. Bentley's emendation is 'on'.

l. 159. *As when to them,* &c.   The fragrance of spice is wafted out to sea for a distance of twenty miles, as is well known to every sailor in the West Indies or in the Indian Archipelago.   But it is impossible that north-east winds could waft scent from the Arabian coast to a ship that had doubled the Cape and passed Mozambique (Keightley).

l. 193. The *lewd* were originally merely the lay people, the ignorant, as contrasted with the clergy.   The idea of depravity became associated with that of ignorance, and at last changed the meaning of lewd into its modern signification of lascivious.

l. 209. The province in which Paradise was situated extended from Auran, a city of Mesopotamia near Euphrates, eastward to Seleucia, a city built by Seleucus, one of the successors of Alexander, upon the Tigris. Telassar (Isaiah xxxvii. 12) is placed by Ptolemy in Babylonia, on the common streams of Tigris and Euphrates.

l. 242. *boon* : kind, bounteous.

l. 255. *irriguous* : well-watered.

l. 264. *apply* : 'join to' the melody of the *Streams* and the *air.*

l. 592. *th' Azores* : these islands lie due west of Mesopotamia.

l. 594. *volubil.* Here the word has the second syllable long, after the Latin accent; in ix. 436 it is short, and the word is written 'voluble'.

l. 603. *descant*: a variation by ornament of the main subject or plain-song.

l. 628. *manuring* : cultivation (Fr. *main, œuvre*).

l. 642. *charm* : vocal noise.

Book V

l. 249. *ardours* : seraphim : for Hebrew *sâraf* = Lat. *ardeo.*

l. 257. From *no cloud* to *interposed* is absolute.   *However small* refers to Earth. Satan sees it, though much diminished by distance, and can even distinguish the garden of God. The following comparison illustrates the meaning.

l. 265. *Samos* is not one of the Cyclades.   It is farther east, off the coast of Ionia.   *Delos* is the smallest of the Cyclades.

l. 272. *sole bird.* There was but one phoenix at a time.   Herodotus relates that every five hundred years the new phoenix rose out of the nest in which the former one had died in Arabia, and carried its predecessor's body to Heliopolis in Lower Egypt. Milton here places the sun's temple in Thebes, the capital of Upper Egypt.

l. 274. *Egyptian*: to distinguish this city from Thebes in Boeotia.

l. 285. *grain*: see note on Il Penseroso, l. 33.

Book IX

l. 5. *unblam'd*: see note on L'Allegro, l. 40.

ll. 14–19. In allusion to the subjects of the Iliad, Odyssey, and Aeneid. Neptune persecuted Ulysses, and Juno Aeneas.

l. 26. In Milton's extant MSS. are many sketches for dramatic poems on Scripture subjects. In his youth he had proposed to write an epic on the theme of King Arthur. Aubrey asserts that Paradise Lost was begun about two years before the Restoration.

l. 33. *races and games* are described in Iliad xxiii, and Aeneid v; *tilting* by the Italian poets and by Spenser.

l. 35. *Impresses* (Ital. *impresa*): the devices and emblems on the shield.

l. 36. *Bases*: the mantle, hanging from the middle to the knees or lower, worn by knights on horseback.

l. 37. The 'marshal' set the guests in order of rank; the *sewer* placed the dishes on the table. The *seneschal* was originally 'the senior servant', the major-domo.

Book XI

l. 389. *Temir*: Tymûr Lung, commonly called Tamerlane. His first seat of dominion was Samarcand, which is the region between the Oxus and Jaxartes, but not near either river (Keightley).

l. 390. *Paquin*: Pekin. The *Sinae* (mentioned by Ptolemy) are the Chinese.

l. 392. *The golden Chersonese*: Malacca and the Birman empire.

l. 395. *Bizance*: Byzantium. The Turks came from Turkistan, a province of Tartary.

l. 397. *Negus*: the King of Abyssinia, who was called by Europeans Prester John. 'Negus' in Ethiopic signifies 'king', and is therefore a title, like Pharaoh.

l. 398. *Ercoco*: Erquico or Harkiko on the Red Sea, the northeast boundary of the Abyssinian empire.

the less maritime kings: i.e. the lesser kingdoms on the sea-coast.

l. 399. These places, on the east side of Africa, first became known to Europe by the voyage of Vasco di Gama. Purchas and others thought Sofala to be Ophir, from the resemblance of the names, and because gold was obtained at Sofala. But the real Ophir seems to be Ofir, on the coast of Oman, in Arabia.

l. 403. *Almansor* was one of the Almohade sovereigns, whose dominions extended over the north-west and a great part of the north coast of Africa. *Fez* is in Morocco; *Sus* on the Atlantic, and *Algiers* and *Tremisen* on the Mediterranean coast. *Tremisen* is named from its capital, which lay inland to the south of Algiers.

l. 410. Sir Walter Raleigh's last voyage was to *Guiana*, for the discovery of a gold-mine which he asserted to be there. Wonderful traditions had been current of a golden city, El Dorado, in the interior.

Geryon's sons: Spaniards. The fabled monster Geryon was king of Spain.

l. 414. *euphrasy*: the eye-bright, so named from its supposed effect upon the sight. *Rue* is 'herb of grace'. Both plants are affirmed by the old herbalists to have the virtue of purging the eyes.

Book XII

l. 589. *speculation*: observation (Lat. *specula*, a watch-tower). Cf. Paradise Regained, iv. 236.

l. 629. *meteorous*: lifted off the ground, high in air (μετήορος).

l. 630. *marish*: marsh.

l. 635. *adust*: scorched.

l. 640. *subjected*: lying beneath.

l. 643. *brand*: sword. Its proper meaning is 'torch', and it is thence used for the gleaming sword, both in Saxon and Icelandic.

PARADISE REGAINED

Book IV

l. 51. *imperial palace*: that built by Nero after the burning of Rome. *Turrets, terraces*, and *spires* belong to modern architecture.

l. 59. *hand*: handiwork.

l. 66. *turm*: coined from Lat. *turma*. The regiment (*ala*) was composed of *turmae* (troops).

l. 68. The Appian road led to the south, and the Aemilian to the north. The nations on the Appian road are included in ll. 69–76; those on the Aemilian in ll. 77–9.

ll. 70–5. *Syene*: a city of Egypt on the confines of Ethiopia. *Meroe*, an island and city of Ethiopia, on the upper Nile. Meroe being within the tropics, the sun, after being vertical, passes north of it; so that the shadow falls then to the south at noon, whence ' it both ways falls ' (Keightley). The *realm of Bocchus* is Mauritania. The *golden Chersonese* is Malacca (Paradise Lost, xi. 392). *Taprobane* is Ceylon.

l. 77. *Gades*: the modern Cadiz, here put for that part of Spain most distant from Rome, Hispania Inferior.

l. 78. From the mouth of the Danube to the Palus Maeotis, all

218 NOTES

along the Euxine, lay the European Scythians, and beyond them northward the Sarmatians.

l. 219. *Moses' chair*: Matthew xxiii. 2.

l. 234. *idolisms*: false ideas, fallacies. The word was apparently first used by Milton in this sense (probably from Bacon's *Idola*); it had been used before this in the sense of 'idolatry'.

l. 235. *evinc'd*: subdued; a Latinism.

l. 240. The Spartans, when urged to destroy Athens, refused to put out one of the two eyes of Greece.

l. 244. *Academe*: called after the Attic hero Academus. It was the favourite resort of Plato, and hence his followers were called Academics.

l. 245. *Attic bird*: the nightingale. Philomela was the daughter of Pandion, king of Athens. Near the Academy was Colonos, which Sophocles has celebrated as the haunt of nightingales.

ll. 247–9. Mount *Hymettus* was famous for its honey. It is about three miles south of Athens. The *Ilissus* rises on the north slope of Hymettus, flows through the east side of Athens, and is lost in the marshes of the Athenian plain.

l. 251. Aristotle was the tutor of Alexander the Great.

l. 253. *Lyceum*: Aristotle's 'school' at Athens, *outside* the walls, just above the Ilissus. His followers were the Peripatetics.

Stoa: the painted portico adorned with pictures of Marathon, by Polygnotus. In this portico Zeno conversed with his disciples, thence called Stoics.

l. 257. *charms*: i.e. songs, *carmina*. Alcaeus and Sappho were both of Mitylene in Lesbos, and wrote the 'Aeolium carmen' (i.e. 'Æolian charm') which Horace boasts to have introduced into Italy.

Dorian: the poems of Pindar are meant. See p. 46, l. 25.

l. 259. The life of Homer, attributed to Herodotus, says that Homer was born near the river Meles, and thence called Melesigenes, and that afterwards when blind and settled at Cumae he was called Homer (quasi ὁ μὴ ὁρῶν) from the term by which the Cumaeans distinguished blind persons.

l. 260. In allusion to the epigram in which Apollo says 'I sang, Homer put it in writing'—Ἤειδον μὲν ἐγών, ἐχάραασε δὲ θεῖος Ὅμηρος.

l. 261. *the lofty grave Tragedians*: Aeschylus, Sophocles, and Euripides.

l. 267. *the famous Orators*: Milton is thinking chiefly, as the following lines show, of Pericles and Demosthenes.

l. 271. *To Macedon*: in the Philippics of Demosthenes.

l. 274. Socrates was so pronounced by the oracle, because, though equally ignorant with others, he knew that he was ignorant, while they esteemed themselves wise.

l. 278. The three phases of Academic philosophy were the old, under Plato (died 347 B.C.); the middle, under Arcesilas (died 271 B.C.); and the new, under Carneades (died 128 B.C.).

SAMSON AGONISTES

l. 1512. *inhabitation*: inhabitants, community.

l. 1519. This and the next line rhyme, as also ll. 1525, 1526.

l. 1529. *dole*. There are two words *dole*—(1) that which is dealt out, and (2) pain, grief (Lat. *doleo*). In a prose pamphlet Milton uses the phrase 'to deal about this dole of laughter'. But here *dealing dole* has the subsidiary meaning of pain, punishment, transfused in it.

l. 1541. *O whither*, &c. So the messengers in Greek tragedy enter with loud exclamations, when they have to announce some dire calamity.

l. 1554. *needs*: is needed.

l. 1608. *of sort*: of quality.

l. 1619. *cataphracts*: heavy-armed cavalry, the horses being protected by mail as well as their riders.

l. 1667. *in number more*: Judges xvi. 30.

l. 1674. *In Silo*. The ark remained in Shiloh from the time of Joshua to that of Eli, more than four hundred years.

l. 1695. *villatic fowl*: equivalent to 'barndoor fowl'.

l. 1699. *self-begotten bird*: the phoenix. Cp. Paradise Lost, v. 272 note.

l. 1700. *embost*: hidden in the woods.

l. 1702. *holocaust*: a whole burnt offering.

l. 1707. *secular bird*: because it was fabled to live for a thousand years. Lactantius uses 'seculum' for a thousand years. In classical Latin it is nearly equivalent to our 'century'. Herodotus gives five hundred years as the age of the phoenix.

l. 1713. *Caphtor*, the mother country of the Philistines (Jeremiah xlvii. 4). According to modern scholars, it was a part of the Nile delta, called by the Egyptians *Keft-ur*, i.e. 'Greater Phoenicia'.

AREOPAGITICA

PAGE 174, l. 10. *those fabulous dragon's teeth*. See the story of Jason, how by Medea's direction he sowed the teeth of the Colchian dragon, and there sprang up men all armed. Ovid's Metamorphoses, vii. 121, et seq.

PAGE 175, l. 4. *an elemental life*, &c. Cf. Paradise Lost, iii. 714-21:

> 'Swift to their several quarters hasted then
> The cumbrous element, earth, flood, air, fire;
> And this etherial quintessence of heaven
> Flew upward.'

So Uriel, the sun-angel, to Satan, of the creation of the world. 'This notion our author borrowed from Aristotle and others of the ancient philosophers, who supposed that besides the four elements there was likewise an ethereal quintessence or fifth essence' (Newton).

PAGE 175, l. 11. *those confused seeds*, &c. See the story of Cupid and Psyche in The Golden Ass of Apuleius, books iv–vi. Psyche has fallen into the hands of Venus, who is wroth with her for having won the love of her son Cupid, and afflicts her grievously. She bids Anxiety and Sorrow scourge and torment her. After further abuse, Venus 'flew upon her, tore her clothes in a great many places, pulled out her hair, shook her by the head, and grievously maltreated her. Then taking wheat, barley, millet, poppy, vetches, lentils and beans, and mixing them altogether in one heap, she said to her: "You seem to me, such an ugly slave as you now are, to be likely to gain lovers in no other way than by diligent drudgery. I will therefore myself, for once, make trial of your industrious habits. Take and separate this promiscuous mass of seeds, and having properly placed each grain in its place, and so sorted the whole, give me proof of your expedition by finishing the task before evening." Then having delivered over to her the vast heap of seeds, she at once took her departure for a nuptial banquet. But Psyche, astounded at the stupendous task, sat silent and stupefied, and did not move a hand to the confused and inextricable mass. Just then a tiny ant, one of the inhabitants of the fields, became aware of this prodigious difficulty, and pitying the distress of the partner of the mighty god, and execrating the mother-in-law's cruelty, it ran busily about and summoned together the whole tribe of ants in the neighbourhood, crying to them, "Take pity on her, ye active children of the all-producing earth. Take pity, and make haste to help the wife of Love, a pretty damsel, who is now in a perilous situation." Immediately the six-footed people came rushing in whole waves, one upon another, and with the greatest diligence separated the whole heap, grain by grain. Then having assorted the various kinds into different heaps, they vanished forthwith. At night-fall Venus returned home from the nuptial banquet, exhilarated with wine, fragrant with balsams, and having her waist encircled with blooming roses. As soon as she saw with what marvellous expedition the task had been executed, "This is no work of your hands, wicked creature", she said, "but his whom you have charmed, to your sorrow and his", and throwing her a piece of coarse bread, she went to bed' (Bohn's Class. Lib., Apuleius, p. 116).

l. 13. *from out the rind*, &c.: see Genesis iii. 5 and 22.

l. 16. *that doom*, &c.: see Genesis ii. 16, 17.

l. 23. *the true warfaring Christian.* In the edition of 1644 the reading is *wayfaring*. The warrant for the change is to be found in a copy of the Areopagitica presented by Milton himself to George Thomason ('ex dono Authoris' is written in Thomason's hand on the title-page), now preserved in the British Museum, where the 'y' is crossed out and 'r' written above, credibly by the author himself.

l. 33. *a blank virtue*: a colourless, neutral, ineffectual thing.

l. 34. *excremental* : superficial.   *Excrement* = excrescence, an outgrowth.

PAGE 176, l. 1. *our sage and serious poet Spencer*, &c.   Milton told Dryden that Spenser was his ' original '. (See Dryder 's Fables, Preface.)   Without any such confession, it would have been evident from Milton's earlier works how great was the influence of Spenser over his youthful mind.   To say nothing of numerous Spenserian echoes that may be detected, it is to the Faerie Queene that he especially alludes in Il Penseroso after his mention of the Squire's Tale of Chaucer.

l. 2. *Scotus* : John Duns Scotus, the famous schoolman, born circ. 1265, died at Cologne 1308.

Aquinas. ' The Angelic Doctor ', born circ. 1224, died 1274. On certain radical questions of thought his views were exactly opposed to those presently urged by Scotus.

l. 3. *Guyon* : see Faerie Queene, II.

with his palmer : the Palmer was *not* with him in the Cave of Mammon ; see II. viii. 3. For a description of the Palmer see II. i. 7.

l. 4. *the Cave of Mammon* : see II. vii. 26–66.

l. 5. *the bower of earthly bliss* : see II. xii.

l. 18. *what I have heard*, &c. : see his account of his travels in his Second Defence.

l. 27. *fustian* : originally a sort of coarse cloth, then stuffing, padding ; in literature it denotes words without force, mere verbiage.

l. 28. *Galileo*, born 1564 (the year of Shakespeare's birth), died 1642.

prisoner to the Inquisition. He seems at the time Milton visited him (1638) to have been in what the Latins called *libera custodia*, i.e. not confined in any dungeon, but only kept under a certain restraint, as that he should not move away from a specified neighbourhood, or perhaps a special house.

l. 29. *for thinking in astronomy*, &c. As is well known, he held that the earth moved round the sun, and not the sun round the earth. Milton himself can scarcely be said to have accepted his views, but evidently they attracted him. See Paradise Lost, iv. 591–7 and viii. 122–58 :

' What if the sun
Be centre to the world, and other stars ', &c. ;

PAGE 177, l. 6. *discourse* : reason.

l. 10. *that writers*, &c. In the notes to Drayton's Polyolbion, song i, we are told that ' Lipsius doubts whether Pythagoras received ' the doctrine of metempsychosis ' from the Druids, or they from him, because in his travels he convers'd as well with Gaulish as Roman philosophers '. For *the Persian wisdom*, see Pliny's Nat. Hist. xxx. 4 : ' Britannia hodieque eam attor ite celebrat tantis caeremoniis ut *dedisse Persis videri possit.*'

l. 14. *civil*: cultivated. *Julius Agricola* (A. D. 37–93) governed here from 78 to 85 for Vespasian, Titus, and Domitian. See the 'Agricola' (his life by Tacitus, his son-in-law), ch. 21.

l. 17. *the grave and frugal Transylvanian.* Many Transylvanians went abroad in the seventeenth century to study at the great universities—at Paris, at Prague, in Holland. Some came to England.

l. 19. *the Hercynian wilderness*: the mountains and forests in Germany from the Black Forest to the Harz.

l. 28. *Wicklif*, John (*c.* 1320–1384), the first of the great English reformers of the Church.

l. 30. *Huss*, John (*c.* 1373–1415), Bohemian reformer, burned at the stake.

Jerome : i.e. Jerome of Prague, burned at the stake 1416.

l. 31. *Luther*, Martin (1483–1546), the leader of the German Reformation.

Calvin, John (1509–1564), Swiss divine and reformer.

PAGE 178, l. 14. *the plates and instruments*, &c.: i.e. defensive and offensive armour. *Plates* = breast-plates, almost the only defensive armour still worn in Milton's time.

l. 25. *We reckon more than five months*, &c. Cf. St. John iv. 35. The Areopagitica was published in November 1644. Perhaps 'the harvest' means the successes to be achieved, as was hoped, by the new modelled army in the campaign of 1645.

PAGE 179, l. 12. *he would cry out as Pirrhus did*, &c., after the battle of Heraclea (280 B. C.). Florus' version is—Pyrrhus of course would speak Greek—'O quam facile erat orbis imperium occupare aut mihi Romanis militibus aut me regi Romanis' (I. xviii. 17).

l. 33. *wherein Moses*, &c. See Numbers xi. 24–30, especially 29: 'And Moses said unto him, Enviest thou for my sake? Would God that all the Lord's people were prophets, and that the Lord would put his spirit upon them.'

PAGE 180, l. 10. *maniples* = companies. A technical term in the Roman army. The size of it varied at different times. In the fourth century B: C. it consisted of sixty privates, two centurions, and a standard-bearer. Strictly, the word is supposed to mean a number of men serving under the same ensign, *maniplus* signifying originally 'a handful' or wisp of hay, straw, fern, or the like which, primitively, did duty as a standard.

l. 18. *when a city*, &c. See in Knight's Pop. Hist. of Eng. iii. 498, second edition, 'a Plan of the Fortifications and City of London'. There were forts from Whitechapel Road to Hyde Park Corner, and on the other side of the river from Vauxhall to 'near the Lock Hospital in Kent Street'. The order for this fortifying was issued by the Parliament in September or October 1642. 'The population, one and all, men, women, and children, turned out day by day to dig ditches, and carry stones for their bulwarks' (Knight). See May's History of the Parliament. On November 12 the Royalists occupied Brentford ; on the 13th they advanced to Turnham Green, when, faced by Essex, they fell back without fighting to Colnbrook and so through Reading to Oxford. In this November Milton wrote his sonnet, 'When the assault was intended to the City'.

l. 24. *should be disputing*, &c. About this time certain eminent men of science were beginning to hold those meetings which eventuated in the formation of the Royal Society.

PAGE 181, l. 4. *pertest*: sprightliest, proudest, highest.

l. 16. *like a strong man.* He is thinking of Samson, long years after to be the hero of his noble drama. See Judges xvi. 13, 14.

l. 18. *muing*: literally = renewing by moulting. Commonly *mue* or *mew* = simply, 'to moult', specially of hawks: strictly, to change, Fr. *muer*, Lat. *mutare*.

l. 24. *a year.* He is thinking of the almanack-makers and their prophecies.

l. 28. *engrossers*: an engrosser or grocer means properly one who buys in large quantities.

l. 35. *your own mild*, &c. Even Hume admires ardently the early career of the Long Parliament ; see History of England, chap. 54. Hallam, who considers that in the end it 'subverted the constitution', speaks of 'those admirable provisions by which' in the beginning 'this Parliament restored and consolidated the shattered fabric'. See Constitutional History of England, chap. ix.

PAGE 182, l. 2. *purchased* = procured.

l. 5. *the influence of heaven.* See Christ's Nativity, l. 71, and L'Allegro, l. 122.

l. 18. *an abrogated and merciless law*, &c. 'From the most remote ages the power of a Roman father over his children, in-cluding those by adoption as well as by blood, was unlimited. A father might, without violating any law, scourge or imprison his son, or sell him for a slave, or *put him to death*, even after that son had risen to the highest honours in the state. This 'ius vitae et necis' by degrees 'fell into desuetude ; and long before the close of the republic the execution of a son by order of his father, although not forbidden by any positive statute, was regarded as something strange and, unless under extraordinary circumstances, monstrous. But the right continued to exist in theory, if not in practice, for three centuries after the establishment of the empire, and was not formally abrogated till A.D. 318.' Ramsay's Roman Antiquities.

l. 21. *for coat and conduct*, &c.: i.e. to resist illegal taxation for the clothing and conveyance of troops, and also for the provision of a navy.

his four nobles of Danegelt: i.e. ship-money. The noble, first struck in Edward III's reign, and current till that of Elizabeth, was worth 6s. 8d. *Danegelt* = Dane-money, was the name of an ancient land-tax levied to provide means for bribing off or for repelling the Danes. It was 'first raised by Ethelred II in 991'. Upon this highly dubious precedent the King's advisers greatly relied in their advocacy and exaction of ship-money.

l. 22. *Although I dispraise not*, &c. Milton never actually fought in the Parliamentary ranks. So much might be suspected from the passage in the text; but there is also quite direct and decisive evidence on the point. In the Defensio Secunda Milton defends himself against the possible imputation of cowardice or sloth because he had not served. He claims no share, he says, in the glory of those who by their most honourable arms had repelled slavery. Far other were the weapons of his warfare.

THE REASON OF CHURCH-GOVERNMENT

PAGE 183, l. 6. *preventive*: simply 'going before', without any sense of hindrance. Cf. Christ's Nativity, l. 24.

l. 14. *equal*: impartial.

l. 15. *exigent*: time of pressing need.

l. 16. *elegant*: correct and delicate in taste.

PAGE 184, l. 30. *much latelier*. Milton set out for Italy in April 1638, and reached England on his return in August 1639.

private academies. 'Seven Florentines, most of them young men, leaders in the chief Academies or literary clubs of Florence, are particularly named by him as friends whose merits, and whose courtesies to himself, he could never forget' (Masson).

PAGE 185, l. 17. *Ariosto*. See p. 59, l. 3.

l. 18. *Bembo*, Pietro (1470-1547), cardinal, poet, and scholar.

l. 23. *That what*, syntactically in continuation of 'these other: That if', l. 10.

l. 32. Many writers at the beginning of the seventeenth century had lamented the absence of worthy histories of the 'noble achievements' of England; see, for example, Bacon, Advancement of Learning, Bk. II, ed. Aldis Wright, pp. 92-5.

PAGE 186, l. 4. *Tasso*. See p. 55, l. 23.

l. 6. *rules of Aristotle*. There are no 'rules' in Aristotle's Poetics, but what he had said in that work about the epic was transformed into rules by the Italian critics of the sixteenth century.

l. 24. *Origen* (*c.*185—*c.*254), the famous theologian and commentator.

l. 29. *Pareus*, David (1548-1622), Calvinist controversialist, professor at Heidelberg.

l. 31. *Pindarus*. See p. 46, l. 25. *Callimachus* (*fl.* 250 B.C.) was the chief poet of the Alexandrian school. Six of his hymns are extant.

l. 33. i.e. most of them faulty in their matter and end (purpose). The original has 'an end'.